The Complete Motorcyclist's Handbook

The Complete Motorcyclist's Handbook

SIMON AND SCHUSTER

NEW YORK

Published by Simon and Schuster
A Division of Gulf & Western Corporation
Simon & Schuster Building
Rockefeller Center
1230 Avenue of the Americas
New York, New York 10020
SIMON AND SCHUSTER and colophon are
trademarks of Simon & Schuster
10 9 8 7 6 5 4 3 2 1
Manufactured in the United States of
America
Library of Congress Cataloging in
Publication Data
Minton, David.
The complete motorcyclist's handbook

Includes index.
1. Motorcycling. 2. Motorcycles. I. Title
GV1059.5.M46 1981 796.7'5 81-14421
ISBN 0-671-44118-3 AACR2

Edited and designed by
Marshall Editions Ltd,
71 Eccleston Square,
London SW1V 1PJ

Editor: Graeme Ewens
Art Director: Paul Wilkinson
Editoral assistant: Gwen Rigby
Picture researcher: Mary Corcoran
Production: Julia Lewis
Artwork: Hayward and Martin
Retouching and **Make-up:** Roy Flooks
Reproduced by Gilchrist Bros. Ltd,
Leeds
Typeset by Technical Editing Services,
London

David Minton; contributing editor. A motorcycle journalist and broadcaster, Minton has ridden, and written about, most bikes sold throughout the world. He has made marathon road journeys — into the Norwegian Arctic Circle, and from Alaska to Mexico.

Dave Taylor is Britain's foremost display rider and owner/operator of trail parks. He has been a road racer, trials and enduro competitor and is closely involved in the education of young riders.

Graham Bailey is a sergeant in London's Metropolitan Police. He is a driver/instructor and he has contributed to magazines and televison programmes on motorcycle safety. An ex-TT racer, he now rides in enduro events.

Peter Bickerstaff is an electronics engineer and technical writer who contributes regularly to motorcycle magazines. He is technical officer of the Vincent Owners Club.

Allan Ross is a qualified motorcycle mechanic who now writes technical articles for various motorcycle magazines.

— 8 —
INTRODUCTION
by Mike Hailwood

— 10 —
IDENTI-BIKE
anatomy of a motorcycle

— 32 —
BIKER'S CHOICE
a selection of machines

— 50 —
EQUIPMENT
for cycles and riders

— 80 —
MACHINE CONTROL
the basic skills

— 96 —
ROADCRAFT
the golden rules

—— 130 ——
HALL OF FAME
a generation of champions

—— 146 ——
THE SPORT
specialized events

—— 178 ——
TOURING
long distance information

—— 194 ——
CARE AND REPAIR
tools and techniques

—— 230 ——
APPENDIX
facts and figures

—— 234 ——
INDEX

Mike Hailwood, the most respected motorcycle racer of all time, was killed in a car accident just after writing this introduction to The Motorcyclist's Handbook. *He had also chosen the men and machines for our* Hall of Fame *(page 130), an evaluation by "Mike the Bike" of the competition during his 20-year career.*

The publishers have retained his contributions for reasons expressed by his business partner Rod Gould, himself a world champion rider. "The pleasure Mike gained from motorcycling he wished to share; his fears for young riders involved him in their education. For both reasons he endorsed this book. In any case, no book about motorcycling would be complete without him."

Motorcycling is dangerous, and it is much more dangerous on the road than it is around a race track. For the same number of rider/miles the risks on the road are three and a half times greater than those facing racing motorcyclists around the TT circuit in the Isle of Man.

A motorcycle itself is not a dangerous machine, any more than it is complicated beyond understanding. The rider is the key. Of course, most accidents happen to youngsters, who are by their nature pretty wild. But from my own experience as a motorcycle dealer I know that the majority are caused by other road users. Few youngsters have the experience necessary for them to recognize this and ride defensively. I only wish all drivers had to ride a motorcycle for a year before driving a car, then perhaps motorcyclists would be treated more considerately.

Racers are fully aware of the danger they face. Like mountaineers and potholers they take all sorts of safety precautions. But it is strange how few young road riders are aware of their vulnerability or make any allowances for it.

In many respects riders these days are luckier than they were 20 years ago. The machines certainly are better than ever. When I returned to the Isle of Man in 1978, I was astonished at the improvements that had taken place in racing machinery since I last raced over the TT course in 1967. Everything was better — engine torque, tires, brakes, suspension, even the road surface. Most of all, though, it was the power of the engine that shook me. I had never travelled so fast on two wheels.

Road bikes have also improved; and riders now need much more skill to use them hard. Mind you, I do not see how anyone can use the full performance of a 750 for very long in safety these days.

The best way to start riding is to practise when you are really young, and learn machine control by riding an old bike around a field or trail park. It is no good wobbling off into heavy traffic and putting all your concentration into operating the clutch and gears when you should have your mind on what is going on around you. New riders should also take proper riding instruction.

Becoming a good road user is no easier than winning races and, although the rewards are different, they are just as satisfying. There is satisfaction to be gained from feeling yourself improve, from learning more about your machine, from saving money on maintenance bills and improving reliability, and from lower insurance premiums, of course. I quickly learned in racing that the combination of a good rider and well-prepared machine can improve the performance of an inferior design, but that bad riding and bad preparation will ruin the best bike in the world.

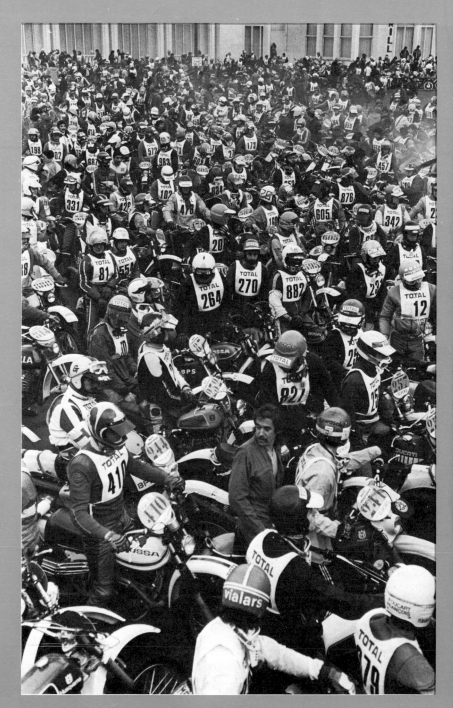

Motorcycle anatomy

The shape of the motorcycle was virtually standardized in 1902 when the German Werner brothers placed the 230cc engines of their heavy, bicycle-type machines low on the front down tube, just ahead of the pedal cranks.

Despite numerous attempts to alter the now traditional man-on-a-horse posture, nothing has fundamentally changed. Until recently the controlling factor in motorcycle design was the necessity for function to override form in all aspects. By the time Velocette introduced the foot gear change in 1928 the entire riding position and control layout system was seemingly irrevocably, and correctly, established.

When America reawoke to the pleasures of motorcycling in the 1950s the *appearance* of a motorcycle suddenly became paramount. Form now frequently preceded function, and this led to some utterly discordant shapes and performances. Impractically small fuel tanks, exaggerated handlebar bends and forward footrests, knobbly tires on roadsters—all are retrogressive yet immensely popular features. Fortunately, the mainstream of motorcycle design continues to progress, although frequently along costly and unimaginative lines. Apart from the radical Quasar concept, the future of functional design can best be seen in Honda's Gold Wing underseat fuel tank and through BMW's R100RS fairing and R80 G/S true swinging arm suspension.

A motorcycle is completely unrelated to a car and presents its builders with a task more formidable than that facing a car's designers. How else can it be when a rider is, almost literally, part of his machine? To each foot a brake or gear control; to each hand a brake or clutch lever; and to each thumb and forefinger, important switches. A motorcycle does not cradle its rider but exposes him to his own shortcomings. Thus a motorcycle is the way it is because of the way man is and it will stay that way until man changes.

1 Warning lights—ignition, battery charge, neutral gear, oil, turn, main beam, etc.
2 Headlight
3 Illuminated tachometer (rev counter)
4 Main lighting and ignition switch

5 Speedometer
6 Brake lever
7 Throttle

12 Seat mount
13 Seat clamp
14 Battery
15 Air cleaner/filter
16 Rubber tank buffer
17 Twin-cylinder 4-stroke sohc engine
18 Wiring harness
19 H/T leads

20 Disc brake assembly fitted to cast aluminium wheel
21 Horn
22 Bottom triple clamp
23 Top triple clamp
24 Clutch lever
25 Steering head

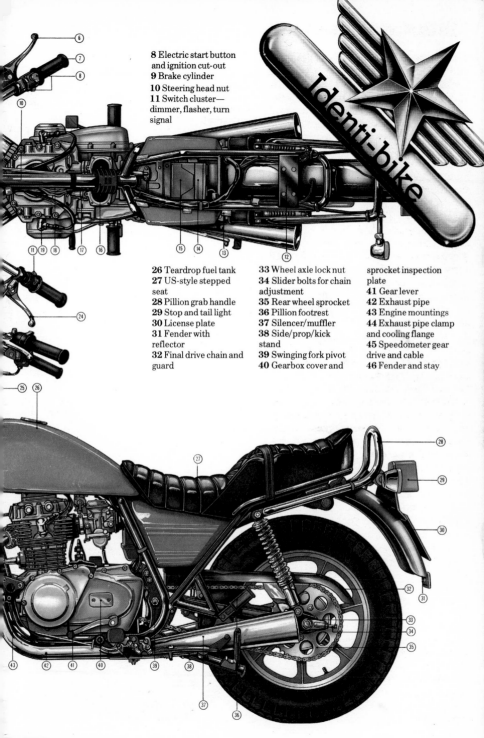

8 Electric start button and ignition cut-out
9 Brake cylinder
10 Steering head nut
11 Switch cluster—dimmer, flasher, turn signal

Identi-bike

26 Teardrop fuel tank
27 US-style stepped seat
28 Pillion grab handle
29 Stop and tail light
30 License plate
31 Fender with reflector
32 Final drive chain and guard

33 Wheel axle lock nut
34 Slider bolts for chain adjustment
35 Rear wheel sprocket
36 Pillion footrest
37 Silencer/muffler
38 Side/prop/kick stand
39 Swinging fork pivot
40 Gearbox cover and

sprocket inspection plate
41 Gear lever
42 Exhaust pipe
43 Engine mountings
44 Exhaust pipe clamp and cooling flange
45 Speedometer gear drive and cable
46 Fender and stay

Motorcycle anatomy/2

Since the turn of the century the weight of the average tourer has increased by a probable 350 per cent.

An old engineering dictum states that machinery can be made more attractive by adding to its complexity, and this is what has happened to the motorcycle. The electric starter motor is a prime example. On its own, it weighs a mere 9lb, but it requires a clutch and drive mechanism, a solenoid, a housing, a heftier battery and a more powerful generator. This leads to beefed-up crankshaft and crankcases and then to heavier frame and suspension, bigger brakes and a more robust transmission.

BMW, almost alone, has remained loyal to traditions of design purity. The brilliantly conceived and spectacular motorcycles from Japan owe their allegiance to consumer desire, not engineering principles.

A Euro-styled motorcycle which is only superficially different from the US version. The design of the twin-cylinder engine and frame is identical. Tank, seat and handlebars are more practical and less flamboyant than those of the American cousin. The traditional spoke wheels and drum brakes are fitted as standard on many machines.

1 Turn signal relay
2 Voltage control unit
3 Air filter/cleaner
4 Carburetor(s)
5 Full loop duplex cradle frame
6 Throttle cable

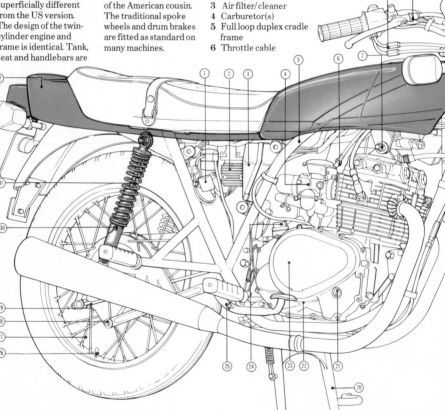

16	Brake shoes and springs	21	Oil level inspection window	25	Rear brake lever	29	Brake rod
17	Brake drum	22	Crankcase including sump	26	Tire valve	30	Suspension load adjuster
18	Hydraulic fluid drain plug	23	Primary drive and clutch cover	27	Wire-spoked wheel. Nipples provide tension adjustment	31	Rear suspension unit/shock absorber
19	Lever to operate brake cam	24	Engine oil filler cap	28	Brake plate and anchor arm	32	Tail locker for toolkit and owner's manual
20	Centerstand						

In the late 1960s Soichiro Honda carried out what must be one of the most successful publicity campaigns in history. He revitalized a dying industry so successfully that a minor social revolution occurred. "You meet the nicest people on a Honda," claimed the advertisements. The world discovered, to its surprise and delight, that it was true. For the first time people went motorcycling with clean fingernails.

Suspension types

A stiffly sprung girder front fork was the only suspension available until 1947—with rare exceptions. Many systems were tried, but after that date the telescopic front and pivoted, or swinging, rear forks dominated.

Girder. High unsprung weight; stiff, heavy action; immense rigidity.

Plunger. Short, stiff action; weak wheel mounting; chain snatch.

Leading link. Difficult to design, easy to build. Light action, strong.

Cantilever. Immense rigidity; single unit; long movement.

Earles type. Excellent suspension but steering is affected by pendulum motion.

Swinging arm (as BMW R80 G/S). Difficult to design, easy to construct.

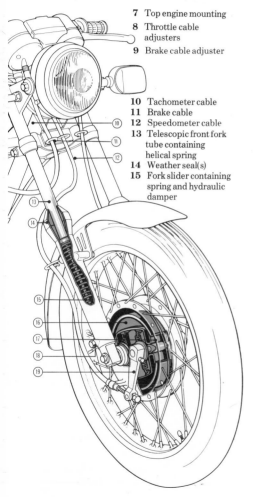

7 Top engine mounting
8 Throttle cable adjusters
9 Brake cable adjuster

10 Tachometer cable
11 Brake cable
12 Speedometer cable
13 Telescopic front fork tube containing helical spring
14 Weather seal(s)
15 Fork slider containing spring and hydraulic damper

The 2-stroke engine

As every piston downstroke is a power stroke, the simple 2-stroke engine has a high power potential. But in the early days of motorcycling, the performance of most 2-strokes was no match for the more complex 4-stroke. Designers, therefore, exploited the 2-stroke's simplicity with cheap, single cylinder engines of modest power and efficiency.

Recent designs, however, feature small, high-revving, multi-cylinder engines producing high power but with increased complication. The inevitable mixing of fresh and exhaust gases leads to high fuel consumption and excessive hydrocarbon emissions. This, together with problems of cooling and lubrication, is the main disadvantage and the reason why modern competition 2-strokes are fuel hungry, noisy and prone to seizure.

On the induction stroke, the rising piston uncovers an inlet port and draws

Compression/Induction

The rising piston compresses the air/fuel mixture in the cylinder and uncovers the inlet port for fresh mixture to enter.

Cylinders are cast, with gas passages, in light aluminium alloy to conduct heat. Hard wearing cast-iron liners have machined port openings.

Combustion

The spark from the plug ignites the mixture in the combustion chamber which expands, pushing the piston down.

A crankshaft-driven disc valve permits independent control of port opening and closing.

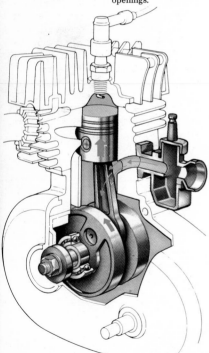

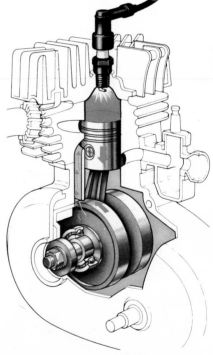

Cylinder heads are finned to dissipate heat. Combustion chambers may be surrounded by squish bands to promote turbulence.

Pistons are cast in 15 per cent silicon-aluminium alloy. Flexible cast-iron rings provide a high pressure gas seal.

Controlled by piston position, transfer ports direct mixture from crankcase to cylinder. Number and position are arranged for best scavenging.

Engine temperatures. Combustion: 3,632°F Piston ring grooves: 392°F max. Piston crown: 572–662°F Bearings: up to 212°F Carburetor: 50°F

mixture from the carburetor into the gas-tight crankcase, while compressing the mixture already in the cylinder. In the last 20 degrees before top dead center (BTDC) the mixture in the combustion chamber is ignited. The expanding, burnt gas pushes the piston back down, compressing the mixture beneath until this is pushed back up into the cylinder through transfer ports, which have been exposed by the piston.

When the exhaust port is uncovered the burnt gas is released. The exhaust shockwave is used to clear the cylinder (scavenging) as more mixture enters, via the transfer port, from the crankcase where it is already half way through its cycle. Additional ports may be included, or transfer controlled by windows in the piston which are angled carefully to chase out residual gas; intermixing of the gas streams reduces efficiency.

Transfer/Exhaust

The burnt gas is released, while the piston compresses the new mixture in the crankcase, forcing it up into the cylinder.

A reed valve, operated by gas flow, reduces blowback through piston controlled inlet ports, improving power and flexibility.

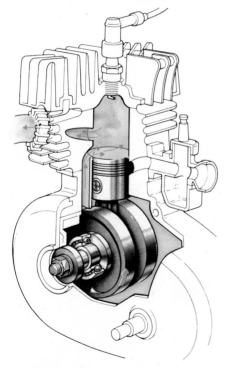

The Wankel engine is not a reciprocating motor. It uses a circular motion but retains the induction, compression, combustion, exhaust cycle. The varying volume above a piston is replaced by three variable chambers formed between a rotor and trochoidal casing. Rotor motion is not purely rotary, necessitating a gear and eccentric coupling to the mainshaft. Inlet and exhaust is controlled by rotor tips passing ports. Suzuki, DKW, Van Veen and Norton are among the few marques to have designed rotary-engined bikes in the 1970s.

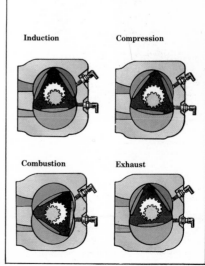

Induction   Compression

Combustion   Exhaust

Oil must lubricate bearings adequately without combustion chamber fouling. The need, in older machines, to mix oil and fuel in the tank has been obviated by a throttle and engine speed controlled pump metering 0.1 to 3 cc/minute directly to the bearings.

The 4-stroke engine

The 4-stroke (or Otto cycle, after its inventor) completes the induction, compression, combustion and exhaust actions in four separate strokes of the piston. This well-defined inlet and exhaust cycle permits the design of engines for flexibility, economy and clean combustion as well as just for power. Weighing against it is the complicated, and therefore expensive, valve gear. The fact that only one in four strokes is a power stroke makes a single cylinder engine run unevenly unless a heavy, counterbalanced flywheel is fitted on the crankshaft.

The early engines were flexible (many veteran bikes were single-speed and clutchless) and simple (gas flow operated automatic inlet valves), but they were slow (cast-iron pistons). Improved technology and racing development over the years have vastly increased performance and reliability (pumped lubrication, improved valve layouts, multi cylinders), although with added complexity.

The inlet and exhaust passages are controlled by poppet valves, which are held against their seatings by springs until pushed open by the camshaft – usually over the cylinder head on modern bikes (ohc).

The obsolete sidevalve (sv) layout was simple to make and maintain, but had an inefficient combustion chamber shape. Retaining the crankcase-mounted

Induction
With the inlet valve held open by the revolving camshaft, and the piston falling, an air/fuel mixture is sucked in from the carburetor.

1 camshaft
2 cam chain
3 rocker
4 inlet valve & spring
5 piston valve
6 needle
7 jet
8 float
9 venturi

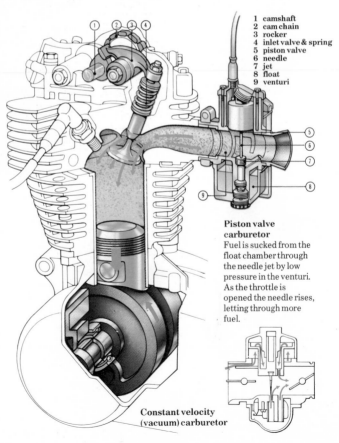

Piston valve carburetor
Fuel is sucked from the float chamber through the needle jet by low pressure in the venturi. As the throttle is opened the needle rises, letting through more fuel.

Fuel injection
Solid-state electronics monitors all engine parameters and calculates the required fuel quantity (less than 1/100 cc) at each inlet stroke. A fine electrical pump injects it into the manifold. Close control for power, economy and clean emissions is possible under all conditions.

Constant velocity (vacuum) carburetor

camshaft but using pushrods to operate valves in the head over the piston (ohv) permits a compact combustion chamber – necessary for minimum heat loss and the avoidance of gas pockets.

The increased valve train weight and flexure of overhead valves can be reduced by using a single overhead camshaft near the valves (sohc). This shaft is driven at half crankshaft speed, often by using a chain and sprockets with 2:1 diameters. The drive from the crankshaft to the camshaft may alternatively be by toothed belt, gears, or shaft and bevels. Drive may be either direct or via intermediate shafts.

Valves wider than half the bore can be accommodated in compact chambers by inclining them to the cylinder axis as in the hemispherical head. Pushrod or camshaft rockers transfer motion to these inclined valves, but to eliminate the reciprocating weight and flexure of the rockers, double overhead camshafts (dohc) are required: one for the inlet, one for the exhaust. This is not too complicated for use on multi-cylinder, in-line engines, where all the cylinders can be served by the two camshafts.

Engines with short strokes (length of piston travel) have larger bores, permitting bigger valves to be housed. Some engines have multiple-valve heads, which offer large port areas, for better breathing, and lower valve train stress and improved cooling.

Compression
Both valves are closed as the piston rises, compressing the mixture to 11.23 kg/sq.cm. (160psi).

Pistons
Modern pistons, made of low expansion, silicon-aluminium alloy run in iron-lined light alloy cylinders. An oil control piston ring below the two plain compression rings scrapes oil from the bore of a 4-stroke and returns it to the crankcase via holes and slots in ring and piston. The oil, which is in contact with the cylinder walls, cools the piston.

Constant velocity carburetor (left)
The choke is restricted by a slide, automatically lifted by a vacuum chamber communicating with the venturi. Total quantity is regulated by a butterfly.

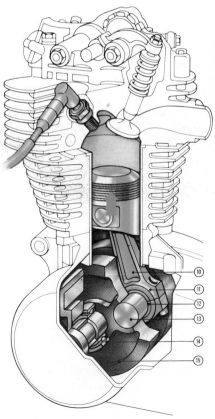

Crankshafts
When ball and roller main bearings and big ends are used (in 2-strokes and many 4-strokes) the crankshaft has to be built up. The bearings are included while pressing together the separate shafts and flywheels. Built-up cranks require little lubrication and are low in friction. The superior lubrication of a high pressure 4-stroke oil system permits the use of split-shell, plain bearings which can be assembled round a one-piece forged and machined crankshaft. One-piece cranks are cheaper, strong and simple to produce, but they require heat treatment for the best compromise of wear and strength properties.

10 connecting rod
11 big end
12 split shell bearing
13 crankpin
14 ball race main bearing
15 flywheel

4-stroke/2

Reduced piston strokes have led to wider cylinder bores and bigger combustion chambers. Yet high octane fuels require *small* combustion spaces for the high compression ratios which produce power and efficiency. The resulting domed pistons, with recessed cutouts for the valves, intrude into the chamber, spoiling the ideal hemispherical shape.

During the few milliseconds when combustion takes place, temperatures in the chamber approach 3,632°F and maximum pressure reaches 14 kg/sq cm (200 psi). High, localized pressures and temperatures cause damage to the combustion chamber, so remote pockets of gas must be avoided. Some pistons are, therefore, designed with flat crowns

and squish bands to produce the turbulence which ensures mixture uniformity.

An alternative is to fashion the chamber in a concave piston crown, leaving more freedom to site the valves in the head for good gas flow. Even parallel, vertical valves can be used, but this results in a piston which is slightly heavier and runs hotter.

To allow time for the gas streams, and the valves themselves, to move there is a period in the 4-stroke cycle known as valve overlap. On the upward exhaust stroke the inlet valve begins to open 35° before top dead center to let in new mixture, while the exhaust valve finishes closing 30° after TDC.

Combustion

The valves remain closed as the spark ignites the mixture, 5° to 35° BTDC. The burnt gas expands to reach maximum pressure as the piston begins its downward power stroke. Before the end of the stroke, the exhaust valve begins to open.

1 H/T lead
2 Squish band

The flame spreads at approximately 8 ft/sec (2.5 m/sec). Combustion temperatures exceed metal melting points and exhaust gas is hotter than 932°F (500°C), yet even hot plugs points and exhaust valves must not exceed 1,472°F (800°C) or damaging premature ignition may occur.

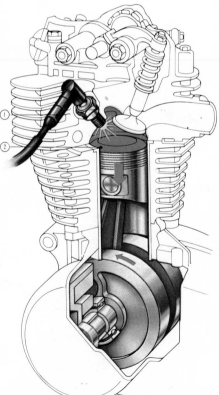

Ignition

In ignition systems using a contact breaker and coil, the electrical current flows from the battery through closed points to the coil. This current magnetizes the coil's iron core. The weak (12 or 6V) current passing through the primary windings creates a strong magnetic field in the coil's secondary windings.

When the contact breaker points are opened, the magnetic field collapses, generating a powerful current (approx. 22,000 volts), which is directed through the high tension (H/T) lead to the plug, where it jumps the gap creating the spark. A weaker collapse occurs in the primary windings, which is stored in the condenser to stop sparking at the points.

Ignition timing

To generate maximum power the spark must be synchronized with the position of the piston. The timing of the spark is dependent on the opening of the contact breaker points, which is controlled by a cam turning with the crankshaft.

As the engine revs rise, the cam is mechanically accelerated a few degrees ahead of the crankshaft. So the faster the engine turns, the earlier the spark must be delivered, increasing pressure and temperature in the chamber as steadily as possible. But if timing is too far advanced, combustion will occur before the piston has reached the top.

On a typically standard engine, timing will vary from 5°BTDC (the retard position) at low revs to 35°BTDC (advance). This applies only to 4-strokes; 2-stroke timing does not vary.

Electronic systems are much more accurate, with none of the inevitable fluttering common to the mechanical operation. Typical is Honda's capacitor discharge ignition (CDI). A special coil on the alternator passes a magnet, each time collapsing the magnetic field and charging a capacitor. A thyristor, or electronic switch, is thereby triggered, passing on the charge to the H/T coil at the correct time.

The faster the engine runs, the more powerful the initial current becomes, so triggering the ignition charge in advance. A limiter cuts in at approximately 4,000 revs to stop the advance.

Exhaust

An upward stroke, with the exhaust valve open, pushes out residual gas and ensures a clear cylinder for a repeat of the cycle.

The 4-stroke's wet sump lubrication system pumps oil to all the engine bearings through oilways, including crankshaft drillings which may receive oil from the main bearings. Oil return is by gravity to the sump, and filtering is done by paper elements, magnetic drain plugs, or centrifugal filters. Plain bearings require a large high pressure, 3.5 kg/sq cm (50 psi), supply to keep the surfaces apart. Cylinder head cooling is impeded by camboxes and so the oil has to remove heat as well as lubricate—maintaining a working temperature of 212–356°F (100–180°C) to evaporate condensation without oxidizing the oil.

Gas is exhausted at 4.2 kg/sq cm (60 psi) and 1,112°F (600°C) into the exhaust pipe, which must dispose of it at low pressure with little heat returned to the already hot valve. Steel pipes, narrow joint faces and a cooling flange are used.

19

Exhaust/silencing

The noise of the explosion leaves the internal combustion engine with the spent gas via the exhaust system. The muffler must accept the slugs of hot gas into a reservoir and use baffles to smooth it into a steady stream. Siamese (two, three or four into one) or balance pipes help to maintain a steady flow, but may affect exhaust pipe tuning.

The release of exhaust gas sets up a high pressure wave, which travels at about 1,500 ft/sec, according to temperature, pressure and pipe diameter. The open end (and siamese or balance pipe junction) reflects this as a low pressure wave and if the pipe length matches engine speed it can be returned, timed to improve scavenging. The design of high-performance exhaust systems is therefore dependent on engine speed.

Some countries and some American states require spark arrestors on the tailpipe to safeguard dry vegetation. With an efficiently silenced exhaust the inlet fluctuations become more noticeable and so large air filter boxes are also designed as mufflers. Without a water jacket to damp out mechanical noise, air cooled engines must be designed for quiet running. Belt-driven cams or rubber damping between fins are often used to minimize engine noise.

Manufacturers build to the most stringent requirements. Bikes for the world market, therefore, comply with US emission regulations and the lowest noise limits.

In the muffler the flow of exhaust gas (indicated by arrows) is strictly controlled. Gas enters each expansion compartment through one connecting pipe and leaves via another; finally leaving the muffler through the perforated baffle tube.

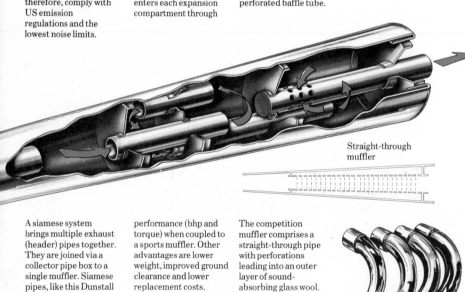

Straight-through muffler

A siamese system brings multiple exhaust (header) pipes together. They are joined via a collector pipe box to a single muffler. Siamese pipes, like this Dunstall set, give improved performance (bhp and torque) when coupled to a sports muffler. Other advantages are lower weight, improved ground clearance and lower replacement costs.

The competition muffler comprises a straight-through pipe with perforations leading into an outer layer of sound-absorbing glass wool.

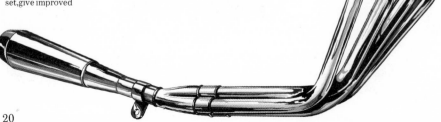

Two-stroke

The piston controlled ports of a 2-stroke can open very rapidly, creating an exhaust shock wave on which power output is dependent. In any engine an open pipe end reflects such a wave as a negative pressure or partial vacuum, but in a 2-stroke a tapered end-pipe is used to broaden this pulse which helps suck out the exhaust gas. (This is not always fully utilized on roadsters because of the increased noise.)

Unfortunately, fresh mixture transferred by crankcase pressure may also flow out of the exhaust port during overlap. The exploitation of exhaust resonance makes this unavoidable. A reverse-tapered section gives a positive reflected pulse, forcing the return of the mixture just before port closure. The two tapered sections form the expansion box. The waves travel at the speed of sound so fixed dimensions can only suit a limited range of engine speeds (the power band).

The expansion chamber forms a reservoir for a muffler, and the reverse taper leads to a restricted output which is not seriously affected by additional baffling to smooth out gas flow at the outlet. A 2-stroke roadster's muffler takes this form and is also tuned to match the engine.

Tuned exhaust pipe
for racing 2-stroke

header   taper   tailpipe
expansion box   reverse taper

The construction of 2-stroke expansion chambers in a straight line is relatively simple. When the pipes have to be fitted to a motorcycle, however, they must be intricately tailored. Construction for optimum tuning then becomes a less-than-exact science.

Off-road machines must wear their pipes high to preserve ground clearance. This bike is fitted with a spark arrestor box on the tailpipe.

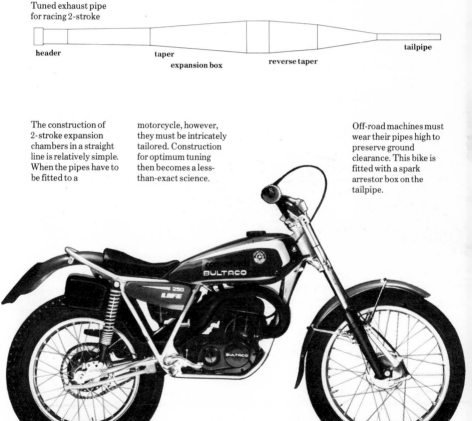

Transmission

The fierce reciprocation caused by explosive combustion forces is transformed into a smooth turning movement by the jointed coupling of the piston(s) to the crankshaft.

On most motorcycles, the turning force (torque) is transmitted by either chain or gear drive to the clutch, which transfers drive to the gearbox mainshaft on which the clutch is mounted. Power is then transferred from the mainshaft to the countershaft by the road gears in the gearbox. It is finally transmitted from the gearbox to the rear wheel by chain, shaft or belt.

The clutch is simply a set of friction plates, splined to an engine-driven outer

drum, driving an interleaved set splined to the gearbox shaft. Its purpose is to interrupt the drive from the engine to the wheel. When pushed apart by a rod through the mainshaft (cable-connected to the handlebar lever) the plates can rotate independently, allowing a gear to be selected. Springs press the plates together to create friction drive when the lever is released.

Each gear ratio is provided by driving through a different pair of gearwheels. Unused pairs remain in constant mesh but one of the pair runs free on its shaft. When a gear is selected a dog clutch, splined to the shaft, slides along until its projections engage with those of the

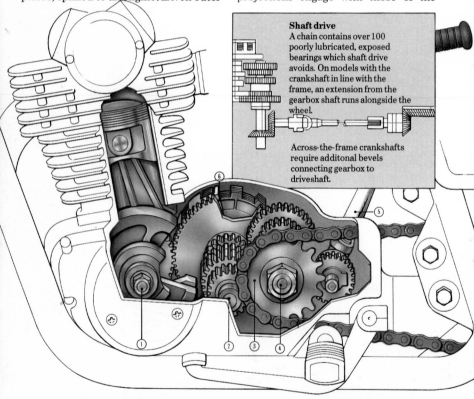

Shaft drive
A chain contains over 100 poorly lubricated, exposed bearings which shaft drive avoids. On models with the crankshaft in line with the frame, an extension from the gearbox shaft runs alongside the wheel.

Across-the-frame crankshafts require additonal bevels connecting gearbox to driveshaft.

1 crankshaft
2 gearbox mainshaft
3 gearbox sprocket
4 countershaft
5 kickstart

6 clutch plates have high-friction surfaces which bind them together when pressed by clutch springs.

Belt drive avoids chain wear, without shaft expense. V-belt drive still finds application on low powered mopeds.

Toothed rubber belting is now strong enough for final drives. Harley-Davidson use toothed pulleys like sprockets.

gearwheel to lock it to the shaft. These dogs are moved by selector forks with pins engaging in cam grooves, usually in the rotating drum. This selector drum is notched to locate the gear positions and rotated by the positive stop ratchet mechanism.

Between two and six gears may be provided, according to engine characteristics. An engine may produce maximum power at 8,000rpm, sufficient to propel the motorcycle on the level at 80mph with a rear wheel speed of 2,000rpm. A top gear ratio of 4:1 is, therefore, required between the engine and rear wheel, and is provided mainly by reductions in the primary and rear

drives. Lower gears permit the machine to be run at slower road speeds in the same rev range.

Automatic transmission

A torque convertor consists of an engine-driven impellor circulating oil through fixed or freewheeling vanes to drive an output turbine. At low output-speed torque is high, reducing as speed rises to that of the input. Clutch and gears are largely redundant, although a two-speed manual gearbox is retained to extend torque range. Several mopeds and heavier machines, including Honda 400s and Moto Guzzis, use this system.

Shock absorber Power impulses, road bumps and gear changes mismatch flywheel and rear wheel speeds, causing harshness and stress.

To absorb these shocks, the rear wheel incorporates a set of rubber blocks, sandwiched between driving and driven vanes.

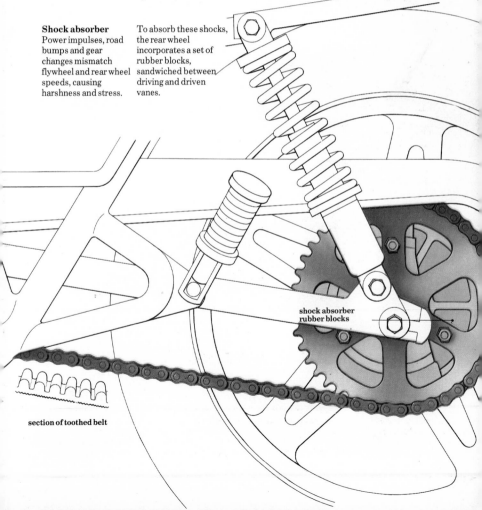

shock absorber rubber blocks

section of toothed belt

Twin-cylinder layouts

The earliest motorcycles had single cylinders and they vibrated. Engine vibration is caused by the reciprocation of the piston assembly as it changes direction at the top and bottom of its stroke. This inertia force occurring in the vertical plane, and another force, which is caused by the horizontal movement of the connecting rod, have the effect of shaking the engine.

If a frame were sufficiently heavy to absorb this vibration the machine would be unridably massive. To avoid such excessive frame adaption, counterweights are built into the crankshaft. Bike designers adjust the crankshaft balance factor and carefully tune the frame to ensure that the vibration frequencies cancel one another.

Parallel twins suffer from an unjustified reputation for strong vibration. This came about largely from the British adoption of single cylinder frames which harmonize with engine vibration. In fact a parallel twin produces half the inertia force of a single at any given engine speed.

The 500cc Triumph Speed Twin of 1937 was so successful because it was almost as cheap to make as a single; was smoother, provided a pleasant torque flow and sounded exciting. Its lighter reciprocating parts permitted higher revs.

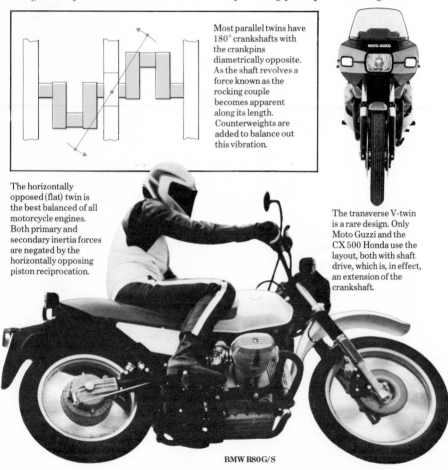

Most parallel twins have 180° crankshafts with the crankpins diametrically opposite. As the shaft revolves a force known as the rocking couple becomes apparent along its length. Counterweights are added to balance out this vibration.

The horizontally opposed (flat) twin is the best balanced of all motorcycle engines. Both primary and secondary inertia forces are negated by the horizontally opposing piston reciprocation.

The transverse V-twin is a rare design. Only Moto Guzzi and the CX 500 Honda use the layout, both with shaft drive, which is, in effect, an extension of the crankshaft.

BMW R80G/S

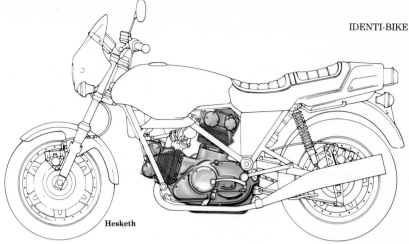

Hesketh

By adding a second cylinder at 90° to the first, a single can conveniently be turned into a V-twin. The primary inertia force that troubles the single is negated by the pistons moving at right angles to each other as in Hesketh and Ducati engines. Other popular V-twins are Harley-Davidson (42°), Vincent (50°) and Moto Morini (72°), but these can never be as smooth as a 90° layout. Many knowledgeable enthusiasts claim V-twins are the finest design of all because they are light, low and have a small frontal area. Others enjoy the irregular heartbeat syncopation of the exhaust note.

Norton Commando

When NVT introduced the 750 (later 850cc) Norton Commando in 1969, they opted for rubber-mounting of the entire engine, transmission and rear wheel systems, naming it the Isolastic principle. The pivoted fork spindle was bolted to the gearbox. High speed stability was excellent until the main rubber mounts became sloppy. The light weight, high torque and smooth ride made the Commando one of the most pleasant of all motorcycles.

In 1946 Sunbeam rubber-mounted their 500cc S7 in-line parallel twin engine. The sohc, 85mph, shaft drive, luxury tourer was as smooth as silk to ride.

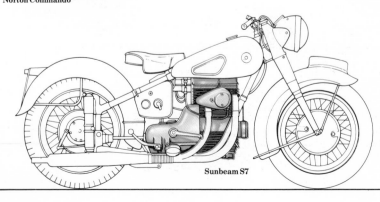

Sunbeam S7

25

Multi-cylinders

A three is probably the finest in-line engine layout of all because it has the best inherent balance. Providing each crankpin is positioned at 120°, no counterweights are required; each piston assembly balances the other.

Four-cylinder engines are not quite the paragons of vibrationless running some people imagine. Their primary inertia force is negated by opposing piston assembly reciprocation and the rocking couple is balanced out, but a secondary inertia force operates.

No motorcycle manufacturer has ever achieved commercial production of an orthodox five, although the German Megola company put a five on the market in the 1920s and Honda raced a 125cc five-cylinder in the 1960s.

A six-cylinder engine develops neither primary nor secondary inertia force, and it runs without a rocking couple. It would be the designer's and rider's dream if it were not for its great bulk.

The Kawasaki range of threes in 250, 500 and 750cc capacity were searingly fast 2-strokes. Triumph and BSA made and raced 4-stroke threes in the early 1970s but Laverda and Yamaha make the only current three-cylinder bikes.

Honda started the current trend for multi-cylinder machines, when they introduced their big road-going fours after an extremely successful racing program during the 1960s.

All the sixes are silky-smooth to ride and, thanks to their lightly loaded reciprocating parts, are mechanically quiet and should last a long time. Their girth could be avoided by using a V layout.

Honda CBX

26

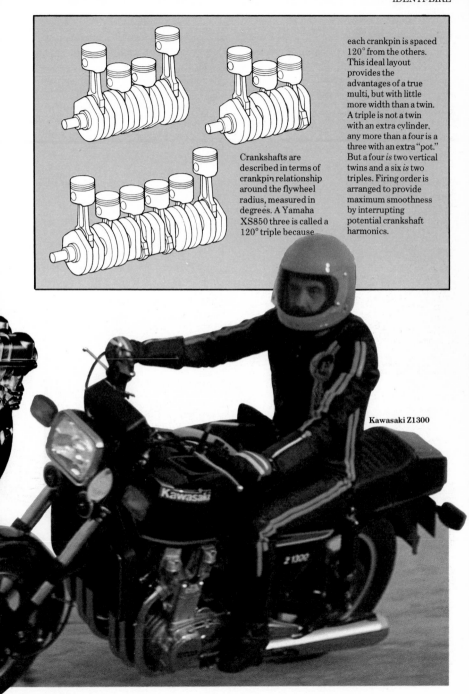

Crankshafts are described in terms of crankpin relationship around the flywheel radius, measured in degrees. A Yamaha XS850 three is called a 120° triple because each crankpin is spaced 120° from the others. This ideal layout provides the advantages of a true multi, but with little more width than a twin. A triple is not a twin with an extra cylinder, any more than a four is a three with an extra "pot." But a four *is* two vertical twins and a six *is* two triples. Firing order is arranged to provide maximum smoothness by interrupting potential crankshaft harmonics.

Kawasaki Z1300

Design for the future

To forecast the future of the motorcycle beyond ten years is impossible. Yet its immediate evolution is open to conjecture.

The principal factor will undoubtedly be fuel shortage and cost. Whatever the fuel of the future is to be, it will be liquid, because gases are unsuited to easy handling. The average big bike will probably use a water cooled engine of about 400cc with one or maybe two cylinders. Four parallel valves per combustion chamber will be operated by a sohc driven by toothed belt. The crankshaft will run on plain bearings requiring 5,000 mile oil changes. All this simplicity will contrast horribly with the means of improving combustion efficiency. To ensure accurate timing of the ignition spark in the correct fresh mixture, a complex system will be controlled by a box of silicon chips.

The current trend towards partial enclosure by way of an aerodynamically stable fairing will continue, but penetration shaping will be improved to reduce fuel consumption. Because of its high cost, plastic will not be as popular as was once anticipated, but its use will have spread to a good many light load-bearing components. It is probable that smaller wheels of possibly 16 inch diameter will be general, and they will be fitted with lock-resistant brakes required by future obligatory standards imposed on manufacturers.

If development continues as it is now—which is *most* unlikely—a typical large tourer of the mid-1990s will probably concede a debt of conception to the Quasar. This machine suffered originally from a fundamental problem in that the technology and production methods available to its creators could not match their ideal.

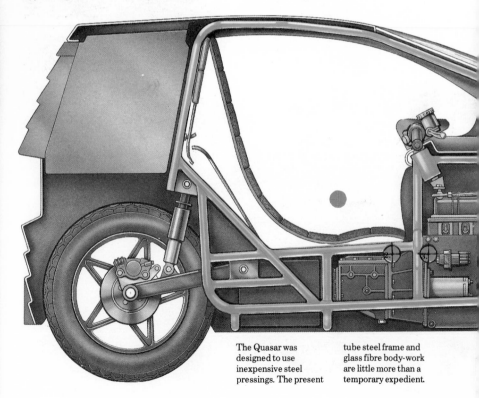

The Quasar was designed to use inexpensive steel pressings. The present tube steel frame and glass fibre body-work are little more than a temporary expedient.

The Porsche Yamaha is a design exercise; but it is no more than a stylishly modern plastic variation on an old theme. Component encapsulation has been attempted since the 1920s but its practical value is minimal.

The radical Elf-X is, however, a truly advanced motorcycle in which function has been given priority over form. This has led to numerous commercial advantages, such as cheap disc wheels. It has hub center steering which is not affected by suspension action. The fuel tank is beneath the engine to keep the CofG low. The lighter exhaust pipes are routed above.

As streamlining follows its predictable path then the shape of the future must resemble that of the Quasar.

An idea of the Quasar's potential can best be appreciated in its comparatively crude construction yet impressive performance. Using an 850cc, 41 bhp cheap car engine (Reliant), Newell and Leaman have built a motorcycle capable of cruising at 100 mph, which will return 50mpg(US) when used a fraction less enthusiastically, despite weighing a gross 780lb with rider.

1. Center of wind pressure
2. Center of gravity loaded
3. Center of gravity static

Frame kits

The average production-line roadster frame is too full of compromises to handle the full power of the engine it cradles without exhibiting some form of high speed waywardness.

Riders with sufficient funds available who wish to ride fast and hard may be tempted by the range of sports/racing frame kits which change completely the manners and appearance of a cycle. But motorcycles of this quality are not built for their aesthetic appeal. They are singularly functional machines and it is this that gives them their form. Unless you are a truly expert rider spend your money elsewhere, because only at the point where ordinary men and machines begin to quail do bikes such as these come into their own.

The basic rules to apply when choosing a racing-type frame are: buy only from a company that relies on a racing program for machine development; buy only a frame manufactured specifically for your particular model (adaptation requires great skill and is expensive); ensure that both you and the frame kit supplier have all the details for assembly immediately at hand.

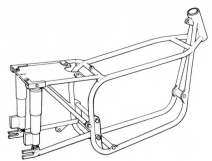

The Norton Featherbed frame epitomizes the cradle type. The frame, which is designed to resist flexure, was frequently used by special builders to house other makes of engine. Most roadsters use cradle frames.

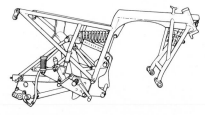

The Swiss-made Moko, or Egli-type frame is designed on the principle developed by Vincent HRD. Since the engine is the most rigid component of a motorcycle it is used as a frame member beneath an upper spine.

The single unit cantilever suspension is adjustable for spring and damping strength.

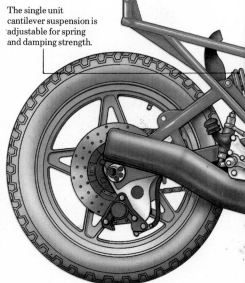

The race-type fairing is fixed to the frame with quickly-detachable fasteners.

Single and double seats can be interchanged.

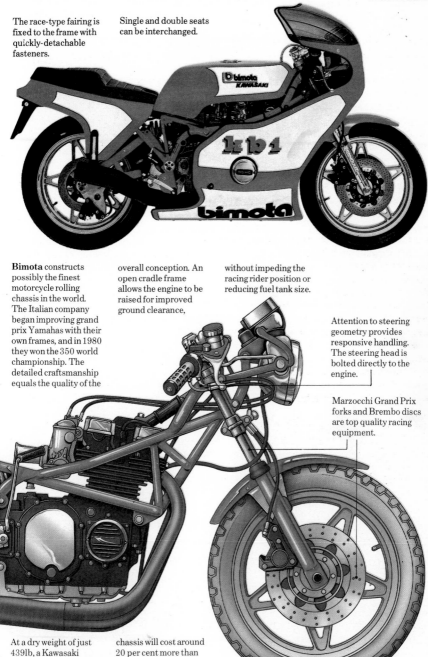

Bimota constructs possibly the finest motorcycle rolling chassis in the world. The Italian company began improving grand prix Yamahas with their own frames, and in 1980 they won the 350 world championship. The detailed craftsmanship equals the quality of the overall conception. An open cradle frame allows the engine to be raised for improved ground clearance, without impeding the racing rider position or reducing fuel tank size.

Attention to steering geometry provides responsive handling. The steering head is bolted directly to the engine.

Marzocchi Grand Prix forks and Brembo discs are top quality racing equipment.

At a dry weight of just 439lb, a Kawasaki Z1000 engined Bimota weighs less than most 500s. But a rolling chassis will cost around 20 per cent more than the complete original motorcycle.

31

The motorcycle market

Never make the fundamental error of assuming that all small motorcycles are utilitarian and that all big motorcycles are luxury sportsters. As with cars, bikes can be classified, although frequently with an apparent subtlety that only knowledgeable motorcycle buffs seem able to appreciate.

To the newcomer, all bikes look alike, and even potentially useful questions are impossible to ask because of the hopelessly alien style of the whole business of motorcycling. On the one hand you face warnings of death-dealing danger from those who dislike it, and on the other an impenetrable mystique of shared secrets by the in-crowd. Take notice of neither party, but go your own way, slowly, one step at a time, at a pace you feel happy with, never moving into areas beyond your understanding or ability to control.

Novice riders who find their choice of bike restricted by law should concede that many lightweight sports machines are too powerful for inexperienced hands.

Once you have a year or two's experience behind you, you will be ready to choose something which matches your real requirements. But beware—this period is only a little less dangerous than your first six months' noviciate, and your roadcraft will not be a match for your apparent machine handling skills. Unless you have developed a sense of total motorcycling awareness in unusually short time, take it easy. Few people at this stage can handle much more than a modern 400cc sports-tourer, used to its performance extremes.

However, few people are willing to put up with the restrictions imposed by a small engine once the honeymoon period is over. Any attempt habitually to force a small machine along at full speed will wear it out prematurely, and overtaking is dangerously protracted in comparison with a larger motorcycle. Heavier bikes are more stable and more relaxing on longer journeys, and their riders experience less bullying by other traffic. It can be appreciated, then, that the

desire for a big bike must be subject to reason. For your own sake, balance lust against practicality and safety.

You will also need to know something about the various classes of motorcycles available. As will be seen in the following pages, the categories overlap, both in design and performance. Engine capacity is connected to, but not responsible for, classification.

Utilities are the cheap machines built to a rock-bottom price with few other considerations. But as dictated by American tastes, street machines can be stylish and fun, if more expensive than bikes for less affluent markets.

Commuters are similar, but good fuel consumption is their primary attraction, as well as a degree of sophistication to make them pleasant to ride in a strictly functional manner. Thus, many mopeds have automatic transmission, and many commuter bikes have electric starters.

Dirt bikes are for fun, pure and simple. The best, such as the Yamaha 175MX, can be used equally well as a heavy traffic commuter and for weekend club enduros. They generally produce less power at high revs than their sports-tourer equivalents, but have better power development at low engine speed. Few will accept pillion passengers, luggage, or weather equipment.

Tourers and sports-tourers form the backbone of motorcycle production. Within this loosely defined classification can be found almost all types of machine. People go to work on them, race them, customize them, drag them, take weekend trips and go round the world on them. A good many have higher top speeds than pure sportsters, while others cost less to run than utilities. An MZ 250/1 is a fine tourer, but it is a utility bike as well, and a commuter. A Kawasaki Z1300 is a tourer, as well as being a megacycle. A tourer must be able to accept weather shielding and luggage, and carry two people for a weekend in comfort at normal traffic speeds.

Sports cycles are lean and hungry

steeds built to encourage high speed rider exploitation in safety. Many, therefore, are functional to the point of starkness and lack the niceties of low speed comfort, starting ease, pillion seats and suchlike. But they are loved by a small minority of knowledgeable and skilled buffs. The rear-set footrests and clip-on handlebars are there to improve the machine's stability and the rider's attitude to speed, *at* speed. And outright speed is of less account than the manner in which the machine deals with it. Most feel raw to use, and are not the nice sort of bike a good boy would take home to his mother.

Megacycles are a peculiar group of machines produced by most manufacturers because they, like so many motorcyclists, are unable to distinguish quantity from quality, and feel that an excess of anything must be better than a limited amount. For all their grossness, such motorcycles can be a delight to use, and offer comfort of a type quite unimaginable by the uninitiated. Harley-Davidson has always been in this league, but probably the first from Japan was that clipper-ship of the world's long highways—the Honda Gold Wing. It seems likely that bikes of this size will become less common as material and fuel costs rise.

Paradoxycles have always been around. The best/worst/most interesting have usually been built by a manufacturer attempting to provide the non-expert with a machine that will outperform an orthodox motorcycle. Most are outstanding in a strictly limited performance bracket, but are horribly disadvantaged in all other areas. The sole exceptions are military motorcycles which are probably the best all-rounders available.

The question most commonly asked by inexperienced motorcyclists is, "Which make should I buy?" There are no rigid rules but your choice should be influenced by the dealer's ability to provide spares.

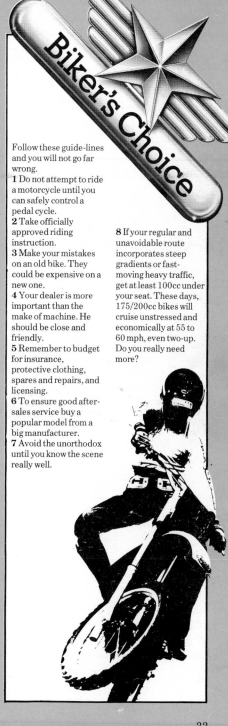

Biker's Choice

Follow these guide-lines and you will not go far wrong.
1 Do not attempt to ride a motorcycle until you can safely control a pedal cycle.
2 Take officially approved riding instruction.
3 Make your mistakes on an old bike. They could be expensive on a new one.
4 Your dealer is more important than the make of machine. He should be close and friendly.
5 Remember to budget for insurance, protective clothing, spares and repairs, and licensing.
6 To ensure good after-sales service buy a popular model from a big manufacturer.
7 Avoid the unorthodox until you know the scene really well.

8 If your regular and unavoidable route incorporates steep gradients or fast-moving heavy traffic, get at least 100cc under your seat. These days, 175/200cc bikes will cruise unstressed and economically at 55 to 60 mph, even two-up. Do you really need more?

Commuters

Honda CG125
A conventional and economical 125 cc air cooled single cylinder bike. The ohv 4-stroke engine produces 11 bhp @ 9,000 rpm. Five speed gearbox. Wheelbase: 47.2 in; curb weight: 232 lb; tank: 2.6 gal.

Simson S 50B
An extremely cheap East German bike which is very economical. The 50 cc single cylinder 2-stroke engine produces 3.6 bhp @ 5,500 rpm. Three speed gearbox and totally enclosed rear chain. Wheelbase: 47.0 in; weight: 172 lb; tank: 1.5 gal.

Suzuki FS50
A step-through scooter with weather protection for the rider's legs and shopping basket as standard. The 40 cc 2-stroke produces 2.5 bhp @ 6,000 rpm, delivered to the rear wheel by two speed automatic transmission. Weight: 152 lb; wheelbase: 43.6 in; tank: 0.8 gal.

Yamaha DT100
The maneuverability of a trail bike is an advantage for certain types of commuting and, unlike most, the wheel sizes of this model allow road tires to be fitted. The single cylinder 2-stroke engine produces 10 hp. Five speed transmission. Weight: 206 lb; wheelbase: 51.0 in; tank: 1.9 gal.

MZ TS 125
A rugged East German machine from the company which led the world in racing 2-stroke development during the 1950s. The 123 cc 2-stroke engine generates 11 bhp @ 6,000 rpm. Four speed gearbox with enclosed chain. Wheelbase: 51.0 in; dry weight: 240 lb; tank: 3.0 gal.

Kawasaki KC 100
A small-sized motorcycle with cradle frame and useful power/weight ratio. Maximum power from the 99 cc 2-stroke single is 10.5 bhp at 7,500 rpm. Five speed gearbox and enclosed rear chain. Wheelbase: 46.0 in; weight: 181 lb; tank: 2.3 gal.

Honda CB400 AT
This medium-weight bike with its automatic transmission is well suited to long distance commuting. The air cooled twin-cylinder ohc 4-stroke engine develops 50 bhp @ 9,000 rpm. Two speed torque converter transmission. Disc brakes. Wheelbase: 54.7 in; weight: 409 lb; tank: 3.6 gal.

Honda C90 Z-Z
The biggest and most powerful step-through built by Honda. Everyone's conception of a commuter bike. The air cooled ohc 90 cc single cylinder engine develops 7.2 bhp @ 8,000 rpm. Three speed gearbox is operated by a handlebar control. Wheelbase: 46.9 in; weight: 194 lb; tank: 1.2 gal.

Dirt bikes

Honda XL 500 S-Z
The largest of Honda's five 4-stroke trail bikes (the XR model is a serious enduro version). The air cooled ohc 4-stroke single has a four valve head and produces 34 bhp @ 6,250 rpm. Five speed gearbox. Wheelbase: 55.1 in; weight: 311 lb; tank: 2.6 gal.

Bultaco Sherpa
Not to be confused with multi-purpose trail bikes, this Spanish trials machine is the one which revolutionized the sport in the hands of Sammy Miller. Trials bikes are road legal. This has a 2-stroke engine with five speed transmission. Curb weight: 216 lb; wheelbase: 51.6 in; tank: 1.3 gal.

KTM 390 GS
Another type of off-road machine which should never be mistaken for a trail bike. The KTM is a professional quality enduro machine from Austria. The air cooled 2-stroke single produces 39 bhp through a six speed gearbox. Wheelbase: 55.0 in; weight: 218 lb; tank: 2.6 gal.

BSA Bombardier
A mongrel with good parents. BSA designed it, Rotax in Austria supplied the engine, Can-Am of Canada built the frame. Over 2,000 have been sold to the British Army. The 250cc 2-stroke single produces 26 bhp. It is reliable and durable. Weight: 274 lb; wheelbase: 51.5 in; tank: 4.2 gal.

Yamaha DT 175 MX

This is the best selling trail bike in the world—for good reason. The 175 cc 2-stroke engine has proved to be equally at home in enduros and traffic jams. Current models feature alloy monoshock rear forks, six speed gearbox. Wheelbase: 53.0 in; curb weight: 221 lb; tank: 1.8 gal.

Suzuki TS 250

An air cooled 2-stroke trail bike in the popular 250 cc class. The single cylinder engine generates 23 bhp @ 6,000 rpm. Five speed transmission. Dry weight: 267 lb; wheelbase: 55.0 in; tank: 2.5 gal.

Kawasaki AR50

Kawasaki's 50 cc, 2.9 bhp enduro-pretender is detuned in Britain to comply with moped laws. A race-styled model, the AE50 and a five speed, 80 cc machine with a 62 mph top speed are also available. Suspension is cantilever. Weight: 169 lb; wheelbase: 47.6 in; tank: 1.7 gal.

BMW R80G/S

This 797 cc flat twin is a gentle trail or ferocious enduro machine. The 49 bhp model reflects BMW's desire to dominate the big bike ISDT class. In fact the light weight and low speed engine torque of all BMWs give them excellent off-road characteristics. Weight: 338 lb; wheelbase: 57.7 in; tank: 5.0 gal.

Tourers

Yamaha SR 500
The model which
revived the big single
concept—once the
mainstay of the British
industry, this 32 bhp
thumper is equipped
for touring, but range is
somewhat restricted by
the small US-style tank.
Weight: 248 lb;
wheelbase: 52.2 in;
tank: 3.1 gal.

MZ TS250 Supa 5
A bike which might be
classified as utility,
except that its stamina
and economy are well
suited to long-distance
work, albeit at a slow
pace. Top speed is 80
mph. The 250cc
2-stroke single gives
21 bhp. Five speed
gearbox. Weight:
322 lb; wheelbase:
52.5 in; tank: 4.6 gal.

**Harley-Davidson
FLT-80**
The Tour Glide uses the
biggest Harley engine
(1340 cc and 70 bhp)
and comes complete
with vast saddlebags and
top box, half fairing,
twin headlights,
footboards, backrest,
grab handles and
running lights. Weight:
774 lb; wheelbase:
60.0 in; tank: 5.4 gal.

Suzuki GSX 400
This twin-cylinder
4-stroke motor,
introduced in 1981, has
double ohc, four valves
per cylinder and twin
swirl combustion
chambers which help it
deliver its 43 bhp
smoothly through the
six speed gearbox.
Weight: 381 lb;
wheelbase: 54.4 in;
tank 4.0 gal.

Moto Guzzi Convert V1000
A 950cc touring version of the Italian Guzzi V-twin. This model features automatic transmission, saddle-bags, footboards, windshield, crash bars and spoilers for comfortable day-long cruising. Weight: 615 lb; wheelbase: 58.0 in; tank: 6.3 gal.

BMW R100RT
The touring version of BMW's 980cc flagship, this model is equipped with the enlarged touring fairing, which includes a quartz clock and ventilation system. The ohv flat twin engine produces 70 bhp. Weight: 478 lb; wheelbase: 57.7 in; tank: 6.2 gal.

Triumph T140E Bonneville
Miraculously, the Bonneville has been in continuous production since 1957. The current 750cc machine weighs about the same as the 649cc stock record breaker but is more suited for touring, and now has electric starting. Weight: 395/440 lb; wheelbase: 56.0 in; tank: 3.4/4.8 gal.

Honda GL1100 K-A
A true heavyweight tourer, the Gold Wing features an engine which is unusual for a motorcycle—a flat four, water cooled 4-stroke. For 1981 the original capacity has been increased by 100cc to 1085cc. 95 bhp is produced; shaft drive. Weight: 639 lb; wheelbase: 63.5 in; tank: 5.3 gal.

Sports cycles

Honda CB1100R
A limited edition replica of the successful Endurance racers, it uses the 16-valve four-cylinder engine. The bike features air suspension in front and oil damped rear shocks. Hp figures are not available but it is claimed to reach 140 mph. Weight: 562 lb; wheelbase: 58.6 in; tank: 6.9 gal.

It is rarely appreciated outside Spain that Bultaco makes a fine range of sports roadsters. The factory's racing background ensures the Metralla is one of the best of its class. The 244cc 2-stroke single turns out 25 bhp. Weight: 267 lb; wheelbase: 52.5 in; tank: 3.4 gal.

Ducati 900 SS
One of the best handling makes of Italian sports bike, the big Ducatis have had consistent success on the race track. The ohc desmo engine produces only 68 bhp, yet the top speed is about 130 mph. A Mike Hailwood replica has full race fairing. Weight: 432 lb; wheelbase: 60.0 in; tank: 5.0 gal.

Yamaha RDL/C
The liquid cooled twins in 250 cc and 350 cc specification are virtually race replicas. The small version is one of the fastest 250s ever. Cantilever suspension, cast wheels and black engine add racy looks to the 35/47 bhp performance. Weight: 340 lb; wheelbase: 52.0 in; tank 4.2 gal.

Moto Guzzi 850 Le Mans II
A sports bike equipped with a wind-tunnel-designed fairing as standard. The big ohv V-twin pumps out 75 bhp through its shaft drive. Guzzi's coupled brake system is used to stop it. Weight: 490 lb; wheelbase: 58.0 in; tank: 6.3 gal.

Laverda Montjuic
Described by the makers as a road-legal production racer, the twin-cylinder 500cc dohc Italian bike generates 50 bhp and is faster than machines of twice the size. It has a six speed gearbox. Weight: 410 lb; wheelbase: 56.0 in; tank: 3.6 gal.

Krauser MKM1000
Krauser, the German luggage manufacturers, market a space-frame chassis kit, or complete machine with a BMW R100CS engine. To ensure registration acceptance by the German government many BMW parts are used. Handling is taut and racer-like. Weight: 467 lb; wheelbase: 59.4 in; tank: 5.5 gal.

Dunstall Suzuki GSX1100
Although they are rebuilt on their way from the factory to the customer, Suzuki offer full warranty on Dunstall bikes. This model can, therefore, claim to be the fastest non-turbo production bike. It produces 114 bhp. Weight: n/a; wheelbase: 60.5 in; tank: 6.3 gal.

41

Utilities

Honda H100
Honda's biggest non-competition 2-stroke is the 99 cc, H100 commuter special. It is not as economical as the 4-stroke equivalents but it is cheap. Top speed is a useful 65 mph. Weight: 188 lb; wheelbase: 48.2 in; tank: 2.5 gal.

Enfield 350
Made in Madras, India, this 348 cc, 18 bhp ohv single was originally a license-built Royal Enfield Bullet. Production began in 1949. Top speed is 75 mph, fuel consumption outstanding. Weight: 172 lb; wheelbase: 54.0 in; tank: 4.0 gal.

Kawasaki Z200
A real little/big bike for economical commuting or long distance cruising, at an easy 70 mph. The 198 cc, sohc, single pops out a useful 18 bhp. Weight: 278 lb; wheelbase: 50.4 in; tank: 2.4 gal.

Suzuki GS250T
Even utilities can have style, for those willing to pay. Typical is the 26 bhp GS250T. The custom styling is hugely popular in America., less so in Europe. Weight: 172 lb; wheelbase: 48.6 in; tank: 2.1 gal.

Dnieper MT10 and sidecar
This 649cc Russian bike is built for sheer strength, but it can be fun. It provides 27 bhp and a top speed of 70 mph solo, or 57 mph with chair or sidehack. A 750cc sv model with side-car-wheel-drive is also available.

Velosolex
Of all the world's utilities this French-made moped is the most basic. It is little more than a robust bicycle with a front wheel driven by a single speed, 2-stroke power pack. Fuel consumption can be as low as 167 mpg (US).

Vespa
Fundamentally, the Vespa scooter has not changed since its conception in 1945. The engine/transmission unit is a miracle of miniaturized, durable engineering. The disc-valve, 198cc 2-stroke single turns out 9.8 bhp. Weight: 110 lb; wheelbase: 48.6 in; tank: 2.1 gal.

Jawa/CZ
The two state-owned Czechoslovakian factories build a range of machines from 50 to 350cc. They are ugly and dull, but rugged and reliable. Weight (with sidecar): 507 lb; wheelbase: 53.1 in; tank: 4.2 gal.

43

Megacycles

Harley-Davidson Sturgis
Harley-Davidson is the first manufacturer to equip its machines with toothed belt drive instead of chains. The 1340cc Sturgis was named after one of America's great cycle rallies. Styling is basically Low Rider. Weight: 575 lb; wheelbase: 63.5 in; tank: 4.3 gal.

Suzuki GSX1100
The fastest accelerating production-line roadster currently available. This 16-valve, 1075cc dohc, four-cylinder bike can cover the standing ¼ mile in less than 11 secs. It has a top speed of over 140 mph and exceptional road holding. Weight: 514 lb; wheelbase: 60.5 in; tank: 6.3 gal.

Kawasaki Z1300
If one word can summarize the Z1300, it is excessive. The performance of the 1286cc, 120 bhp, dohc six-cylinder engine is spectacular but the bike is ponderous. Used hard, it will chew through a rear tire in under 1,000 miles. Weight: 714 lb; wheelbase: 62.0 in; tank: 5.4 gal.

Laverda 1200
This Italian motorcycle has been made famous largely by the publicity given to the British importer's sporting development of the Mirage and Jota. The standard models equal the sophistication of Japanese bikes yet offer the individuality of the Italian. Weight: 487 lb; wheelbase: 58.0 in; tank: 5.2 gal.

Honda CBX
Honda was the first Japanese manufacturer to list a six. The six carburetor, 24-valve, dohc, electronic ignition sports-tourer is probably the most complex machine made. It produces 105 bhp. Weight: 590 lb; wheelbase: 58.0 in; tank: 5.3 gal.

Hesketh
Spearheading a probable British renaissance in the 1980s is the Hesketh. Its 96 bhp Weslake-based 90°, dohc, 8-valve engine is designed for low speed torque, as much as top-end bhp. Handling is light, and high speed stability of rare quality. Weight: 510 lb; wheelbase: 62.5 in; tank: 7.1 gal.

Yamaha TR1
This big V-twin is now available in America in a 920 cc model, along with a custom 750 cc version. The European 981cc model has been developed for economy and longevity and features a fully enclosed chain. Rear suspension is cantilever. Weight: 490 lb; wheelbase: 60.7 in; tank: 5.0 gal.

Munch 4. 1300 TTS E
Munch machines are some of the most rare and highly developed big bikes. Modified NSU car engines are squeezed into Friedle Munch's own chassis. The 1300cc, 104 bhp turbocharged machine is one of the world's great motorcycles. Weight: 659 lb; wheelbase: 57.0 in; tank: 6.6 gal.

Paradoxycles

Rokon 2-wheel tractor
This improbable two-wheel-drive American machine will plough, gang-mow, spray, and do all a normal tractor can. The 134cc 4-stroke single turns out 10 bhp through a torque converter plus three speed selector. Weight: 185 lb; wheelbase: 49.0 in; tank: 1.2 gal.

Honda ATC 110
An all-terrain vehicle designed specifically for soft sand and marshes, where it will out-perform orthodox vehicles of all types. The 105 cc ohc 4-stroke engine turns out 6.5 bhp through an eight speed gearbox. Suspension is provided by super-soft tires. Weight: 236 lb; wheelbase: 40.0 in; tank: 1.6 gal.

Quasar
The British designers rejected tradition and built for the safety, economy and comfort needs of the immediate future. The 41 bhp, 850 cc, water cooled, shaft drive four has a top speed of 100 mph (160 km/h) and consumption of about 50 mpg. Weight: 679 lb; wheelbase: 77.0 in; tank: 4.8 gal.

Shifty
The Italian company has shoehorned a Fiat 127 car engine (four-cylinder, 906cc, 45 bhp) into its own frame with Laverda wheels and suspension. The 105 mph (170 km/h) machine is unusually quiet, flexible and economical. Weight: 626 lb; wheelbase: 60.5 in; tank: 4.2 gal.

Italjet 50
This Italian company was responsible for the early popularity of junior trials and moto-cross. Three-to-six-year-olds can begin on garden bikes like this 30 mph 2-stroke. The 2 bhp, 50cc engine transmits power through a single gear auto transmission. Weight: 62 lb; wheelbase: 33.0 in.

Hard-tail chopper
Choppers are highly stylized, nostalgic symbols of 1950s Americana. Thus, a hard-tail (no rear suspension) represents the classic chopper. This American show prizewinner is Roadrunner, a low rider built by one of the very few British chopper craftsmen, Uncle Bunt.

Italjet Pak-a-way
High density, load-bearing plastic was used to construct this folding 50, intended for use as a transportable tender for light aircraft and boats. Metal is too heavy, too hard and corrodes. Weight: 86 lb; wheelbase: 39.0 in; tank: 0.8 gal.

Testi Militaire'
No more ruggedly functional lightweight is available than this army-designed 50. It has eight gears, moto-cross tires and heavy-duty suspension. Optional extras are ski rack and rifle scabbard. Weight: 159 lb; wheelbase: 46.1 in; tank: 1.8 gal.

Pre-purchase checks

The used motorcycle market is full of traps for the gullible and bargains for the wily. Unlike the good old days when British, Continental, and American bikes held sway, today's Japanese motorcycles are neither simple nor built of material of a quality that encourages unending rebuilds. Some are not repairable because they have been designed that way; they are virtually sealed units with no user-serviceable parts inside. Because of this, the cheap and scruffy, but basically sound bike bargain rarely exists.

Motorcycling's innocents usually fare best in the used departments of major companies. With a brand reputation to uphold, few dare upset customers for fear of reprisal from their machine supplier. In consequence, the used machines they are left with as trade-ins from new machine sales are carefully checked before sale. Second-rate bikes are sold to the secondhand motorcycle trade, while the best are displayed, frequently with guarantee, on their own showroom floor. As such machines are the real "cherries" of the motorcycle world they usually cost a little over the odds, but in the long run undoubtedly save inexperienced riders money.

Dealers specializing in nothing but secondhand motorcycles are frequently cheaper but can rarely offer any after-sales service. Trouble occurring with a bike obtained from a source like this is invariably expensive to remedy.

Private deals are fine if you know the ex-owner and his or her riding methods, or if you are a skilled enthusiast yourself, or can obtain the assistance of one. In all other cases stay clear, because the law is unlikely to help you in case of post-sale disasters. When only a small amount of money is involved, then the chance of getting a bargain is probably worth taking.

Dealers are by no means the crooks some people would have you believe. If you buy from a local dealer, it is unlikely he will try anything but honest money-making from you. The same applies to the reputable major dealer offering a guarantee with the bike of your choice. In these cases a detailed examination is probably unnecessary, but the decision is yours. At all other times, follow this routine and you should stay clear of trouble.

1 Either pay for an engineer's report from a major motoring organization, or employ the services of an experienced and skilled motorcyclist who knows something about the model you are considering.

2 Ask for a history of the motorcycle and the previous owner's name and address. Then contact the ex-owner and talk to him or her.

3 Place the machine on its centerstand. Check wheel alignment with a string along the wheels: uncorrectable misalignment suggests a bent frame and/or forks. Lift tank, remove side panels and lift seat to check for weld repairs and repaint marks: these suggest a crash repair. Previous owner quality can be judged by electrical wiring and connection condition, control cable routing and lubrication, or battery terminal corrosion marks. All controls, including switchgear, should operate lightly and smoothly. There should be no play in either front or rear forks or their respective wheels. Control pivots should be damp with a little oil.

4 Request that the machine be started, which it should do instantaneously. Once warmed up, after a few minutes it should idle reliably at no more than 1,000 rpm. All lights, instruments and warning lights should work correctly; check especially the ignition warning light. Then blip the throttle lightly a few times: modern 4-strokes should emit neither black (rich mixture) nor blue (burned oil) exhaust smoke. Mechanical noise should be little more than a loud, sewing machine-type noise.

5 Roll the bike off its stand and sit astride it after the seat and tank have been replaced. Pump the front forks, which

should smoothly resist both down and upward movement. If they, or the similarly treated back end, appear to resist either movement, suspect a bent tube or damper rod, and if the machine bounces on its springs then the dampers are shot. With a dead engine (to avoid any suspicion of intent to steal the bike) check through the clutch and gear shift movement.

6 Ask to ride, or see the machine ridden. It should accelerate sharply in top gear from low revs without hesitation, and generally appear to look balanced and perform willingly. Keep a look-out for brand new components, which indicate crash damage repair; scarred bolt or screw heads around a particular area,

which indicate habitual component unreliability or ham-fisted treatment. Brakes should work well repeatedly.

7 Avoid non-standard machines, apart from those with sports exhaust systems, alternative touring handlebars, or good quality seats and suchlike. These extras are common. Stay clear of high-grade racing suspension or brakes, clip-on bars, rear-set footrests, racing seats, scuffed tires and blue exhaust pipes. Beautifully maintained it *might* be—very hard ridden it has been! Beware of a machine with either dirty, clouded oil, or a white deposit inside the valve inspection covers or oil filler cap. Both indicate condensation contamination from too many short, cold journeys.

Points to check on a used machine

Obtain an engineer's report and check for inept maintenance.

Start engine and check that it idles at low revs.

Exhaust smoke should be neither blue nor black.

Lift tank, seat and side panels to inspect the frame for damage.

All instruments and switchgear should work.

Test fork action for excessive play.

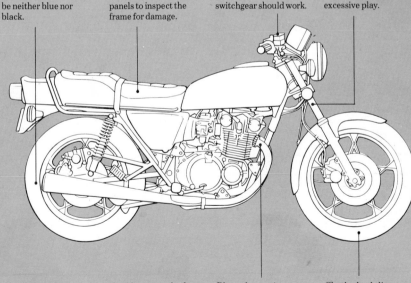

Check wiring and connections for corrosion.

Avoid non-standard equipment, particularly racy extras.

Blue exhaust pipes indicate hard riding.

Check wheel alignment and look for uneven tread wear.

Aerodynamic fairings

The average motorcycle uses approximately 75 per cent of its engine power in overcoming drag—the atmospheric resistance to forward motion. Even at speeds as low as 30 mph, the force of drag can be three times as much as rolling resistance.

As air is not friction-free it clings to the surfaces which pass through it. For the purposes of research it is assumed that the air moves in lines of air stream, or streamlines. Once they are past the moving body these streamlines break up into eddies of turbulence—which causes greater drag than the friction between the air and the surface. It can, therefore,

be appreciated that a naked roadster with rider and multitude of projecting surfaces must have a higher drag coefficient than a car.

Naked touring machines also have a tendency to lift under the effect of frontal wind pressure at high speed. Alteration of the steering geometry and gravity center combined with a frantic tugging on wide handlebars upsets stability, disturbing the vitally smooth gyroscopic forces on the front wheel. An aerodynamically faired machine with low frontal area will, therefore, split the breeze with greater efficiency and stability than an unfaired bike.

The BMW R100S fairing was developed in 1975 at Pinin Farina's wind-tunnel in Italy. Compared to an unfaired touring motorcycle, the RS fairing reduces lift at speed by 17.4 per cent, improves lateral stability by 60 per cent and increases penetration (lowers the drag coefficient) by 5.4 per cent.

An aircraft gains lift by exploiting the shape of the wing which causes air above it to lose pressure and the slower air moving beneath to create pressure. A powerful downthrust is

attained by the BMW R100S whose design uses this principle in reverse. Windscreen, longitudinal ribs and short, tapered seat create the downward pressure.

The stream of air is distorted by the shape of the object passing through it. Air flows at different speeds, depending on how close it is to an object. The closer to the surface the slower it moves. This laminar flow acts as a lubricant.

Equipment

Moto Guzzi used their own wind-tunnel to design the spoilers fitted to their V1000 Convert tourer in 1974. Guzzi's fully-faired grand prix racers of the 1950s were successful, but unstable copies caused full streamlining to be banned from racing.

Fairings on racing bikes are a post-WW II refinement, but full enclosures have been in use for record breaking since the 1930s. The major disadvantage with full fairings is the lack of directional stability in cross-winds.

The loss of stability in cross-winds is due to the Bernoulli effect. As a full fairing is virtually a solid shape, a partial vacuum is set up on the lee side, into which the machine will be sucked. Equally, much effort is required to lean a fully-faired bike into the wind.

Early pioneers of motorcycle record breaking were German. BMW and NSU machines broke speed records on the new autobahns. Ernst Henne and Willie Noll were supreme.

Fairings/2

Touring fairings are available in two main styles: the full fairing, and the handlebar fairing. Both can be further sub-divided: the sports or racing fairing designed to give real or illusory speed and used with clip-ons and rear-sets; and the heavyweight tourer intended to provide maximum protection from wind as well as rain and spray.

Decide what you want the fairing for—think hard about its desired function. If you live in a cold or wet climate, then ensure that your hands and feet are protected; if you live in a hot climate,

ensure adequate ventilation is provided. Full fairings are permanent fixtures. Handlebar fairings can be removed easily when necessary, unless they are motorcycle frame mounted, when they are as permanent as a full fairing. Handlebar models come in two main styles; the sports-styled headlamp cowl and the full-width touring windshield.

Ignore all claims of aerodynamic stability or improved machine performance unless proof of wind-tunnel development can be shown. Assume the worst. Request independently published

The Windjammer fairing is a high-quality item for use on large tourers. The headlight is adjustable. Turn signal/side lights are built in.

The optional stereo sound system, with five-inch speakers, can be incorporated inside the cowl. FM/AM radio, cassette players and CB units can be fitted.

The fairing can be color-matched to suit most popular machines. Gold striping is a standard feature.

test reports before buying, and take special note of comments on high speed stability. Ignore all fairings without heavyweight fittings specifically designed for your model of motorcycle—and those that do not guarantee total fitting rigidity.

Top quality fairings are frequently the most difficult to fit because they are designed to become part of the motorcycle: unless you are a competent handyman, leave the fitting to a professional mechanic. If you try it yourself allow a clear weekend for a full fairing and a

whole day for a handlebar model fitment. First remove all trim and fittings, including screen, and protect all high spots, edges and fitment areas with masking tape. If drilling is necessary, mask the vital area generously with masking tape to stop it splintering. If possible, borrow or rent a light hoist to support the fairing weight: they can weigh up to 22 kg (50 lb) stripped. Anchor the motorcycle *securely* on flat ground. Study the instructions in detail the day before and attempt nothing until you understand them fully.

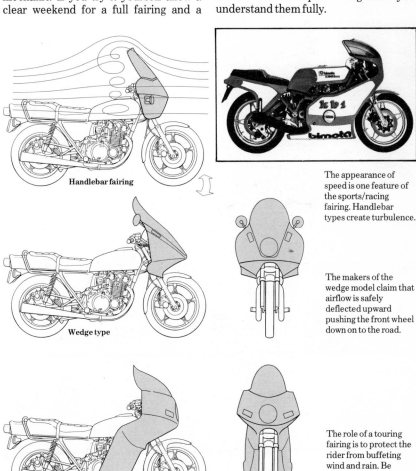

Handlebar fairing

Wedge type

Touring fairing

The appearance of speed is one feature of the sports/racing fairing. Handlebar types create turbulence.

The makers of the wedge model claim that airflow is safely deflected upward pushing the front wheel down on to the road.

The role of a touring fairing is to protect the rider from buffeting wind and rain. Be prepared for an increase in engine noise, which is reflected by the fairing.

Luggage

The popular assumption that carrying luggage on a motorcycle is made problematical by the machine's single track characteristics is untrue. The difficulties imposed by load carrying—which are mainly those of instability—are almost solely due to a short wheelbase.

Placing anything but a pocket-sized package ahead of the steering axis can induce a dangerous pendulum effect in the front wheel. A heavy load behind the rear wheel axle can reduce the vital lateral damping effect of the front tire's contact patch to zero and cause uncontrollably violent steering wobbles. The lighter the motorcycle the more sensitive it is to poor weight distribution. Ultra-heavyweights such as Harley-Davidson Tour Glides (approximately 795 lb road-equipped) are much less disturbed by poor weight distribution because the luggage/machine mass ratio is so great. To avoid instability problems: keep loads inside, or as close to, the triangle as is practicable; fasten loads securely so they neither shift nor wobble over even the worst roads.

Top box (trunk). A more convenient yet

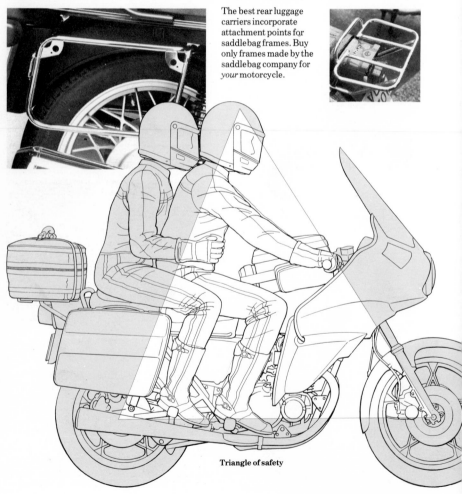

The best rear luggage carriers incorporate attachment points for saddlebag frames. Buy only frames made by the saddlebag company for *your* motorcycle.

Triangle of safety

more dangerously unstable method of luggage carrying could not be devised. These rear-mounted boxes will hold the bulkiest of objects, such as full-face helmets, but they place weight where it does most harm—above and behind the rear wheel axle.

Hard saddlebags. Krauser-type hard saddlebags offer the best compromise between excellent load carrying and acceptable stability. Ensure they fit as low and far forward as the pillion rider's legs will allow.

Soft saddlebags. The sling-over bags are one of the finest and cheapest methods of luggage carrying. They absorb road shocks as no hard mounted bag can, and they can be stuffed full of awkwardly shaped loads.

Tank top bag. Without doubt these provide the safest heavy load carrying capability. They are most popular with European high speed tourists because the bags keep the weight in the right place and make an excellent windbreak and body rest. They are less popular in America because of incompatible machine styling and lower speeds.

Two sets of saddlebags can be carried—one on the tank and another on the seat. Both should be fastened with bunjees.

Top quality tank bags incorporate strong carrying handles for use when off the bike.

Load within the triangle, if possible— especially if you ride fast. Krauser, the luggage makers, do not recommend travelling at over 80 mph (129 km/h) on BMW's with their saddlebags fitted because of instability.

Large trunks and hard saddlebags should be fitted only to the heaviest machines. Several models, such as Vetter and King of the Road, have lights and chrome guards which add to the weight.

Extras

Do not waste money on purely cosmetic extras. Equip your motorcycle only with functionally efficient accessories that improve safety, reliability or comfort. Accessories that increase power output or fuel economy have yet to be made: these are tasks of *alternative* equipment.

Heavy gauge crash bars generally do more harm than good in a crash. They twist expensive frames and break riders' legs. Engine protection bars are different altogether and are designed to crumple and bend under heavy impact. By so doing they absorb sharp, damaging impact and resist high speed abrasion.

Essential equipment for regular pillion users is a grab handle on to which the passenger can hold securely during acceleration. It stops him loading the rider during braking and generally inspires confidence.

Mirrors are obligatory in some places: essential everywhere. Convex mirrors (illegal in Australia) display the biggest, wide-angle, image. Long-stemmed mirrors frequently vibrate too much. This may be cured by sleeving the top end with an inch or two of lead tube.

Ammeters were phased out in the 1960s by red "idiot" lights providing retrospective information. Fortunately, ammeters and voltmeters (which perform a similar task) are still available as extras. They indicate the state of health of the electrical system.

Water cooled engines use temperature gauges for monitoring thermal efficiency. Users of air cooled engines can fit oil and cylinder head temperature gauges. Oil pressure gauges used to be common on plain bearing engines, but they went out of fashion after complaints from owners needlessly frightened by the inevitable loss of pressure on overheated or worn engines.

Instruments monitoring battery condition, voltage and charge, and those indicating broken circuits can provide an insight into the workings of the electrical system.

A pillion grab handle inspires confidence in a passenger, especially during acceleration.

Crash bars, designed to protect riders' legs, may lead to frame damage in the event of a fall.

Unless you are an exceptionally hard rider living in an exceptionally hot country, do not fit an oil cooler. Unless they are fitted as original equipment most do more harm than good. Overcooled oil in a hot engine causes condensation contamination.

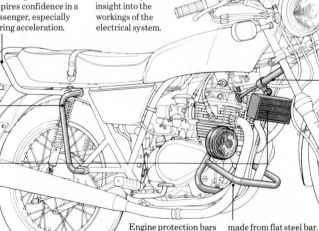

Engine protection bars should be designed to crumple under heavy impact. The best are made from flat steel bar. Buy only close-fitting types with round frame clamps.

Motorcycles cannot be made entirely theftproof. Professional thieves can simply power-lift a chosen machine into a waiting truck in seconds. The only guard against this form of theft is never to park regularly in the same place. Anti-theft devices are no more than deterrents. An electrically powered audio alarm is of no value on its own because the machine can still be ridden and few people will notice its plaintive bleeping. But thieves dislike being delayed and joy-riders rarely bother with anything too complicated to start easily. Never rely on the standard steering locks: they are fragile and can be broken by a quick handlebar twist. Do not encourage scavengers by removing obviously visible parts.

SECURITY CHECKLIST

1 Park only in open, well-lit places.
2 Never leave the machine in one place outdoors for more than two days at a time.
3 Secure the bike with a high quality padlocked chain or wire rope with a written guarantee.
4 Remove the battery earth (ground) strap.
5 Cover the bike with a heavy waterproof cover padlocked into place.
6 Fit an electrical audio alarm with its own battery.

If the bike is to be left for a long time, or in a thief's paradise:
7 Fit and hide a small on-off switch to the low tension ignition circuit.
8 Fit unserviceable but visibly complete spark plugs.
9 Remove or block the fuel supply line after draining float chambers.
10 Select first gear and remove gear and clutch levers if possible.

Bar-end mirrors give the best view but are vulnerable to impact damage. Good mirrors have thumb press adjustable glass, which is also replaceable.

An adjustable steering damper minimizes front wheel flutter during fast cornering on rough roads.

Fog lamps give a wide, flat beam; one spotlight beam is too narrow. Handlebar lights should be central and not rigidly mounted. A crash bar is a good mount but there are legal restrictions on the height of a light. Auxiliary lights must be extinguished when dip beam is selected.

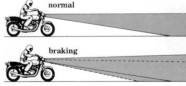

Under braking or acceleration, a motorcycle dives or rears up and the headlight beam follows. The Cibié automatic levelling system uses hydraulic sensors to monitor suspension travel and actuate an adjuster which maintains a level beam. Prototype systems have given no problems when cornering.

Power tuning

The simplest and least expensive way to get more power out of your bike is to sell it. Then buy a bigger one. Modern motorcycles leave the production line in a high state of tune, and in standard form they offer useful power characteristics within socially acceptable limits of noise, safety and fuel consumption. If you want more power out of your engine then be prepared to spend much time and money to maintain even some of that useful balance. Buy only equipment which has been race-proved, such as that from a maker like Yoshimura or Moriwaki.

Not all motorcycle engines are suitable for power tuning and often roadster frames are incapable of handling the increased power. A new frame will allow you to use the added power, but the resulting speed will have you searching desperately for improved brakes and suspension.

The best starting point is blue-printing. This entails checking every aspect of the bike to ensure it operates at maximum efficiency — the way the designer intended. First, the frame must be tuned to improve high speed stability. Engine modifications will include the re-aligning of cylinders to combustion chambers and carburetors to their induction tracts. Unless such care is taken it is pointless fitting power equipment.

Most original mufflers strangle an engine's full potential, so choose an exhaust system that provides a less restricted gas flow but which still silences sufficiently well. The carburetors will then require re-jetting to compensate, especially if the air cleaner is removed, as the resulting weak mixture will burn holes in your pistons. By now you should have gained 12-15 per cent more power in the middle of the engine's rev range, which will provide a much quicker throttle response and acceleration.

Turbochargers are simply turbines which are driven by the exhaust gas to force-feed fresh fuel mixture into the combustion chamber at above atmospheric pressure.

Mixture is forced into the chamber at pressures that vary from 0.28 kg/sq cm (4 psi) to as much as 0.84 kg/sq cm (12 psi) on roadsters. The force of each combustion stroke is, therefore, enormously increased.

The advantages are many. Turbos eliminate the need for high quality and expensive internal engineering. Engine power can be increased by up to 40 per cent, without extensive modification, which means that engine capacity and, therefore, weight can be reduced. The increase in combustion efficiency almost balances out the increased fuel used to obtain the speed.

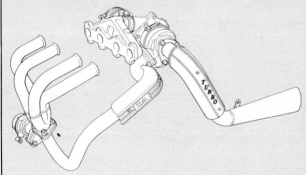

Because they are turned by fast-moving exhaust gas, turbos do not come into use before about 6,000 rpm. When they do switch in the power often hits with a wallop.

If the engine has not responded in this manner then have the ignition timing checked on a stroboscope. A contact breaker point system might flutter at a particular engine speed. If so, replace it with electronic ignition.

The next step is to fit a big-bore kit — and inform your insurance company of the fact. A simple overbore will usually provide a capacity increase of no more than 10 per cent, and a top-end power increase of two or three bhp. Anything more requires special cylinder liners, or even new barrels. Such big-bore modification not only enlarges cylinder capacity, but also combustion chamber capacity — in effect reducing carburetor size and producing higher induction speeds at lower revs.

Your machine should now be providing more power for less fuel, simply because it is breathing more freely. Similar benefits can be obtained from properly gas-flowing a cylinder head. But modern heads are already well gas-flowed, and only the best engineers should be allowed near an expensive cylinder head. Internal polishing is of no value whatsoever. A set of improved racing carburetors of slightly enlarged bore will pass more mixture.

High compression pistons increase top-end power and acceleration, but at this stage power tuning shows its unacceptable face — silencing, smooth running, flexibility, and low speed power begin to suffer, while costs soar. Increasing compression ratios reduces the shape of the combustion chambers and, therefore, their efficiency.

Finally, there is the heart of all power tuning, the camshaft. If you fit a full race camshaft to a roadster it will make more noise, use more fuel and produce less effective power. Always fit a half-race, or sports camshaft, which will be designed to cope with the restricted gas flow and lower engine speeds of a roadster.

A Yoshimura-Kawasaki ported race head, 998 cc piston kit and racing camshafts.

1 is a mild cam giving bottom-end power. Valves are opened and shut quickly. 2 is a medium cam for normal use. 3 is a race cam, which holds valves open longer, giving more top-end power but less tractability.

Buy equipment only from suppliers with a racing development program. A dynamometer in the shop shows they are serious about engine efficiency.

Tires

Tires are the most important piece of equipment on your motorcycle. They rank third on the list of life-preservers, after a reasoning brain and a disciplined right fist. They precede good brakes by one place because tires are in use *all* the time. The contact patch printed over this page in blue is life-size. In conjunction with that of a smaller front tire, it represents the only connection between machine and road.

The original pneumatic or inflatable tire was invented by John Dunlop in 1888 when he glued together a circle of garden hose and attached it to a wooden bicycle wheel rim. By 1891 the Michelin brothers had developed the world's first detachable pneumatic tire, and in 1902 cotton-wound fabric tires were introduced. Until World War I, tires were secured to the rim by air pressure which forced a bead under the rim. By 1920 tires with high tensile wire inside their beads had replaced the bead-edge, or clincher, tires.

For almost four decades tires were refined around these existing principles, but in 1961 the Avon tire company introduced the cling, high-hysteresis or low-bounce tires. The adoption of rubber that resisted bouncing as it rolled across micro-irregularities improved wet weather adhesion by up to 26 per cent, compared with previous tires.

Five years later Dunlop introduced the Trigonic or semi-triangular section tire.

The first job of a front tire is to resist the potentially powerful lateral flutter of a front wheel which is caused by its trailing castor action behind the steering head. This is frequently felt during deceleration between 55 and 25 mph when tires are incorrectly inflated. Incidentally, the most influential damper at such times, and one gladly exploited by designers, is the rider's arms!

A rear tire is designed first and foremost for durability. Although the rear wheel of a motorcycle is also a trailing castor, the high mass of the machine itself resists strongly the natural impulse to flutter. The rear wheel follows a line dictated by the front wheel so it therefore requires neither the same high degree of side-slip resistance nor water-draining qualities. As a rear wheel brake is comparatively ineffective, high braking adhesion qualities in a rear tire would be lost.

A wet road is almost completely drained along the rear wheel's track by the pumping action of the front tire.

The front tire has to provide a low rolling resistance and to resist side-slip during cornering, when the rear wheel is attempting to force it to follow its line, rather than the new one.

The high power-to-weight ratio of a motorcycle encourages wheel spin. This normally takes the form of a powerful dragging motion during acceleration which twists pieces from the tire, and wheel-hop at high speed which abrades the tire. Thus, durability is of paramount importance in a big bike tire.

Cornering adhesion and stability were improved by increasing the size of the contact patch during acute angles of lean. This design has since been forced into obsolescence by the current trend for big bikes—which need a bigger contact patch when upright to handle the power and weight. The Trigonic tire also provided insufficient lateral stability. The answer was the low profile tire. This provides a big contact patch without increasing tire section depth. Flexing is reduced which aids stability and limits heat generation.

Until recently the Japanese designed tires almost solely for the dry-road American market, with durability as their main aim. The Europeans designed their tires for winter wet-road riding. This posed problems when trying to match tires. Further complications arose from the Japanese practice of building in strong directional stability to keep the wheels of a comparatively soft-chassis motorcycle in line. The Europeans built in cornering and direction change ability with little thought for straight line stability, which was provided by stiff frames and suspension systems.

Now that European manufacturers are familiar with the need for directional stability and the Japanese have begun to make excellent wet-weather tires, few of the early problems remain.

Tire Tips

1 Learn to fit your own tires. It will teach you to respect and understand them.

2 Check tire pressures at least once a week and inspect the tread for stones, nails, wire, etc., which may be embedded. Pry them out carefully.

3 Do not mix tire brands, or low profile and ordinary tires.

4 Do not fit tubeless tires without expert advice.

5 Do not fit a specifically designed rear tire to a front, or a front tire to a rear wheel.

6 Do not fit fat-section tires unless a guarantee of safe compatibility can be obtained from wheel *and* tire manufacturers.

7 Do not fit tubeless tires to cast wheels unless the wheel and tire makers recommend it.

8 Do not expect off-road tires to perform with guaranteed safety at high speed on paved roads.

9 Tires with less than 2 mm tread depth have impaired adhesion and stability. REPLACE THEM.

10 Read the tire manufacturer's performance limitations and pressure recommendations— exceed them at your peril.

The reason motorcycles can be banked to such incredible angles, apparently defying the laws of physics, is that only the part of the tire in contact with the ground skids. The tread about to contact the ground does not skid, and when it first does make contact it strongly resists skidding and attempts to follow its original line of travel, which is rotational. If the influence of the tire's rolling direction and lateral cornering force is equal, a drift or partial skid occurs, which can be controlled by a skilful rider. If the lateral cornering force overcomes that of the tire's direction of rotation, a skid occurs. If the force of rotation overcomes the lateral cornering force, the skid stops.

The rubber part of a tire is made from a polymer, the main constituents of which are natural rubber and butyl plastic, or synthetic rubber. The tread contains anything up to 100 per cent butyl, while the sidewalls are comprised of up to 60 per cent natural rubber.

Butyl is used for the tread because it is stiffer than natural rubber and wears better. The sidewalls are mainly natural rubber because this has great flexibility, does not generate excessive heat, and remains durable under stress. An impermeable butyl coating envelops the inside of a tubeless tire, while a soft butyl coats the bead. These ensure air tightness.

Until recently the fibre used to weave the fabric material in a tire's carcass was best Egyptian cotton. In the past few years this has been superseded by less expensive synthetic fibres like rayon or nylon. Initially these fibres were too stiff and caused a build-up of heat, but they have since been refined to exceed the performance of cotton.

Several tire companies have experimented with forms of radial motorcycle tires but the construction encourages wild instability due to the ultra-flexible tire walls. By far the majority of tires have cross-ply type fabric skeletons, but in 1978 the Dunlop company introduced a range of bias-belted tires. In these the tread area is stiffened with two belts, or layers, of fabric. By so doing,

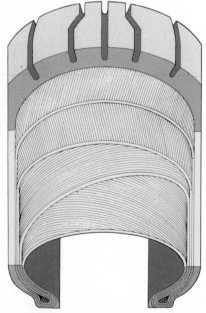

Bias-belted construction.

Most roadster tires are built along similar lines. Four plies, or layers, of fabric form the skeleton of the carcasses. In most cases one, or even two, plies are excluded from the sidewall because only the tread need be very stiff. Sidewall flexibility is a matter of careful tuning because it controls directional stability, shock absorption, and deformation. Around the inner periphery of each wall are the beads.

Under-inflation or overloading causes flexing of the tire casing. This causes instability and leads to irregular tread wear. Due to the distortion of the casing the overheated tire may fail without warning.

Over-inflation causes exaggerated central tread wear. The reduced size of the contact patch can lead to instability, and increased bounce reduces adhesion.

Correct inflation ensures maximum efficiency, longevity, stability and adhesion. Stick to the tire manufacturers' recommendations and remember to increase pressure when carrying a passenger or heavy load.

Dunlop appear to have created a tire that provides improved durability without any loss of wet-road adhesion, and which also offers enough directional stability to discipline the sloppiest chassis. Until now it has been impossible to combine high durability and adhesion satisfactorily in one tire. Durability demands a hard polymer and hard polymers are notoriously slippery in the wet.

During fast cornering all motorcycles drift, however imperceptibly. Tire manufacturers are aware of this and they incorporate a warning zone of progressively increasing danger signals into their tires. As the moment of unavoidable disaster is approached during an ultra-fast corner, so the tires manifest minor symptoms of performance decay. The closer to the absolute limit of recovery, the stronger the signals of danger from the tires.

Racing experiments with tubeless tires during the 1970s have led to their limited adoption for roadsters by some of the bigger motorcycle manufacturers. A tubeless tire is unlikely to cause a dangerous blowout at high speed. It leaks air from punctures only slowly, and does not generate much heat under stressful conditions because there is no heavy and aggravating tube.

The tire of the future for use on most roadster machines will probably be low-profiled and tubeless.

Trials tires have a block tread and are officially recognized for road use. They are designed to run off-road at pressures as low as 0.28kg/sq cm. (4 psi).

Enduro: a new design for fast, heavy enduro bikes, which is speed-rated for road use. The tread provides off-road grip, the round section permits fast road work.

Moto-cross: knobbly tread with lugs to provide maximum traction in soft going. They are unsuited and, in most places, illegal for road use.

Sports roadster rear tires can be used on the front wheels of some machines. The central strip is a water draining groove.

Front ribbed: has five water draining grooves. Cuts across the ribs act as water pumps, clearing the road for the rear tire.

Racing slick (low profile), for use on dry circuits. The tread has no pattern, so maximizing the area of the contact patch. They are illegal for road use.

Helmets

As a safety measure, crash helmets are second-line. Safety lies inside the head, not around it.

In many countries, helmet use is now compulsory, and all major motorcycling nations have laboratories and licensing authorities to inspect, test, reject or approve helmets offered for sale. In the USA the Department of Transportation (DOT) approves helmets which are offered for sale; much higher standards are maintained by the Snell Foundation. In Britain helmets have to be approved by the British Standards Institute (BSI).

Unfortunately, the business of helmet licensing is confused and confusing. Although each nation has its own, there is movement towards an internationally-agreed safety standard, such as the world-wide International Standard Organization (ISO) specification 1511, or ECE (United Nations ITC), which have the same broad aims. But they differ enough to ensure some confusion.

Confusion also exists in most countries over the difference between helmet sales laws and helmet use. In Britain, for instance, BSI test and license

In all probability, shell quality is over-emphasized. The best shells are designed to crumple under heavy concussion in order to allow the energy-absorbing liner to do its job of decelerating the head on impact.

Liners are usually made of expanded polystyrene, a non-elastic, resilient cellular plastic. Some helmets

incorporate a thinner layer of tougher material of the same type sandwiched between the liner and shell. If the liner were

made of a comfortable-feeling spongy foam, the head would literally be bounced back and forth by the foam inside the shell during impact, which might harm the brain more than the hard knock itself.

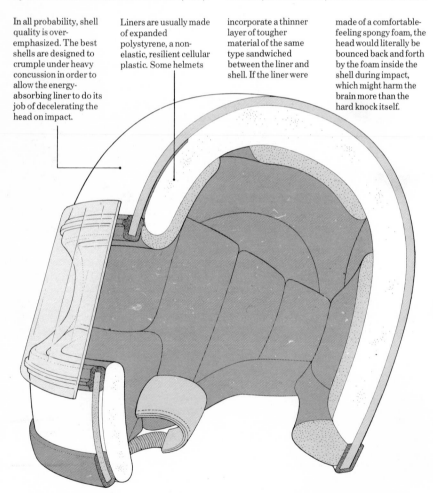

all helmets for sale for road use. The governing body of motorcycle sport, the ACU, stamp-approve all helmets used in competition. The subtle difference between the sales law and the use law leaves a serious gap to be exploited by unscrupulous importers and retailers who claim to sell non-BSI-tested helmets for sporting and competition use. A thoughtless person could, therefore, legally buy a helmet which has been approved only for racing, but which he can then use on the road. In fact, the international racing standards should be at least as good as any other road use standard, although road accidents are a much more severe test of a crash helmet.

Helmets are usually made of glass fibre or thermoplastic. Controversy still rages about the suitability of some thermoplastic (polycarbonate) helmet shells, which may be seriously weakened by strong hydrocarbon-based products, such as spirit cleaners, wax polishes, decals and paint. As these helmets are always sold with large warning labels concerning their treatment, users generally have only themselves to blame if the helmet does weaken.

Polycarbonate helmets, produced under the right conditions and treated correctly, are the equal of glass fibre ones.

Glass fibre comes in two qualities. The cheaper kind uses chopped strand matt. If any gaps or thin areas of glass fibre matt are filled with resin, a weak area is left in that spot because resin is comparatively brittle. Top quality glass fibre helmets utilize layers of resin-bonded glass fibre cloth or woven fabric. This guarantees a uniform measure of known strength throughout the shell. But glass fibre construction is expensive.

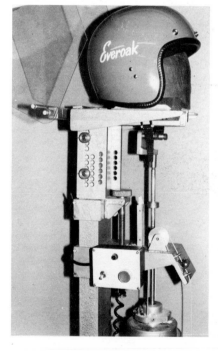

A helmet on a chinstrap test rig: helmets tested under BSI2495 are saturated in water, subjected to 122°F of heat and finally to −4°F of cold for between 4 and 24 hours. Some materials lose their original qualities when used this way. The helmet is put to a shock absorption test, when it must provide a deceleration force of 400g on a weight dropped on the helmet shell. A spiked 4.5lb weight is dropped twice on the helmet. Finally the chinstrap has to resist a heavy dynamic loading without breaking.

The international governing body of motorcycle sport (FIM) recognizes helmets which have undergone a test corresponding to the specifications of at least one of the following standards:
ECE 22 (Europe)
BS 2495 (Great Britain)
AS 1698 (Australia)
DIN 4848 (Fed. Rep. of Germany) only with additional approval of the OMK
Snell Memorial Institute (1975) (USA)
DS 2124 ⎤
SIS 882411 ⎥ Common Nordic
SF 3653 ⎦ standard
Dutch TNO Standard
AFNOR (NF) (France)
JIS T 8133/1978 Class 2 (Japan)

Helmets/2

Walk into your nearest motorcycle dealer and acquire the first helmet that feels comfortable and you will probably be disappointed within a short time. So make sure you choose a helmet to suit your requirements.

There are four main types. The lightweight trials or commuter helmets are designed for maximum lightness and leave the ears free for good hearing. The open-face helmet covers the ears but leaves the face exposed to the elements. Although most countries test them up to the top quality standards, these are now illegal for road racing. Despite rumor to the contrary, and despite the opinions of users of full-face helmets, no facts or figures are available to prove that open-face helmets are any less safe than full-face helmets.

The old type of full-face helmet is not much more than an open-face with a bonded jaw-piece and proud-fitted shield. Until the newer generation of helmet came along these seemed fine, but they are now revealed as drafty, noisy

Early full-face helmets with proud-fitting face-shields were virtually open-face helmets with added chin pieces for facial protection. Wind roar was loud at high speed, and they misted easily at low speed.

The best of the new generation of full-face helmets are wind-tunnel-tested. Face-shields are recessed into the helmets, reducing wind roar, and apertures are bigger than previously.

Trials and/or moped helmets are built to the minimum saftey standards but are adequate for low speed riding. They are extremely light and well ventilated. They are often worn with motorcycle spectacles.

Moto-cross helmets, unlike other full-face types, are designed for use with goggles and are ventilated. Since the shell is perforated they are illegal for road use in some countries.

and, in wet weather, steam-filled antiques. This is not to say the accident protection they offer is inadequate.

Truly modern full-face helmets can be recognized by a smoothly contoured, streamlined appearance in which the shield fits more or less flush with the aperture rim. The best, such as the Nava 11, are equipped with wind-tunnel tested shields that are lowered to the closed position by wind pressure at above 30 mph. Others, like the Kiwi K9, have been designed aerodynamically in a wind-tunnel for maximum high speed comfort and minimum wind roar. Some are provided with anti-misting ventilators, while yet others isolate the rider's nose and mouth from the faceshield to inhibit condensation build-up.

Moto-cross helmets are much fancied by the poseur for their rugged, somewhat flamboyant appearance. They are not designed for prolonged comfort at high speed, but to keep the rider cool while he is being shot-blasted by a hail of flying stones.

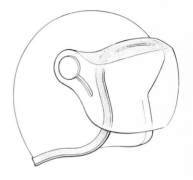

Open-face helmets are now illegal for road racing, but they are still popular with many road riders — including the police. One advantage is that the rider is more aware of his surroundings.

Open-face helmets can be used with goggles or a variety of shields. This bubble type contains a sun diffuser on top. Other types of faceshield can be fitted to helmet visors.

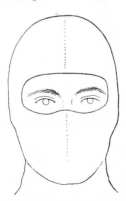

A balaclava is essential wear for motorcyclists in sub-zero temperatures, even with a full-face helmet. The best are made of pure silk and sold as skiing equipment.

1 Helmets should be treated carefully. Read the instructions.
2 Store the helmet right way up so it cannot roll off a shelf and bruise.
3 Never attempt to retailor the liner. Cutting will weaken it, and the application of glue or adhesive might destroy it.
4 Check the chinstrap fixings and ensure the adjusters and fasteners work efficiently.
5 Wash the inside with cold water and toilet soap only. Then rinse it.
6 Wet helmets should be dried in an airy room, away from radiant heat.

Goggles and faceshields

Goggles with glass lenses are still popular with a hard core of motorcyclists who prefer to feel the weather on their faces, and who distrust the degradable optics of soft plastic faceshields. Flat glass lenses are best because they do not distort the vision at all. Soft plastic types are favored by some moto-cross riders who wear them either with full-face helmets or with face protection and an open-face helmet for improved ventilation.

Plastic-lens goggles are generally less efficient than faceshields, following abrasion. This is because no goggles are manufactured with the recently developed scratch-resistant plastics. The advantage is that spare lenses are cheap and can be inserted quickly whenever necessary.

With the enforced use of full-face helmets for racing, the choice of quality goggles has been depleted, although many good goggles are still manufactured. Open-face helmets and goggles are unsuitable for cold weather riding by people used to full-face helmets. The pain receptors in their faces will be too sensitive, making winter riding uncomfortable.

Faceshields scratch easily. Accidental damage can cause heavy scratches which do, at least, encourage the user to replace the shield. The most serious scratching is caused by regular use, when abrasion results in a fine network of micro-scratches. Normally these pass unnoticed by the user, but any attempt to ride into a low sun or vehicle headlights will result in a blinding blaze of diffused light known as starring. Air-blown grit, wet vehicle spray, wiping fingers and careless polishing all scratch.

General Electric has developed a hard plastic film (MR400) for faceshields. It was originally produced as a wear-resistant covering for bullet-proof bank windows, but used on polycarbonate faceshields it is proving to be a valuable contribution to motorcycling safety. Even with regular daily use, one of these shields should last at least a year.

National safety standards institutions are wakening to the need for minimum faceshield requirements. The ironic fact is that the danger of abrasion has been treated casually by comparison with the secondary qualities of impact resistance and light transmission.

Checklist

1 Test goggles for optical accuracy by moving them in front of your eyes. Reject those that distort vision.

2 Ensure goggles fit completely snugly all around your face while you are wearing your own crash helmet.

3 Buy nothing that does not supply a written guarantee of lens quality.

4 Check that spare lenses and straps are available.

5 Check for adequate lens ventilators, if possible with adjusters. Goggles without them mist up.

6 Leather goggles are best because, unlike plastic, they do not split.

Checklist

To ensure your faceshield remains in safe condition follow these simple rules.

1 Clean a faceshield by letting it soak in clean, warm water with a little liquid soap, and then gently wash it in the same water with a soft cotton cloth.

2 Drip dry, then polish it with a clean silicone car wax applied with a camera lens cleaning cloth. The slippery wax film provides a poor anchorage for dirt and rain.

3 Polish the inner surface using an anti-mist chemical.

4 Faceshields should not be cleaned with chemicals unless recommended by the maker. They might spoil the clear surface.

Soft faceshields become scratched during regular use.

Scratches diffuse bright lights into blinding glare.

A clean, clear faceshield gives normal vision. It should not distort the

image at all. Hard plastic resists scratching.

Tinted faceshields are illegal in some countries. They do reduce glare, but

obscure details: under this bridge lurks an unseen car.

The safety glass faceshield is scratch-proof and, therefore, long lasting. It is optically correct and is backed with a non-distorting plastic which prevents splintering under impact.

Leathers

Well-designed touring leathers are the finest clothing investment a big-mileage rider can make. Unless you fall into that category, leathers are a waste of money. They cost approximately three times as much as a storm suit, and only show a return on their outlay after a lot of use. There is no such thing as a set of good cheap leathers.

Leather has excellent insulation properties, is windproof and will resist rain for up to an hour. A good suit reduces wind-drag and improves riding comfort. Expensive wear and tear on ordinary clothes is eliminated yet properly maintained touring leathers will

not, themselves, wear out. In the event of a crash they offer the finest protection.

The best (and most expensive) hides come from horses, mature bulls, mature cows and young beef, in that order. Calf and deer make the softest gloves. Goatskin is light and tough *if* it comes from animals reared in damp, temperate climates. Heat and lack of water cause hides to become thin and brittle.

Makers of top quality suits proudly label the hide type. To test unlabelled leathers, crumple six different spots: if they fold they are good; if they wrinkle they are poor. The larger the unseamed panels are, the better the suit. A lot of

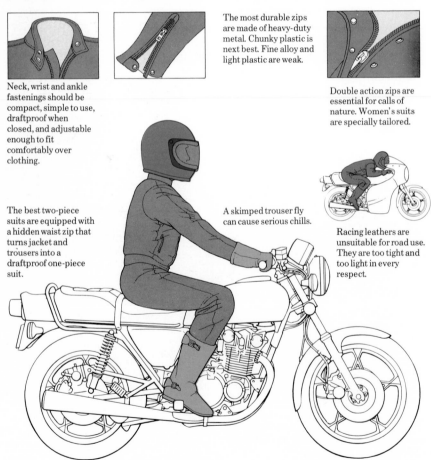

Neck, wrist and ankle fastenings should be compact, simple to use, draftproof when closed, and adjustable enough to fit comfortably over clothing.

The most durable zips are made of heavy-duty metal. Chunky plastic is next best. Fine alloy and light plastic are weak.

Double action zips are essential for calls of nature. Women's suits are specially tailored.

The best two-piece suits are equipped with a hidden waist zip that turns jacket and trousers into a draftproof one-piece suit.

A skimped trouser fly can cause serious chills.

Racing leathers are unsuitable for road use. They are too tight and too light in every respect.

pretty, panelled styling means a lot of unwanted seams. Ensure all colors are dyed; the worst leathers are lacquered.

Decide what you want your leathers for. High speed riding requires a one-piece close-fitting suit; touring, a two-piece; cold climates, a heavy and thermal-lined suit with draftproof fastenings; warm climates, light and thinly-lined leathers, with adequate ventilation control. Unlined leathers are unhygienic and vulnerable to spoiling from constant perspiration.

A leather suit is not an alternative to a weatherproof storm suit, but unless you ride in extreme cold, it is unlikely you will require more than an unlined commuter suit to provide complete protection.

If possible, buy personally adjusted, if not tailored, suits, and never buy without inspecting and trying on the suit.

Good leathers do not hang well on a standing person. (It is vital that women riders buy only suits cut for the female form.)

Always try on new leathers while wearing your personal maximum of undergarments.

Refuse suits that are tight anywhere: they will *not* stretch.

Request, firmly, a written guarantee of dye-fastness in wet conditions.

This is a good quality jacket. Note the protective padding on shoulders and elbows, double-breasted draftproofing of front opening, adjustable hip straps, adjustable neck and gussetted wrist zips. The pockets are completely leather lined to stop wind penetration.

A standing leather-clad rider should expect the suit sleeves and legs to be 2 in (50 mm) too long, the jacket back to be too broad, and the trouser seat to appear baggy. The extra material will be taken up when the rider is seated.

Seams are the weakest point of a suit and should be inspected closely when you are buying. Raised jean-type seams encourage rapid thread wear. Hidden seams are essential on inner trouser legs and jacket sleeves.

Zips on one-piece suits *must* be draftproofed by a snap-fastened outer flap.

Leather is organic and needs much the same sort of care as it had when it was still on its original owner. Use this as your guiding maintenance principle and your suit should outlast you.

1 No suit requires oil-food unless it has been saturated, sun scorched or wind dried many times over. But leather should not be allowed to lose its waxy feel by drying out completely.

2 Apply only natural animal or vegetable-based oil or wax sparingly with a clean, soft cloth. Any attempt to waterproof leather with silicone-based oil might lead to clogging of pores and fibre disintegration. Leather should breathe.

3 Clean a suit by scrubbing it with a soft brush lightly damped with clean, cold water and a little pure toilet or saddle soap. Pay special attention to seams where abrasive grit and acid dirt collect. Detergents and spirits in unskilled hands ruin leather.

4 Wet suits should be dried in an airy, cool/warm atmosphere away from radiant heat and fierce sun.

5 Lubricate zips and snap fasteners with a candle stump.

71

Boots and gloves

It is suspected by some authorities that damage to riders' legs accounts for 60 per cent of all non-fatal motorcycle injuries, if all sporting and non-reported injuries are considered. It is foolish, therefore, to ride without some form of leg protection. Even in hot climates a pair of light boots and jeans should be worn.

Purpose-designed motorcycle boots offer the best protection, but the traditional cowboy boots can make a fine alternative, although they frequently come off in accidents. Choose boots with secure fasteners.

Lined leather boots will keep your feet warm, but no amount of treatment will ever make them waterproof for long. Zip back boots are convenient to fit, but the zip encourages loss of heat and allows the entrance of water unless it is flap-covered.

When buying boots, remember to leave room for extra winter socks in cold climates, or ventilation in hot climates, although the boot should fit well enough to make walking comfortable.

Scrub dirty boots clean of salt and mud while they are still wet. Dry them in a warm, ventilated room.

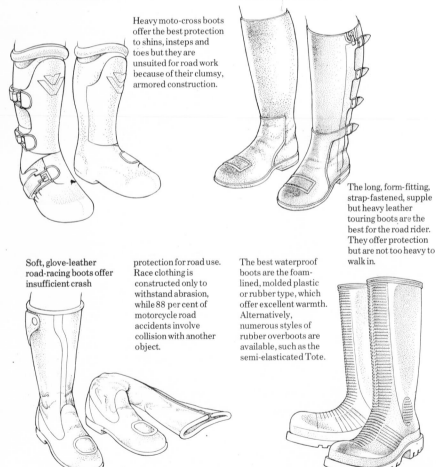

Heavy moto-cross boots offer the best protection to shins, insteps and toes but they are unsuited for road work because of their clumsy, armored construction.

The long, form-fitting, strap-fastened, supple but heavy leather touring boots are the best for the road rider. They offer protection but are not too heavy to walk in.

Soft, glove-leather road-racing boots offer insufficient crash protection for road use. Race clothing is constructed only to withstand abrasion, while 88 per cent of motorcycle road accidents involve collision with another object.

The best waterproof boots are the foam-lined, molded plastic or rubber type, which offer excellent warmth. Alternatively, numerous styles of rubber overboots are available, such as the semi-elasticated Tote.

Riding without gloves is fine — until you fall off. The result can be indescribably painful, and may preclude motorcycling for a month or two.

Riders living in warm climates need to wear only short, light and well-ventilated gloves — with a guarantee of dye fastness, or perspiration will cause indelible stains.

In cold weather separate pure silk liners, with an ultra-thin foam layer between two silk layers, make the best hand warmers. Cheap, imitation silk liners are a waste of money. For long rides in sub-zero weather, especially in damp air, mittens are advisable. Do not use leather mitts because they are too heavy and stiff. Buy an Arctic type made of heavy nylon waterproof cloth, with soft leather palms and thumb pads for good grip. Inside, wear heavy shrunk-wool mitts. It is vital that the cuffs can be strapped shut to retain warm air.

Prolonged heavy rain invariably penetrates the finest waterproof glove by working through the cuff. Most waterproof gloves are plastic, or rubber; few last longer than one or two winters' riding. Stitch light elastic around the cuff to stop rain trickling in.

Moto-cross

Touring

The best gloves for cold and wet weather riding have the following features. 1) Soft, pliant, but not thin leather. 2) Internal seams — exterior seams encourage thread wear and tear. 3) Adjustable, weather-resisting and warmth-retaining straps around the wrist and cuff. 4) A plastic foam lining. Genuine lambskin is too heavy unless the fingers are tailored to a curve, and synthetic wool is a poor insulator. Check that the lining fits right around the fingers and is not a useless fold-over type which leaves the sides uninsulated. 5) Fingers should not feel restricted when gripped around a handlebar.

Arctic mitts

Heavy wool mitts

73

Oversuits

Motorcycle riding suits are a post-World War II invention. Even as late as the 1960s, the monstrously ugly but supremely comfortable storm coats reigned supreme among the year-round riders. The best of these relied on an inner, detachable lining of heavy wool for warmth. Then came a layer of soft but heavy cotton that covered the water-proofed undercoat of oilskin (a tar/rubber-impregnated light canvas). Over that was the outer garment itself, usually a super-heavy cotton twill or gabardine. The coats buttoned in a flap across the front and could be clipped around the legs as far down as the calves.

Trials riders began using waxed-cotton suits, like the Barbour International, in the early 1950s, and a new trend was set. These suits ruled until the mid-1970s when gum-backed, heavy nylon cloth suits with thermal linings became popular among road riders. By the end of the 1970s leaking seams, the bugbear of nylon suits, were virtually eliminated and some manufacturers started to give one year waterproofing guarantees with their suits.

Current styles fall into five main categories: the traditional baggy, belted two-piece with large patch pockets and plain trousers; form-fitting suits with

Buy your suit one size too large to allow extra clothing to be worn without stressing seams. Ensure it comes with a written guarantee of waterproofing.

Test all fastenings for simple closure, adjustment and release while you are fully kitted.

Ensure all pockets are weatherproofed with fold-over bellows flaps.

Trousers without braces and/or a chest-high waist will allow chilling around the waist gap. Elastic waists are useless.

Welded seams are necessary. Check for them. Gum-painted seams will quickly lose their waterproofing.

A thin layer of plastic foam can be glued inside the lining at the knee to make trousers warmer.

Cuffs must be gusseted, or wind and water will penetrate.

Ankle cuffs must fit snugly around boots or warm air will be sucked out from the legs.

elasticized jacket waists and chest-high trousers with slim legs; thermal-lined variations; unlined, commuter suits and one-piece oversuits.

The list of materials used is endless. Most suits are made of a synthetic cloth, coated with a watertight and flexible plastic. The best ones use plastic impregnated cloth which seems to be more durably waterproof.

To stay warm in any but a mild climate, a heavy thermal lining is a prerequisite. Tourists should concentrate on two-piece suits for the sake of convenience. Fast riders are better off with snug-fitting one-piece suits.

Before buying a storm suit, test it for a good fit over your normal riding gear.

Modern plastic suits are prone to condensation dampening unless they are aired thoroughly after use. Turn them inside out and hang them to dry.

Even the cheapest unlined one-piece suit should have at least one pocket.

The form-fitting two-piece suit is a recent invention. The main advantages are a smart appearance and reduced wind drag.

One-piece suits should have a double-action zip for calls of nature.

Wash suits in warm, soapy water occasionally. Do not use spirit or strong detergent which might spoil the material.

Before buying, ask about a repair service. If you tear the suit, contact the manufacturer or dealer for advice about a suitable adhesive for mending. The wrong adhesive might melt the material or coating. Apply the patch from the inside. If necessary, cut carefully through the lining, which can be resewn. Do not stitch plastic-coated suits.

Stay clear of hot engines and mufflers. They melt synthetic materials.

Moped commuters do not require expensive motorcycle clothing. Whatever the advantages of racing crash helmets, they cost half the price of a moped.

The most practical moped helmets are the lightweight, trials-type. Never ride without a helmet or eye protection; the smallest piece of wind-blown grit can momentarily blind you. Always wear gloves

In the wet, moped riders are best protected by an unlined, waterproof raincoat. Do not wear yachting gear because the baggy styling gathers wind and causes instability in gusty weather.

Neat commuter suits like this woman's outfit are fine lightweight alternatives to heavy riding gear. They are not effective at speeds of over 30mph (50km/h), but they can be used for non-motorcycle activities. Skirts offer no leg protection from weather or injury. Long boots must be worn.

Conspicuous clothing

A motorcyclist is a soft-skinned, defenseless but quick mammal living in a world of ponderous, short-sighted, armored dinosaurs. He or she lives on wits alone.

Most other vehicle users fail to see motorcyclists. Not only is a motorcyclist comparatively unusual but he is small and rarely where other vehicle users expect to see a vehicle; he reacts to potential hazards in a manner beyond the understanding of other vehicle users, and is unlikely to hurt the other driver.

Various survival techniques are available for the bike rider. The most valuable are those that make him conspicuous. Inconspicuousness is the main cause of road accidents involving motorcycles and other vehicles. Government traffic/safety departments the world over have established that in over half the accidents involving other vehicles, the other driver did not see the bike.

A daytime-lit headlight is favored by many authorities. But experiments have shown that the use of a single daytime headlight encourages other road users to underestimate the speed of oncoming lit vehicles. A recent Japanese accident survey put the figure of motorcycle speed underestimation by other vehicle users as high as 62 per cent. In Britain, the Transport and Road Research Laboratory (TRRL) discovered in one typical accident survey that "the motorcycle was going ahead, and the other vehicle maneuvering, in 72 per cent of multi-vehicle junction accidents."

Even more disturbing is the American Motorcyclists Association (AMA) refer to "the Greensboro experiment," in which it was made clear that other vehicle drivers can see motorcyclists *if* they expect to be heavily penalized for not doing so.

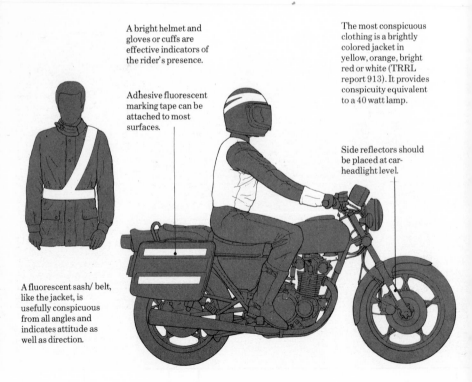

A bright helmet and gloves or cuffs are effective indicators of the rider's presence.

Adhesive fluorescent marking tape can be attached to most surfaces.

The most conspicuous clothing is a brightly colored jacket in yellow, orange, bright red or white (TRRL report 913). It provides conspicuity equivalent to a 40 watt lamp.

Side reflectors should be placed at car-headlight level.

A fluorescent sash/belt, like the jacket, is usefully conspicuous from all angles and indicates attitude as well as direction.

The advantages of a daytime headlight are arguable, but in poor visibility a dipped beam is essential. Bright clothing and equipment also help the rider's conspicuousness.

The periods of half light between day and night are the most dangerous for bikers. Without lights or bright clothes you can easily be lost.

When riding across the traffic flow, a motorcyclist may well be obscured by a dark or busy background. Reflective materials and/or a light colored helmet make the rider and his machine stand out in the lights of another vehicle. Even in daylight it pays to wear bright clothing. Make sure you can be seen.

Special clothes

Fortunately low temperatures usually involve low humidity as well; rainproofing is unnecessary, and dry air is less conductive than damp air.

Strangely, one of the greatest dangers in really low temperature motorcycling (—22°F) is that of condensation, or perspiration, in extreme cases. Clothing that cannot breathe collects condensation which saturates and freezes thermal linings, not only spoiling the insulation properties but dangerously chilling the atmosphere inside the suit.

Where snow and ice lie thick, tumbles

are all part of riding, but the clothing needed to keep a rider warm while sitting stock-still in what amounts to an Arctic gale is too much for walking, or struggling to heave machines upright again. It is then that sweat condenses and freezes in ordinary riding suits. Never travel without alternative clothing.

Boots are a problem. "Moon boots" are warm enough but unable to stand the rigors of motorcycling. Arctic walking boots are clumsy and lack vital ankle protection. So invest in a pair of sheepskin-lined moto-cross boots, or

The warmest underclothing is the spun, synthetic fibre, Damart type. The thickest prevents adequate air circulation next to the skin. The best is the cellular type. But it chills dangerously when wet, while wet wool retains around 50 per cent of its insulation properties.

Over the underclothing wear a thermal undersuit, a heavy wool shirt and mountaineering sweater. Damart-type socks must be covered by heavy, knee-length, pure wool socks to absorb perspiration, then knitted wool or foam knee-warmers. A body belt is vital for internal warmth. The next layer should be a thermal oversuit.

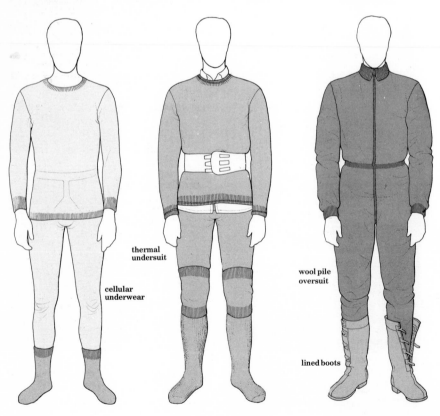

thermal
undersuit

cellular
underwear

wool pile
oversuit

lined boots

buy a pair three sizes too large and have them lined, including the soles. The sole tread must be smooth so as not to pack with foot-freezing ice. Cover with canvas overboots.

A full-face helmet is vital, preferably with an electrically heated faceshield, such as fitted as an extra to Griffon helmets, to prevent condensation freezing. Demister chemicals do not work in these temperatures. One or two silk balaclavas must be worn beneath the helmet. The danger of frost-bite when wearing an open-face helmet is very real.

Electrically heated clothing is good — but never rely on it because it can break down and then, with insufficient insulation, you will become dangerously chilled. Elements which are subject to flexing will break.

In these temperatures, nylon crackles like cellophane, clear plastic splinters like glass, engines puff condensation all day and remain constantly cool to the touch. A pair of thin leather, warm-lined maintenance gloves are essential. You cannot work on a motorcycle in heavy mittens or with bare hands.

An Arctic survival suit such as that made by Karrimore, will keep you warm down to —76°F. The warmest are quilted with goose down, but synthetic material, while not quite as warm, is more robust and is not affected by wet. Goose down is useless when wet.

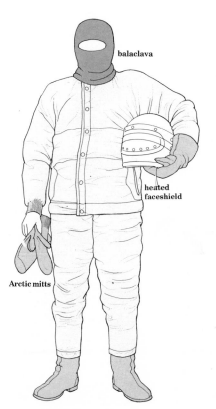

balaclava

heated
faceshield

Arctic mitts

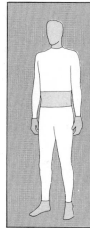

Body heat is lost mainly from the head, the wrists, ankles, and lumbar region. At all these places blood runs close to the skin and is subject to quick chilling (or warming). It then carries the chill (or warmth) to the rest of the body which reacts accordingly. If you must wear electric heating elements, place them around these areas.

Once the temperature rises above 122°F you lose energy rapidly. The sun burns unprotected skin with radiant heat, and the average person requires at least a gallon of water daily.

Use an open-face helmet — white with a dark visor to reflect heat and shade the eyes. Wear loose fitting, well ventilated, tough clothes for protection from the sun and against a fall — jeans and a denim jacket or a moto-cross jersey at minimum.

Adjustment

Machine control involves a feeling of one-ness with the bike; a confidence in, and knowledge of, the bike's and your ability; a partnership between rider and machine. This relationship extends from the rider's dependence on tire adhesion to the engine's facility for high speed cornering or slow "plonkin" — when high torque is demanded at low revs.

Machine control cannot be taught, it has to be learned by experience, thought and even pain. But thought is the key. To ask why? is as important as asking why not? when learning the capability of a motorcycle. The answers to the why nots are normally found in crashing — an activity to be indulged only in off-road conditions to which the novice should confine himself. Mastering the fine distinction between why and why not gives a rider the necessary confidence.

Before a rider can even consider himself in total control of a motorcycle it must be adjusted to suit his size and shape. The natural riding position is designed into a motorcycle and is difficult to alter, except for the handlebar and footrests which can be adjusted or replaced.

If the bars are too high you will not be able to lean into the wind at speed; if they are too low the spine will suffer on a long journey. Wide straight bars are useful for trials and moto-cross riding, where extra leverage is required, but they can be a liability for the road rider. Low bars are either dropped units or separate clip-ons which are bolted to the fork legs.

The throttle is undoubtedly the most important control on a motorcycle because its action determines not only road speed and personal safety, but engine speed, which is important for gear changing and cornering. Adjust the throttle cable so that the least movement of the twistgrip operates the throttle slide, but not so tightly that, when the handlebars are turned on full lock, the pulling of the cable causes the throttle to open. Remember, too, that the throttle works both ways.

The sports or café racer riding position involves rear-set footrests and clip-on bars. These are available for most sporty machines or they can easily be made up by an engineer.

Footrests should not be farther back, or higher, than the swing arm pivot. For long-term comfort the position of bars and footrests should be carefully tailored. Low bars and normal footrests cause excessive strain on the rider's back.

The clutch and front brake levers should be at the same angle to the bars as the arms. When outstretched, the fingers should rest easily on the levers.

Position the gear lever level with the big toe joint when seated in the normal riding position. A simple movement of the foot gives both up and down gear changes.

The American-style upright riding position is dependent on pull-back bars and low, stepped seat. The rider's weight is dispersed only through the base of the spine, which feels the strain after a few miles. He has to hold himself upright with the bars. Highway pegs allow the legs to be stretched forward but this does not contribute to stability.

Machine Control

Keep shoulders and elbows relaxed or they will stiffen up. Steer the bike with the knees which should lightly grip the fuel tank.

Never allow the front brake cable to have too much play: when the lever is squeezed hard, it may come right back to the handlebar without using the full capability of the brake. If you use only two fingers to operate the front brake, leaving two fingers wrapped around the twistgrip, then a slack adjustment not only impairs braking but in an emergency can leave you with two bruised fingers squashed between handlebar and lever.

Some riders prefer the rear brake pedal to be higher than the ball of the foot so they have consciously to lift the foot over it to brake. Others like the pedal just under the foot.

Starting

Many people with non-electric start bikes have trouble starting, and usually this is unnecessary. If the machine is properly maintained, with ignition timing and carburation spot on, then it should start without much effort. Needless to say, most problems stem from a poor kick start technique.

First turn on the fuel; switch the choke to the on position, then turn the motor over a couple of times. Turn on the ignition and with the throttle twisted just a fraction, give a healthy kick. While kicking, do not operate the right wrist, giving big handfuls of throttle — it doesn't aid starting. When the engine does fire, do not scream it to high revs; back the choke off so as not to inject straight fuel into the cylinder, thereby weakening the oil on the cylinder walls.

Some Japanese electric start models with sophisticated carburetors tend to be slow to start if left for a few days. The best technique is to turn the engine over with the fuel and choke on and a wide throttle opening. Then close the throttle completely and the engine should fire sufficiently to keep going. Be careful not to keep the starter button depressed so that the engine drives the starter motor. Engines idle fast when the choke is out and, therefore, need delicate throttle control at low speeds.

When engaging gear to pull away, it is important not to have the motor revving too high; one reason being that the clutch plates sometimes tend to stick. If the bike has not been used for some time, banging it into gear with a high revving motor and a sticky clutch means you will

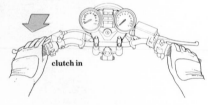

clutch in

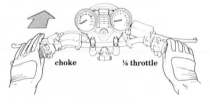

choke   ⅛ throttle

Kick starting
If the machine has been standing for some time, it may be necessary to free the clutch plates before starting, otherwise the machine may lurch forward when first gear is engaged. Pull in the clutch lever and kick the engine over once — after checking it is in neutral.

With the engine in neutral, open the throttle about ⅛th and engage the choke. Bring the engine up to compression — where the kickstart meets resistance at the top of the piston stroke. Ease over compression and the bike is ready to start. Switch on ignition and lunge down with your full weight.

engage drive instantly, lunging forward and possibly losing control. It pays, also, to be kind to the gearbox; whenever you engage first gear, have the motor running as near to idle as possible.

The coordination of clutch and throttle control is often the biggest obstacle to be overcome by the novice. The technique when starting is to rev the motor gently and ease the clutch out slowly. When you start moving forward, slow down the rate at which you are easing the clutch and slightly increase the revs. You will gently pull away and you can then release the clutch lever completely. Do not — as so many novices do — ease the clutch gently until it bites and then simply let it go, causing an uneven, jerky pull away, and possibly stalling the motor.

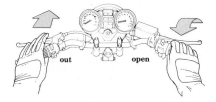

out   open

Pulling away
With the engine now running, squeeze the clutch lever in and engage first gear. Then simultaneously release the clutch and gently open the throttle. Make sure it is safe to go before moving away.

To bump start a motorcycle you must be fairly proficient in machine control. Never do it on the road with traffic passing as it is easy to overbalance and fall off. Even the experts do that sometimes, often in the most embarrassing situations.

1 Make sure that fuel and ignition are on.
2 Engage second or third gear.
3 Pull the machine back on compression (if it is a single cylinder bike).
4 Pull the clutch in and push as hard as you can.
5 When you feel you have enough momentum, jump aboard, aiming to land your butt on the seat. At the exact moment your backside hits the saddle, release the clutch all the way. When the engine fires, either pull the clutch in sharply and cock your leg over, or use the nearside footrest to take your weight.

It is possible to jump on the bike into the riding position with a leg either side, but this can be painful, and it stops you getting straight off to continue pushing if necessary. Always be ready to pull the clutch in instantly and do not take great handfuls of throttle or you could lose control. The safest procedure is to sit astride the bike in the normal position and get someone to give you a push.

Changing gear

A proficient motorcyclist is always in the right gear at the right time. Changing gear correctly is a matter of coordination between the clutch, the throttle and the gear pedal. That coordination is dependent on an awareness of the engine's work load, which can be felt and heard. An insensitive rider (or one whose bike is ultra-sensitive — like a racer) can rely on the rev counter alone.

The procedure may sound long-winded when broken down, but it can and should be done in a fraction of a second. Always use the clutch even though it may be possible to change gear without it. When changing up, the throttle and clutch movements should be made together. Never change up until necessary.

There is no point in being in too high a gear; the engine will slog and you will lose the delicate balance of throttle control.

With any gear change it is mainly the use of the clutch which determines whether it is a smooth or jerky change. The gearbox will clunk if, for instance, you have not pulled in the clutch sufficiently, or if you forget to close the throttle, leaving the revs too high. Operate the clutch, therefore, smoothly and progressively. It is not an on/off switch but a soft graduated link between engine and gearbox.

Master a neat art of gear changing and you will enjoy the full benefit of the bike. Make gear changing a chore and you will never be a proficient motorcyclist.

The downshift is a little more difficult because you have to blip the throttle for a sweet change. The idea of blipping is

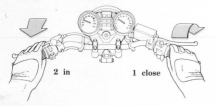
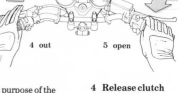

2 in   1 close   4 out   5 open

Changing up
Change up when the engine is spinning freely and before it is revving fast. Refer to the maker's handbook for recommended rev levels for gear changes, until you are familiar with the feel of the engine.

1 **Close throttle**
2 **Pull in clutch**
3 **Select gear with foot. pedal**

The purpose of the gears is to match the engine speed with road speed. An understanding of this relationship and smooth changes are crucial to good riding. Let out clutch smoothly and accelerate.

4 **Release clutch**
5 **Open throttle**

to get the engine up to the rev range required for running in the lower gear so the gear change will be smooth. It will not jerk or harm the gearbox. After blipping the throttle, operate the gear pedal while the revs are dropping (throttle shut), not when the revs are rising (throttle open).

Never change down when you know the road speed is really too high for a lower gear. This will over-rev the engine and with heavy flywheel bikes such as Harley-Davidson, will cause the rear wheel to hop, which diminishes deceleration and promotes skidding. If you happen to miss the gear, the soaring revs can cause serious engine damage.

Whenever you do accidentally miss a gear and select a false neutral between the gears, change *up* to a higher ratio before continuing.

The red zone on the rev counter is not a target to be achieved before changing gear. It indicates the maximum safe revs. The gearbox is used to keep the engine spinning in its useful torque range— for durability and fuel economy. Refer to the handbook for optimum torque range. A good rider can be recognized by the ability to coordinate the actions of feet and hands.

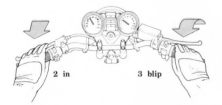

2 in   3 blip

Changing down
Never change down at high revs. Ease off the throttle. Then, with the clutch in, blip it to avoid a surge of revs in the lower gear. While the revs are dropping, slip into the lower gear, matching the engine speed with road speed.

1 **Close throttle**
2 **Pull in clutch**
3 **Blip throttle**
4 **Select gear**
5 **Let out clutch**
6 **Open throttle**

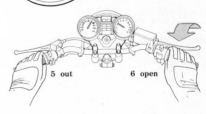

5 out   6 open

Balance

For an insight into the use of balance and distribution of body weight, it is worth watching the top competition riders in action. Roadracers, moto-cross and trials aces all use a great degree of body movement. While they certainly look spectacular, the acrobatics are not for show but to make the most efficient use of their machines.

Even on the road, riding a motorcycle requires more than just sitting on the bike like a sack of potatoes while moving your extremities to operate controls. The steering of a bike is not controlled totally by the handlebars, but also by pressure on the footrests, pressure from the knees on the tank, the leaning of the trunk and the feeling in the seat of the pants. Most of the body movement is from side to side, but off the road great use is made of the front-back movements.

Confidence comes only with experience and thought, but lessons can be learned by watching the movements of the professionals. Trials riding is the slowest sport and in some ways the best test of a rider's ability. As it is an off-road sport, many lessons can be learned painlessly on soft, forgiving soil. Do not imagine, however, that serious trials riding is for any but the strongest of heart. A trials rider has to negotiate incredibly difficult terrain at a slow speed; control is by throttle, brakes and, most importantly, by weight distribution. The rider utilizes his weight to the full by standing on the footrests virtually all the time.

To tackle a steep, muddy hill you must have as much weight as possible over the

Dave Taylor exhibits supreme control of his machine. A master of the wheelie, Taylor has ridden a 37¾ mile I.O.M. TT lap on his rear tire.

The importance of body lean is demonstrated by Taylor, here riding a trials machine at his motorcycle park.

A forward body stance keeps the front wheel down on steep climbs. Keep weight over the back wheel for traction. on a steep descent.

rear wheel for grip, but at the same time appreciate that if you lean back too far, the front wheel will lift and steerage will be lost. To go down a steep hill as slowly as possible (which is often more daunting than going up), you also need to get weight over the rear wheel to use the braking ability of the dirt bike's large-section rear tire, while lessening the risk of a front wheel slide.

When riding across a hill, or against a strong camber, the bike should be leaned out and the body in, so that the wheels are as close as possible to perpendicular to the surface, for maximum grip. The body should be as close to vertical as possible.

While trials riding presents the best examples of body lean, at a speed which allows the style to be studied, the road racer's technique equates more with road riding. Remember, though, that racers will never come across traffic heading the other way. Ace riders such as Kenny Roberts lean incredibly low into corners and can flick their bikes several feet across the track in an instant to overtake another rider. The flick is a body movement rather than a handlebar action and, in a sense, the bike is directed by force of will. This action can be called on as a defensive measure on the road when, perhaps, the door of a parked car is opened in your path. It may look and feel exciting but in normal conditions it is no more than showing off and can be dangerous.

Good riders, who have developed empathy with their machines, are able to ride harmoniously and unobtrusively.

For riding off-road, the ability to stand on the machine is vital. The technique remains the same, whether your bike is a tourer or an off-road bike.

Low speed control

Master throttle control and you will soon master low speed riding. Habitually use a snappy right wrist and you will never be adept at slow riding. Smooth, gentle throttle operation is imperative. It is impossible actually to teach anybody low speed control because it calls for practice and patience. It is not a knack, but a gradual learning process.

When riding slowly, you have more control if you can keep the throttle at an even setting rather than blipping it the whole time. Slip the clutch only when the speed is so slow that the bike will not pull evenly in first gear, and when you do so try to keep the revs even, although not

low enough to cause a stall, which is not only embarrassing, but can be dangerous in traffic.

The amount of power delivered to the rear wheel at low speed has a great effect on where the bike will go, certainly if you are cranked over for a corner. Imagine turning off a main road into a side street; you slow down before taking the turn, crank slightly into the bend and then open the throttle. The amount of throttle/power determines where you will be when you come out of the bend. Too much throttle/power will take you wide, and with too little you will be tight into the side of the road. With no

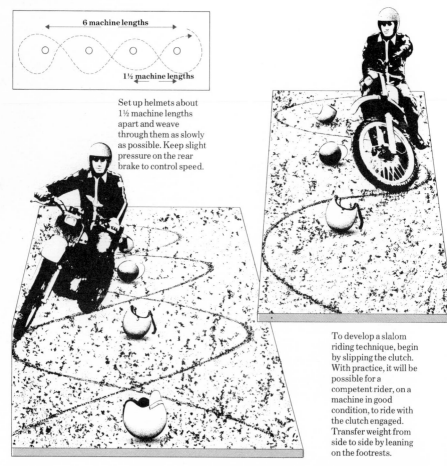

Set up helmets about 1½ machine lengths apart and weave through them as slowly as possible. Keep slight pressure on the rear brake to control speed.

To develop a slalom riding technique, begin by slipping the clutch. With practice, it will be possible for a competent rider, on a machine in good condition, to ride with the clutch engaged. Transfer weight from side to side by leaning on the footrests.

throttle/power at all you will have difficulty lifting the bike up from its leaning attitude.

Weight or pressure on the footrests also has an effect on steering which has to be learned by experience. Practise riding at the slowest speed possible while keeping your feet on the footrests. Steer with the handlebars and by shifting your weight on the rests. Think about it while you practise and try to understand the relationship between balance and steering ability.

Many riding tests incorporate a slow-riding slalom through cones, involving lock-to-lock turns at very low speeds, with the space between the cones about 1½ times the wheelbase of the bike. This is an easy exercise to set up on a piece of waste land. The technique is to have the clutch out all the time and not to be tempted to pull it in and slip it. You need a constant throttle opening which is often difficult when you are moving the

handlebars from left to right. If necessary, it is easy enough to adjust the carburetor to increase the idling speed, so that it will pull evenly in first gear without stalling, while still running slowly enough to tackle the test.

Another variation is the figure-eight test. This is more difficult, in that one has to ride so slowly that clutch slipping is essential. The knack here is to have an even throttle opening and to maintain your speed using the clutch and rear brake. The rear brake can be used during any low speed maneuvering, but always be gentle — don't stab at it. Apply slight pressure to the brake pedal so that if you ease the clutch out too quickly you will not shoot forward and flunk the test.

As final proof of your low speed control skills, try the police test of riding through a succession of 360 degree turns on continuous full lock. Use clutch, throttle and coordinated transfer of body weight to remain upright.

Full-lock turns can be done sitting down on a road bike, but the clutch will have to be slipped.

A trials or trail bike can be turned easily without using the clutch. But because of the wide bars

it is easier to ride standing up. Practise both ways, until you can turn continuous circles

on full lock in both directions without footing.

Cornering

The art of cornering is demonstrated at the highest level by the top road-racers. Their techniques have varied over the years, due mainly to improved frame design and the adhesive properties of modern racing tires, which allow the bikes to be cranked over to incredible angles. Freddie Frith, a master of many years ago, used to crank the bike over more than his body; Geoff Duke rode as though his body was a permanent fixture of the bike and he was one of the neatest riders ever. Modern aces hang off the bikes spectacularly. But do not try to copy them. Let your own style develop as your ability improves.

Extensive scratch damage from grounded stands, exhaust pipes and footrests demonstrates nothing more than the stupidity of a rider who is exceeding the machine's safe limits when cornering.

The modern motorcycle is a reasonably stable vehicle at over 20 mph. If you relax and take your hands off the bars the bike will continue in a straight line. But it is not only the handlebars that determine the path into corners. Weight placed on a footrest will gently turn the bike in that direction. Pressure on the handlebars mainly determines the path in and out of a corner, but this depends also on throttle control.

Many bikers find it hard to understand that to take a left-hand bend one first turns the bars to the right — this has

Riders' attitudes in corners vary with their experience and feel, and the condition of the road. Rider **a** is at one with his machine. The others, **b** and **c**, are apprehensive and overzealous respectively — their centers of gravity are not aligned with those of the machines.

centrifugal force

weight

a
b
c

At speeds of over 20mph a motorcycle is made stable by the gyroscopic force of the revolving wheels. Cornering is done by banking the machine, rather than turning the bars into the corner. The weight of the rider and machine counteracts the outward centrifugal force.

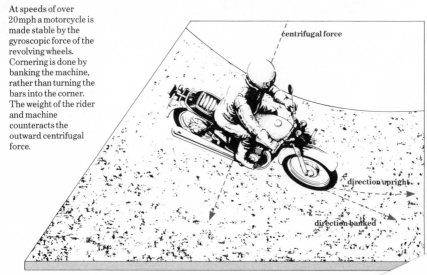

centrifugal force

direction upright

direction banked

the effect of tipping the bike to the left. The bars must then be turned to the left to maintain direction. The more pressure applied to the bars the harder and quicker you drop into the corner and come out of it. The higher your speed the more pressure you need to drop into and pull out of a bend. This is due to the gyroscopic power and, to some extent, the weight of the wheels. The heavier the wheels and tires, the more powerful the gyro effect and, therefore, the more pressure you need to make the turn.

How hard you can ride round a corner is determined by the tire adhesion and road surface. Braking hard when cranked over will make the tire slide, as will too much power or a jerky gear change. The idea is to pick the correct gear for the bend and stay in it until you are lifting out of the bend.

If a gear is missed just before you dive into a bend, it is sometimes wiser to freewheel rather than risk jerking, which will break traction. When this happens and the back of the bike does begin to move out, steer into the slide. Get all your weight off the saddle and on to the footrests so you can vary your weight distribution.

It is a good idea to work on one particular corner, so you know every ripple and every line of the road, until you have it perfect — that does not mean fast, but smooth and effortless. Make that corner your standard.

Checklist
1 Position yourself to the outside of the lane for the best vision throughout. Be able to stop within the limit of your vision.
2 Travel at the right speed. Brake early.
3 Be in the correct gear before banking over. Do not change gear during the maneuver.
4 Maintain an even speed.
5 Accelerate gently through the exit.

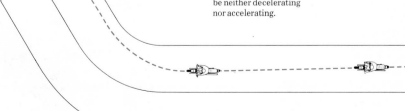

Adopt a cornering position which gives the best visibility throughout the curve. Do not imitate racers. Only straighten the exit of a bend.

The cornering procedure is to size up the corner for speed and line; do your braking and down shift before the bend. At the apex you should be neither decelerating nor accelerating.

After the apex straighten up and slowly accelerate. Too much power will take you wide; too little will keep you too tight.

Stopping

Stopping a motorcycle in the shortest possible distance is a test of the rider's reflexes and ability to assess tire adhesion on a particular surface.

Braking techniques vary slightly for differing surfaces, but the basic rule is to apply the front brake fractionally before the rear one and always to use both brakes together. There are a few circumstances in which only the rear brake should be used (on a slippery surface or in an emergency when cranked into a bend) but generally the rule is use both brakes. Never get into the appalling habit of using just one brake. If you rely on body reflexes to get you out of an emergency, it is possible that the most-used brake (usually the rear one) will be applied too hard and that will promote skidding.

The front brake and the grip of the front tire do most of the work of stopping. On a good, dry surface apply about 70 per cent pressure on the front brake lever and 30 per cent on the rear brake pedal, although without using pressure meters you will have to guess.

The best practice is to stop hard, using both brakes, while noting the amount of pressure you can put on the foot pedal without locking the rear wheel. The harder you use the front brake, the more weight goes on the front wheel and the sooner the rear wheel will lock.

On a wet road, use both brakes at the same pressure, to lessen the possibility

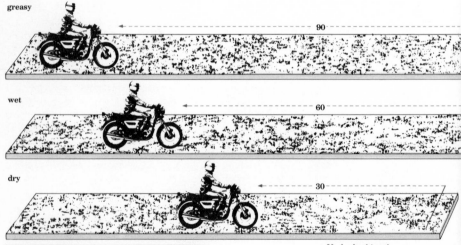

greasy 90

wet 60

dry 30

Checklist
1 Anticipate the need to brake, rather than leave it too late.
2 Watch the road surface and apply brakes smoothly.
3 In most circumstances, apply the front brake just before, and twice as hard as the rear.
4 Always brake with the machine upright, travelling in a straight line.
5 In the wet, apply occasional pressure to keep brakes dry.

Under braking the weight is forced forward. The forks compress, increasing the front tire grip. The rear wheel may hop on a rough surface.

of locking the front wheel. On really slippery surfaces, use engine braking helped by a gentle rear brake action. Always brake smoothly and progressively. Never stab at the rear brake pedal nor grab at the front brake lever.

Always brake when travelling in a straight line, never on a bend. It is possible to use the brakes on a bend but the degree of control necessary is only learnt by experience and the ability to recognize surfaces for their grip value develops slowly.

Most modern, large capacity motorcycles have disc brakes which, unlike those in cars, are not power-assisted. When the discs and brake pads are wet they are inefficient — in fact, in really

heavy rain the brakes sometimes just do not work when applied. A novice will press the brake lever hard in this situation — this is logical but dangerous because when the disc/pad clears the water film, the brakes will grab. With pressure applied on the brake lever it is easy to lock the wheel and lose control. Wet weather disc pads are available for most models, but if you have the standard pads it is wise, in heavy rain, to apply occasional pressure to the brakes to keep them free of water.

Downhill riding

It is easy to collect too much speed when riding downhill. This is not only dangerous but could also see you in trouble with the law for speeding.

When travelling down a steep hill change down a gear or two so as to use the braking power of the engine. Four-strokes have good engine braking capability and no harm is done on constant over-run. Two-strokes, however, do not have good engine braking and when the throttle is closed, not only is the fuel cut off but so is the oil supply, which is metered by the throttle. On over-run blip the throttle occasionally to deliver some oil to a 2-stroke engine.

A 2-stroke's engine braking can be improved by the fitment of a decompression valve to the cylinder head(s). These are worthwhile investments for 2-stroke owners who ride regularly in hilly country. Decompressors slow the movement of the piston by making it squeeze combustion gas through a valve into the atmosphere.

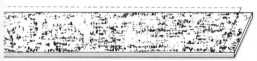

Braking distances are doubled on wet roads and at least tripled if they are greasy as well. In the wet, apply equal pressure to front and rear brakes. On greasy roads use the back unit more, as the front wheel is likely to break away. Remember that reaction times may also be increased by poor visibility.

Once at a standstill (but not before) select neutral. Apply both brakes and release the clutch.

Wait to move off with both feet on the ground, front brake on and gearbox in neutral.

Skidding

Many motorcycle accidents are the result of skidding, the main cause of which is panic braking. If the brakes are hit too hard the wheels will lock and a skid will develop. A skid can be avoided by smooth, skilled braking but if it does happen, let the brake off instantly then put it on again; if the wheel locks again, repeat the action. The new anti-lock braking systems do just that about four times each second. A human being cannot work as quickly so it is best to prevent the skid starting.

Skidding most commonly occurs when braking on wet off-camber surfaces; on greasy road sections such as the approach to traffic signals; under any tunnel when it is wet (tunnel washing maintenance), and on diesel fuel patches, autumn leaves, frost patches,

mud, cowpats or gravel on bends.

The ability to recognize surfaces for their grip value and assess the possibility of skid situations is knowledge gained mainly through experience. A thinking, alert rider constantly collects information about possible danger areas.

A front wheel skid is the hardest to control. All you can do is let the brake right off and try to ride it. A rear wheel skid can be mastered — again let off the brake and hold tight; if necessary, steer into the direction of the slide. It sounds difficult but it is, in fact, a strangely natural reaction. A front wheel slide while cranked over is usually caused by braking. You only realize what is happening as you hit the ground — it happens so fast. Experienced rough riders can kick themselves up if they are

A rear wheel skid on a muddy surface poses few problems if off-road tires are fitted. If the locked wheel continues to break away, the bike can often be kicked upright.

On wet pavement a skid at speed is almost impossible to control. Relax as you hit the road. This racer is kicking his bike away and protecting his head, while sliding.

quick. The skills acquired through regular off-road practice are worth having.

Another frequent cause of skidding is over-exuberant earoling — cranking over at an angle too great for the grip available, or meeting, while cranked over, a tire lubricant — diesel, mud, water, cowpat, gravel, oil. To survive this type of slide, lightning reactions and a natural machine control ability are needed. Your protective suit and helmet will probably be put to the test. A rear wheel slide can be controlled by steering into it and, again, a smart kick can get you out of trouble. When skidding, never give up. Fight it and you will find that usually you will stay aboard.

If you must crash, try to relax when you hit the road. This is easier said than done, but it is a fact that a sliding body suffers less than a tumbling body — tumbling breaks bones. If the bike slides and lays itself down it is imperative to get your leg out from underneath it before the bike actually hits the ground. If you are not pitched away from the bike hold on to it and try to climb on to the side of it. The extra weight will probably cause more damage to the sliding bike but it will stop quicker and you will not be injured. This may sound impossible, but it can be done.

The brain can work quickly when in terror; utilize it, don't throw away the ability by hollering in blind fear. DO NOT PANIC. Panic kills. Try to anticipate skid situations. Think how you would like to react then, if the situation occurs, put your thoughts into action.

Too much power can cause the rear wheel to break away. On a loose surface this can be controlled and used to broadside the machine round a curve in dirt-track style.

If you are separated from the bike, try to keep your eye on it and keep out of its path, perhaps by rolling. If it doesn't have crash bars it will stop quicker than your body—if it does have crash bars or a fairing it may slide for a long way. A tumbling bike can kill you if it hits you. Strong protective clothing such as a leather suit will resist penetration of sharp components.

During a skid the inside leg is in immediate danger of being crushed. Extract it as soon as you know the bike is falling. Either ride the sliding bike like a sleigh, or kick it away from you. If the bike and rider tumble together, the softer of the two will come off worse.

Observation

Of the many abilities a motorcyclist must develop, observation is one of the most essential. It is central to the police driving practices discussed in this section.

To gain maximum benefit from observation it must be combined with concentration and anticipation. These natural faculties should be developed to the level of skills. Observation means more than just looking—it involves looking at the right thing, intelligently. It is crucial that a motorcyclist is seeing and being seen at all times, not merely to promote general harmony among road users, but also as a basis of self-preservation.

If you wore spectacles to obtain your driving license, you must wear them when driving. Take note of any deterioration of your eyesight and visit an eye specialist if you have any doubts. Do not wear scratched faceshields or goggles or shaded ones in bad light. Adjust handlebar mirrors so that they provide a useful view of the road behind, and take steps to reduce vibration of the mirror lens, which confuses the image.

If you do not know your way, do not assume that you will find it. Plan your route beforehand and decide which roads you intend to use.

Good riding is dependent at all times on the correlation between position, speed and gear.

To see best what lies ahead, correct positioning is important. Always travel at a speed which allows you to stop safely within the distance which you can see to be clear. Look ahead to analyze the situation, and anticipate the actions of others. Ride in the appropriate gear for the speed so that the engine responds immediately to the throttle; whether you are about to accelerate or slow down will depend on what you have observed on the road ahead. Remember that speed affects vision. As you travel faster you focus farther ahead and foreground detail becomes blurred.

In city driving it is possible to watch car drivers in close proximity and anticipate their intentions from a slight movement of the head or hand. If a driver is in animated conversation with a passenger, give him a wide berth. His concentration will certainly be diverted from his driving. Puffs of smoke from a parked vehicle's exhaust, or movement within, will warn you that it is about to move off or discharge a passenger into your path.

Passengers moving inside a bus indicate a stop approaching. The sight of feet moving about beneath parked vehicles warns of pedestrians about to step into the path of traffic.

When approaching a road junction on your right, vision into the adjoining road can be improved by taking a position near the center of the road. A quick scan of the junction area before making the turn should include a look over the tops of parked cars or hedges and at any store windows which might bounce the reflection of an otherwise obscured vehicle.

Watch the road surface carefully at all times. Near bus stops, filling stations, road junctions and other places where vehicles brake to a standstill, tire rubber and brake dust are deposited, along with drips of oil, providing a treacherous surface for the bike rider. When the road is slightly wet (before it has been rinsed by the rain) it takes on a surface like ice. Similarly, a road which is drying out can be extremely slippery.

Freshly spilled diesel fuel from commercial vehicles is most common around the outside edges of curving traffic lanes. Bus and truck depots are invariably surrounded by heavy deposits of slippery fuel oil.

The usefulness of road signs is negated if they are not observed, understood and acted upon. Pay attention to signs and markings on the highway and think about what they mean, even if you are thoroughly familiar with the road. Read the road in all its aspects whenever you use it. Treat it with the greatest respect.

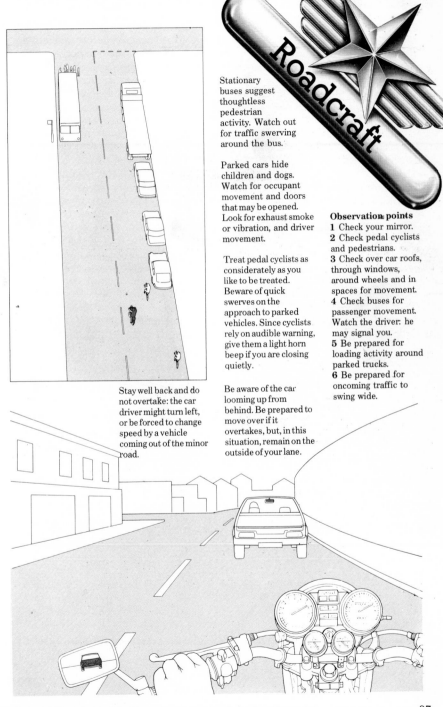

Stationary buses suggest thoughtless pedestrian activity. Watch out for traffic swerving around the bus.

Parked cars hide children and dogs. Watch for occupant movement and doors that may be opened. Look for exhaust smoke or vibration, and driver movement.

Treat pedal cyclists as considerately as you like to be treated. Beware of quick swerves on the approach to parked vehicles. Since cyclists rely on audible warning, give them a light horn beep if you are closing quietly.

Stay well back and do not overtake: the car driver might turn left, or be forced to change speed by a vehicle coming out of the minor road.

Be aware of the car looming up from behind. Be prepared to move over if it overtakes, but, in this situation, remain on the outside of your lane.

Observation points

1 Check your mirror.
2 Check pedal cyclists and pedestrians.
3 Check over car roofs, through windows, around wheels and in spaces for movement.
4 Check buses for passenger movement. Watch the driver: he may signal you.
5 Be prepared for loading activity around parked trucks.
6 Be prepared for oncoming traffic to swing wide.

Positioning

The first of the golden rules of roadcraft is: *be in the right place*. Positioning is crucial, both for immediate survival, and to make steady progress with consideration for other road users.

Being in the right position means that you will be unimpeded and conspicuous, with the best all-round vision and the space to maneuver and stop safely.

To pick a riding line that gives the best surface, the fewest obstacles, and the best vision under normal circumstances invariably means riding to the outside of the traffic lane—away from the curb, towards the center of the road. Think yourself into position before and during every maneuver, then follow through like a sportsman hitting a ball.

Never ride too close behind another vehicle. Your vision ahead will be reduced. Being able to see over the roof of a car is not sufficient because a pedestrian may step out from behind the vehicle before you can react. Riding too close also robs you of any safety braking distance. If your vision is limited give yourself more room for braking and maneuvering.

Incorrect position
This rider is in trouble. He is too close to the truck to see oncoming traffic, and to react safely as the truck brakes and swerves around the parked car which is pulling out.

Correct position
By holding back, the rider can contain the entire traffic scene in line-ahead vision, and is ready to take avoiding action, if required. He is also outside the braking line of a following vehicle.

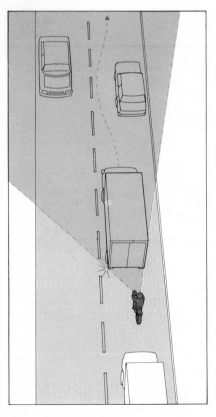

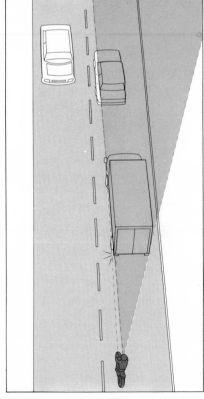

In slow moving city traffic allow at least one foot per mile per hour between you and the vehicle in front. As your speed rises above 30mph, increase the distance to one yard per mile per hour, under normal conditions.

It is foolish to sit squarely behind a vehicle you are following. This also limits your field of vision and the driver may be unaware of your presence. Positioning yourself slightly to one side of a vehicle gives a safety margin for observation and evasive action. Most vehicles have blind spots but if you can see the driver's face in his own rear view mirror, he will be able to see you—if he should chance to look. This applies particularly when riding behind a truck.

At road junctions and traffic signals, occupy a space in the center of your lane, so other traffic does not try to squeeze alongside.

Do not take curves too tight. Leave yourself room to see out of a bend. For a left-hand curve, move towards the right side of your lane. Begin a right-hand curve from the left. This will give you the best sight-line throughout the bend.

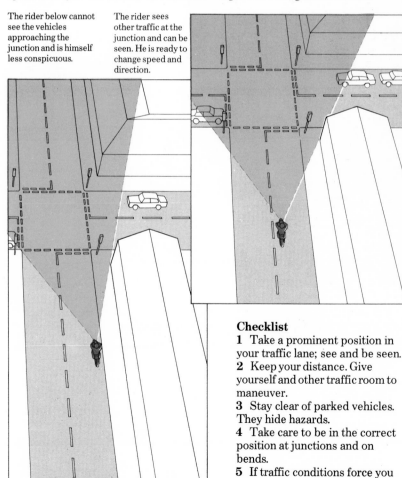

The rider below cannot see the vehicles approaching the junction and is himself less conspicuous.

The rider sees other traffic at the junction and can be seen. He is ready to change speed and direction.

Checklist
1 Take a prominent position in your traffic lane; see and be seen.
2 Keep your distance. Give yourself and other traffic room to maneuver.
3 Stay clear of parked vehicles. They hide hazards.
4 Take care to be in the correct position at junctions and on bends.
5 If traffic conditions force you out of position, slow down.

Overtaking

Overtaking is a skill to be learned, not hit upon by chance. It is one of the most frequent traffic maneuvers, yet one which can go dangerously wrong.

As vision ahead is opening up, you should be reading the road as far as you can see and analyzing the situation. Once aware of a vehicle ahead which you will want to pass, set yourself on the course to overtake as early as possible. Never leave it until the last few yards before committing yourself.

Remember, the vehicle ahead is a mass of moving steel, which can alter course or speed in an instant. Its driver is probably unaware of your presence. The vehicle is in your path and, as you close on it, so your braking distance is being reduced. Should a vehicle come from the opposite direction while you are passing, a fast-moving steel barricade will be closing in front of you.

Never pass a moving vehicle on a bend, the brow of a hill, a junction or on the approach to any hazard. Wait until it is safe to pass before overtaking. Obey road markings and signs. It is unwise and illegal to ignore them.

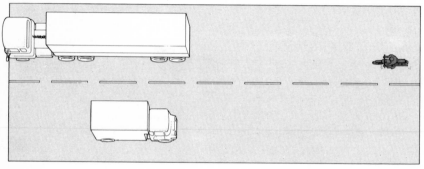

1 Move on to the course which you have selected for your overtake. Do this as early as the conditions allow, bearing in mind that a straight course is the only safe one.

2 You should be as aware of what is going on behind you as you are of what is ahead. Check behind and, if necessary, give the following traffic a signal of your intention to overtake.

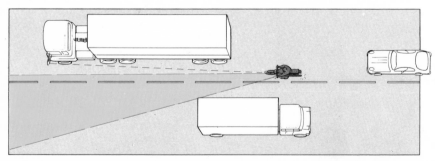

5 Does the vehicle ahead know that you are there? Be conspicuous. A flashed headlight could be misunderstood. A constant headlight is better.

6 Before you begin to pass, take a final lifesaver look behind, just to be sure that there is nothing trying to pass you.

The key elements of overtaking are:

Position. To overtake safely the machine must always be upright, travelling in a straight line.

Vision of the road ahead and behind.

Correct speed, which might change throughout the maneuver.

Correct gear for the speed. The machine must be able to respond instantly to the will of the rider.

Judgement of speed and distance. You must be able to assess the speed of the vehicle to be passed, and that of any oncoming traffic, relative to your own speed. Pass as quickly as possible.

DO NOT go when you cannot see. Always have a clear piece of road to ride on to after the overtake.

DO NOT change gear when alongside. A sudden loss of acceleration, or a missed gear, could be fatal.

DO NOT sweep in and take the other vehicle's braking distance.

DO NOT accelerate into a closing gap. Never begin to overtake when an opposing vehicle is closing on the vehicle you want to pass. You will become the meat in the sandwich.

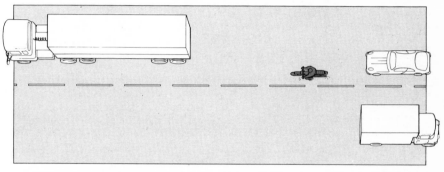

3 As you close up on the vehicle to be passed, balance your speed with his and select the appropriate gear for the speed.

4 Check behind once more. The situation is always changing, and a vehicle unaware of your intentions may have closed up on you. If necessary, signal your intentions.

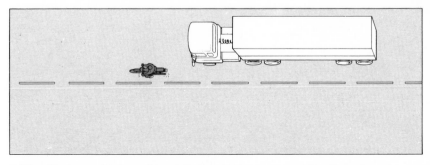

7 When all is clear, accelerate smoothly and crisply past the vehicle.

8 Resume your correct position on the road.

Road junctions

Let's say it again: position, speed and gear. Be in the right place on the road, travelling at the right speed for the situation, with the correct gear engaged. This rule applies at all times, but is of the utmost importance at road junctions, where traffic converges from all points of the compass and diverges in all directions. Remember that it is at road junctions where most accidents occur.

Concentrate and observe. Read the road ahead, picking up early clues even before you see the junction sign. The glare of brake lights, the movement of vehicles or the brightness of headlights at night can give you an early indication that a junction is ahead and may even give you some idea of its type and layout. A flashed glimpse through a gap between buildings or a field/garden gateway will often show you that a road is joining your route, how much traffic there is and how quickly it is moving.

Apart from the movement of wheeled traffic, you will have to contend with pedestrians waiting to cross the road, some with strollers, or trying to control children who have little idea of road sense but who possess phenomenal acceleration from a standstill.

The cross roads

Whether you are on a major or minor arm of such a junction, the basic rules apply. Never take it for granted that because you are on a major road you can blast through the junction. Bring into play that precious life-saving skill known as anticipation. Whatever your immediate riding plans are, they must always be based upon what you can see, and situations which might reasonably be expected to develop, even if they are not plainly visible immediately.

Take up position well before the junction. Early positioning not only puts you right for the situation ahead but also indicates your intentions to other traffic. For instance, if you are going straight on, the ideal position is just to the right of the center line (other traffic conditions

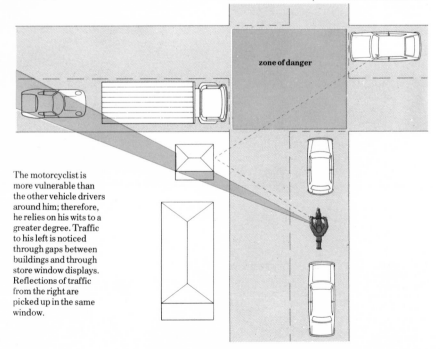

zone of danger

The motorcyclist is more vulnerable than the other vehicle drivers around him; therefore, he relies on his wits to a greater degree. Traffic to his left is noticed through gaps between buildings and through store window displays. Reflections of traffic from the right are picked up in the same window.

permitting). You will now be riding in a position which will give you earlier vision into the junction on your right than would be the case if you clung to the right side gutter. Thus you will get that vital early warning of a vehicle which may be approaching the junction too quickly and you will be able to take the necessary action.

Your vision into the junction on your left will be as good as is possible. Your speed of approach must always be such that you can stop safely within the distance of the road which you can see to be clear; so that if a "clown" enters the junction from a side road, you will be able to stop safely, almost without a change in your heartbeat!

The gearbox on your machine is a great friend, if used properly, and by selecting the appropriate gear for the speed at which you are travelling, you will ensure that the engine responds instantly to your control, enabling you to accelerate or decelerate quickly and safely, whatever emergencies may arise.

There is a point in any road junction, often called the zone of danger, where vehicles from all directions meet. It is the area where you will have finished with your braking, selected your gear, summed up the situation and be preparing to accelerate through the junction. A systematic approach to a junction must always be adopted, therefore, because when you reach that zone, vehicles are either coming to a standstill or accelerating away. To stagger into a junction in top gear is one way to get caught out. Finding yourself stationary in top gear and wanting urgently to clear the junction, you would be in dead trouble.

If you approach a junction on the minor road, be prepared to halt even if there is no Stop sign. Yield or give way markers should only be passed once you are positive that no traffic is coming your way: even if a car is indicating a turn it may continue straight over the junction.

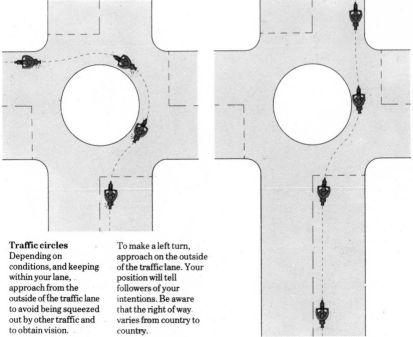

Traffic circles
Depending on conditions, and keeping within your lane, approach from the outside of the traffic lane to avoid being squeezed out by other traffic and to obtain vision.

To make a left turn, approach on the outside of the traffic lane. Your position will tell followers of your intentions. Be aware that the right of way varies from country to country.

Road junctions/2

The left turn is the maneuver which results in most accidents on the road because you must cross the path of traffic passing in the opposite direction. Other traffic may also approach from right angles.

1 As you approach the junction take up position — just to the right side of the crown of the road, having signalled your intention to turn.

2 Check behind and, if necessary, signal to following traffic that you intend to deviate and to reduce speed. Constant rear observation is as important as forward vision. Now reduce speed, using your brakes.

3 Select the correct gear for your speed.

Second gear will probably be the best for this maneuver as it will give you good control for the turn and, if you have to stop, the gear lever is only half a movement away from neutral.

4 Have another look behind (the picture may well have changed) and, if necessary, repeat your hand turn signal. Flashing signals should have remained in operation from the start of the maneuver.

5 Check if there is any vehicle or pedestrian nearby who should be told of your approach; if so a horn note should draw you to their attention.

6 Now you have reached the junction, take up a position opposite the center of

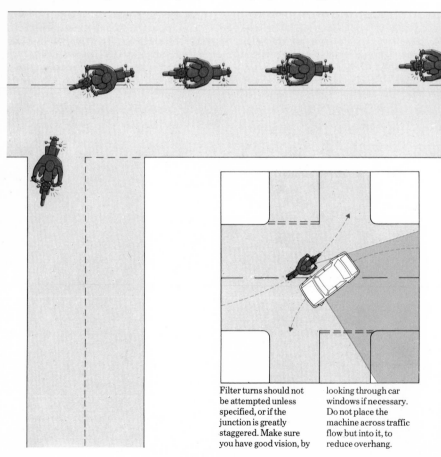

Filter turns should not be attempted unless specified, or if the junction is greatly staggered. Make sure you have good vision, by looking through car windows if necessary. Do not place the machine across traffic flow but into it, to reduce overhang.

the road into which you are turning. Never cut a corner.

7 Check that the road ahead is clear, but before completing your turn, look behind once more. This look is known as the lifesaver. There is always the impatient driver/rider who will rush down the left side of a line of vehicles waiting behind you and attempt to cut into the turning. He will be unaware of the presence of a motorcycle until it detaches itself from the other traffic. If you don't see him, he will scoop you up.

8 If it is safe, complete the turn, watching the road surface. Hard acceleration on a loose or slippery surface can do wonders for the seat of your pants!

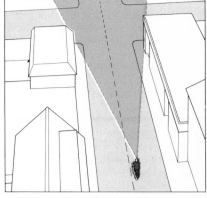

Position yourself for best visibility and conspicuity. As you decelerate adopt a line toward the center of the road. This also gives you extra room to maneuver.

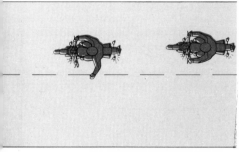

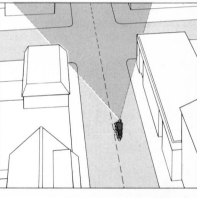

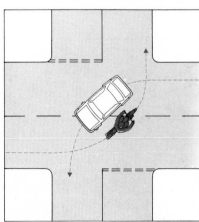

Most left turns are the cross-over type, in which vehicles are expected to cross each other's path. This is to provide both drivers with a clear view of oncoming traffic.

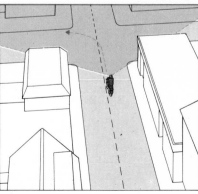

The field of vision improves as you approach the junction. Study other road users.

Help other drivers to anticipate your intentions. Use hand signals and the horn.

Urban hazards

City driving might appear to the novice to be smooth and trouble free. But, because of the mass of traffic moving along roads already crowded with parked vehicles and intersected by junctions which are often unsighted, everything tends to happen at once.

The pace and standard of driving vary from town to town and even change drastically from block to block. Emerging from the darkness of a high speed underpass into the stop-start bustle of a commercial district calls for keen observation. When pedestrians are added to this turmoil, the importance of the golden rules about position, speed and gear becomes vital.

The correct position is the one which enables you to obtain the best view and to place your machine correctly for the course you have planned. By taking a position away from the right-side curb, you will keep your machine off slippery drain covers and oil deposits at bus stops and keep clear of parked cars, the doors of which are so often opened thoughtlessly. You will gain extra vision ahead into those gaps between parked vehicles where impatient pedestrians often hover, and out of which pedal cyclists wobble. You will be away from the path of vehicles which might begin to pull into the line of traffic, and you will avoid being boxed in by traffic.

To ride close to parked vehicles not only means that you have to brake suddenly or alter course should a vehicle or pedestrian move into your path, but you may have robbed yourself of an early opportunity to see a road sign or junction.

When vehicles are travelling at similar speeds, many of the potential road emergencies are avoided. Should you, however, be blasting down the outside of traffic or forcing your way along a street crowded with pedestrians, you will have increased the speed differential between yourself and others, so reducing the safety factor — whether or not you

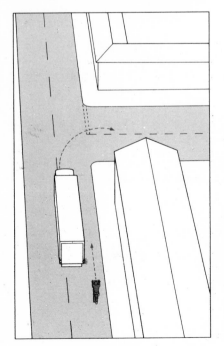

Big trucks are forced to swing wide for a tight turn. Many inexperienced riders drive down the right side and risk getting crushed. Once the turn is under way, the truck driver's mirror will not reflect any useful images.

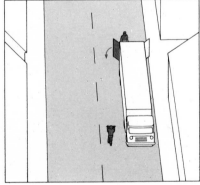

Trucks are frequently parked carelessly and doors are often swung wide into the traffic stream. Motorcyclists should watch for pedestrian movement close by, and be ready for sudden braking and/or direction changes.

are riding within the prescribed speed limit. Compare walking through a crowded pedestrian area with running through a similar crowd and you will understand how much harder it is to avoid collision when moving fast. Cars, trucks and buses are even harder to avoid and the truck driver, seated high in his noisy cab, can easily miss the racer who dives out from under his right side.

Do not emulate the motorcycle messengers, common to most cities, who ride on their nerves. These riders know the city well; they ride for money and therefore have their own equation for calculating the risks.

Local knowledge of an area is of great benefit but the skills of concentration, observation and anticipation must be honed to their finest. Remember that where vision is reduced things seem to happen more quickly.

The correct gear for the speed will ensure that your machine responds to your wishes, either delivering instant acceleration or added control when reducing speed.

Concentration can be reduced by your state of mind as well as your state of health. If you are tired, concentration is hampered and your reaction time is increased. Tired commuters riding home through the evening rush hour traffic may be in far from peak condition. The risks of riding to work in the morning can also be magnified by the after-effects of a heavy night out.

Look out for the tell-tale danger signs of increased pedestrian activity from factories, theatres and sports grounds disgorging their human contents.

Car drivers who have been sitting in lines of slow-moving traffic all day become frustrated and are likely to make irrational or desperate moves. Be prepared for the sudden, frantic U-turn by the driver who wants to chance his luck in another direction. Taxi drivers are notorious for their unorthodox maneuvers; treat them with caution.

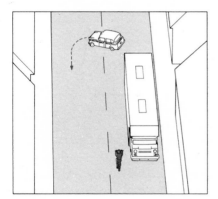

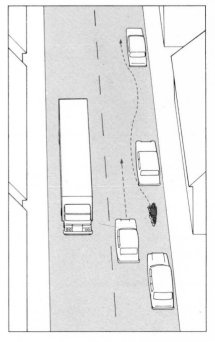

U-turns are common in cities, however unlawful they may be. Riders should expect the unexpected from taxi drivers who are accustomed to other vehicles giving way.

When two vehicles meet in a narrow road, one gives way. Motorcyclists who ride on the right should be prepared to accept the consequences of being trapped.

Rural roads

The experience of riding the open road, with its lighter traffic and lack of restrictions is a sensual one — almost without parallel. It is here that the motorcycle returns the best value. None the less, it should not be taken as an opportunity to switch off the brain and senses. The rules of riding still apply. .

A winding lane can hide all manner of hazards which can catch out the unprepared. The rider who is concentrating will observe the smallest details and prepare for what could otherwise be difficult situations. Newly cut grass on the verge, cuttings blown on to the road or smelled in the air, warn that a mower may be just out of sight, working its way along the road.

When vision is lost and position on the road cannot be modified enough to improve it — reduce speed. Never bore along until the hazard comes into view. At 30 mph (48 km/h) you will be covering 46 ft/sec (14 m/sec). With the average reaction time of 0.75 sec, a rider will have covered around 33 ft (10 m) before he can do a thing about slowing his bike — or notice the driver coming the other way, passing the mower.

Riding blind into an unknown curve is fraught with many possible dangers. Never guess at the line of the road regardless of what unforeseen obstacles may await you. Bends on country roads are frequently tighter than at first they appear. On hilly ground be prepared for ever-tightening hairpin bends.

Note the shadows thrown across the road on a bright day. You can then be prepared for the blinding shaft of sunlight which will hit you as you turn a bend or breast a slope. Even the shadow of a horsebox or combine harvester can be thrown on to the road ahead. The vehicle may be unsighted to you but the shape will be enough to indicate its approach to a bend or road junction. Watch the lie of the land, the run of the hedgerows, and the severity of the undulations. There is nothing worse than

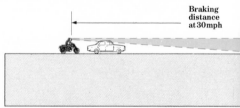

Braking distance at 30 mph

Learn to detect hazards before they arise. This rider has slowed for the fresh muddy tracks across the lane, and will be inspecting both gateways to ascertain the cause of them.

Country roads dip as acutely as they curve; riders who make a guess at the depth and length of dips and the vehicles they hide risk their lives as surely as they would speeding around a blind bend on the wrong side.

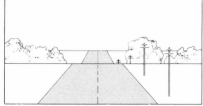

coming upon a sudden drop with 10 mph (16 km/h) too much on tap.

Long straight roads with many undulations can hide large vehicles in the dead ground at the bottom of the dip. Do not imagine it is safe to pass.

The keen eye will spot the changes in direction evidenced by the line of the hedgerow or telegraph poles striding off into the distance. But reading the road involves interpretation of the various details observed — telegraph poles may suddenly take a different path from the course of the road. On a hilly route the severity of a gradient can often be gauged by noting roadside properties. If you can only see the tops of roofs or trees a short way ahead you will know that the road drops steeply. When you can see the lower branches of trees or most of a telegraph pole the hill is less steep.

The road surface itself can contain some nasty surprises. Wet leaves beneath trees or neatly placed road apples (cow pats) make good lubricants between road and tire. Road apples also warn of trouble ahead. Always treat animals with respect. Pass them slowly, or stop and wait. Dirty tire tracks may herald a farm or field entrance where the road grip is reduced. Damp conditions make even old deposits of mud lethally slippery. Observe, react and remain aboard.

Fords, puddles or pools of water left in the dip of a country lane are to be avoided. If that is not possible then ride through as slowly as you can. The water may not look deep but it may obscure a jagged-edged pothole beneath the surface. Flooded electrics are trouble. If you have to ford water, however shallow, always run for the next few hundred yards with the brakes lightly applied.

Respect the pace of country living. Do not antagonize the locals who might resent the presence of fast traffic —they might also be inexperienced at driving in traffic and, therefore, be potentially dangerous.

Speed over dead or lost ground (a series of acute dips) should be limited by what is visible within your braking distance. Look far ahead for other vehicles before they enter the dips.

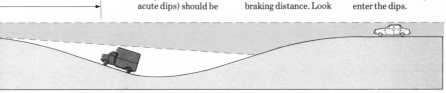

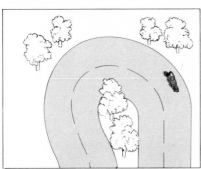

Bends on country roads often tighten unexpectedly. Position yourself to see through a bend. Take the entrance wide and do not cut the corner until you can see a clear exit.

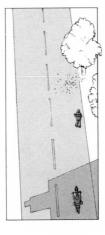

In damp climates the area beneath trees is often slippery with fallen leaves or sap. This is dangerous on corners.

Walkers usually look after their own interests by facing oncoming traffic, but novices sometimes walk with their backs to oncoming traffic.

Shadows may hide hazards. In this case the rider will soon face a flash of sunlight.

Freeway riding

On a freeway the normal advantages of riding a motorcycle — its superior mobility and the rider's greater awareness — are negated by the unavoidable regimentation of many vehicles in close proximity at high speed. The higher volume of fast-moving freeway traffic in Europe has led to drivers having a much less benevolent attitude to other motorists than they do in America. Driving standards are frequently worse on controlled-access highways because people are easily lulled into a sense of false security.

Freeway accidents might be fewer per vehicle/mile but statistics are rarely specific about motorcyclists' injuries, which must inevitably be serious or fatal. In dry daylight, conditions are comparatively safe. Should a rider fall off in darkness or bad weather he surely will be killed or maimed because he will not be visible to other drivers.

Most freeway accidents are due to insufficient braking distances and loss of maneuverability. A motorcycle is further disadvantaged because it cannot be stopped dead instinctively, as it is inherently unstable and requires much greater skill to brake than a car. Neither can a bike be maneuvered as quickly at speed.

Alternative routes usually exist, so use them. Unless you are willing to suffer the dangerous consequences of arousing other drivers' impatience, it is unwise to use a freeway unless your motorcycle cruises relaxedly at a minimum of 70 mph (120 km/h). Despite legal limits, normal fast vehicle speed is highest in Germany at 110 mph (180 km/h), followed by France at 90 mph (145 km/h), Britain at 85 mph (133 km/h) and America at 65 mph (105 km/h).

In practice rear glances and hand signals are unsafe. At 110 mph (180 km/h) a usefully long three-second glance will take you about 1,500 ft (450m), and this is much more than the probable distance between you and the

Use the access lane, or on-ramp to a fast highway, to accelerate up to traffic speed. It is dangerous to hesitate or ride it like an ordinary road junction.

In bad weather, do not travel on the central strip of any lane used by heavy trucks: they drip oil from chassis lubricating points, leaving a slippery track. The lane edges are cleaner and more adhesive.

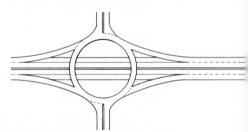

car in front, which might crash-stop.

1 When joining a freeway, accelerate along the access road to match the speed of the first-lane traffic. Study this traffic carefully and ease into it, using turn signals.

2 Use twin mirrors constantly and turn signals for every lane change. Never cruise in an overtaking lane — and leave no room for impatient drivers to bully past you in the same lane. Keep well clear of dangerous close formations of other vehicles.

3 Stay well clear of non-adhesive rubber and oil deposits in the centers of first and second lanes, especially in wet weather when you should ride along the clean lane edge. Be wary of rain grooves. Some cause instability with certain tires.

4 Be patient. Wait for long lines of vehicles ahead to clear naturally. Your flashing headlight may only antagonize other drivers in the same position as you. But move over for the impatient headlight flashers yourself.

5 Overtake fast-moving trucks — only after checking behind to make sure it is safe to do so — with a full lane between them and you to avoid the powerful turbulence. This is vital when strong cross-winds are blowing.

6 Study the wind and be wary of deep cuttings, exposed high bridges, gaps in woods, hills and banks, etc.

7 In dirty weather avoid following other vehicles closely. Their road spray will coat your faceshield or goggles. Tie a cotton rag or piece of chamois around your left forefinger to wipe shields clean.

8 Check your brakes frequently in wet weather.

9 In heavy fog ride without faceshield or goggles at low speed. Enquire about the weather ahead at the next service area, and/or leave the freeway.

10 When leaving the freeway do not rely on instinct to gauge speed. Use your machine's instruments, which are more reliable. Prolonged high speed riding dulls the senses.

High bridges generate turbulence. Relax: it usually feels worse than it really is.

Powerful cross-winds blow through gaps in cuttings and hills. Watch for clues.

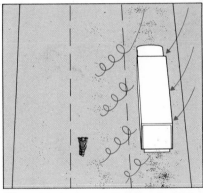

When passing trucks on windy days, leave a lane width between you to avoid the turbulence.

Fast riders should rely on mirrors and turn signals. Backward glances take time, and hand signals at high speed induce instability.

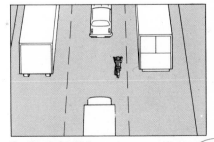

Bunching is the chief delight of some drivers: stay well clear of these dangerous groupings.

Bad weather

Bad weather is bad news to all road users, but riding in wet or cold conditions need not hold any fears for the careful rider who takes precautions.

First of all, ensure that you are properly dressed to combat the elements. A rider who is cold or wet finds it more difficult to concentrate and to react properly and promptly. Not only should your clothing be water- and wind-proof, but it should be roomy enough to prevent too tight a fit at elbows, knees, seat and shoulders; otherwise the insulation provided by warm air pockets inside the suit is impaired at such places. Ensure a good overlap between gloves and sleeves and trousers and jacket. Seal the collar at the neck with a comfortable scarf. Good, sound boots keep out the weather and protect the lower limbs from injury in the odd bump or slither. Trousers must overlap your footwear well to keep out damp or cold drafts.

The condition of the machine is particularly vital during the winter months. Electrical components should be waterproofed, and tires in prime condition.

In wet conditions the most immediate problem is the potential loss of adhesion. Roads are most slippery after the first rainfall, before the grease has been rinsed off. A balanced riding position is all important. As soon as the machine is moving, get your feet up on the foot rests and keep them there. A trailing foot will unbalance the machine. Never ride on slippery surfaces with feet down. Try to keep your machine as upright as possible and coordinate the operation of the controls so that changes of gear or the application of brakes or throttle take place smoothly. Operate each control on the bike as gingerly as possible. Accelerate only when the machine is upright, and then lightly and smoothly.

Ride in as high a gear as is practicable. Throttle variations will not then be transmitted too sharply to the rear wheel and cause it to break away. Speed

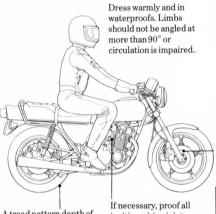

Dress warmly and in waterproofs. Limbs should not be angled at more than 90° or circulation is impaired.

A tread pattern depth of at least 2mm is vital for adequate adhesion.

If necessary, proof all ignition wiring joints with special sleeves or adhesive tape.

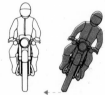

Cornering should be the same as in the dry, but with more delicate control. Watch for deadly rainbow-colored diesel spillage on the road.

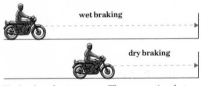

wet braking

dry braking

The harder a front brake is used, the more water is squeezed from under the tire. But if the road is at all greasy the front wheel will skid. Rear wheel skids are less serious, so use the rear brake more than normal.

The assumption that drum brakes are inherently superior to disc brakes in wet weather is wrong. When drum brakes do get wet, they require a long period of careful drying out. Test brakes regularly.

As a general rule do not attempt to ride far without eye protection, unless it is inescapable — even a fogged-over faceshield or goggles can be smeared clear with saliva. Heavy rain can penetrate the tear ducts, chill, inflame, swell and finally block the sinuses. This can lead to sickness if the sinuses are not free to drain.

reduction using the brakes should also be carried out smoothly. Lightly apply both brakes equally, with the bike upright. When moving at a crawl in traffic, however, light application of the rear brake will often suffice.

Sadly, although disc brakes are superior to drum brakes in many ways, some manufacturers have yet to master the wet efficiency of disc brakes in the rain. Bear this in mind when on the move and give the brake an occasional squeeze. A warm disc is less attractive to flying spray and will be more immediate in its response. Be warned; if the brakes slip, do not grasp the lever in a desperate vise-like grip, or when the brake eventually does bite you will be spat off as the front wheel locks up. Needless to say, a similar firmly applied back brake will lock up the rear end in an instant.

In the wet, braking distances are greatly increased and if vision is reduced things can go wrong quite suddenly. Clean but wet pavement offers half the coefficient of friction of dry pavement.

Avoid riding on the greasy strip in the center of a lane. Raised, painted lane markings and studs, railway tracks and manholes should be avoided or ridden over cautiously.

Defensive riding and early analysis of the road conditions is of paramount importance. Pick up clues from whatever useful source there is. On the open road, early observation of spray ahead will warn of other traffic and can even indicate the force of the wind. If the traffic ahead is passing an open space you will be forewarned of cross-winds and be ready for any blinding faceful that might be coming your way. The same is true of deep puddles ahead which could flood your electrics, or unseat you by causing the bike to aquaplane.

Spray obscures vision and can cause faceshields to mist over. An anti-mist or soap solution rubbed over the inside will prevent this. If vision is impaired, reduce speed.

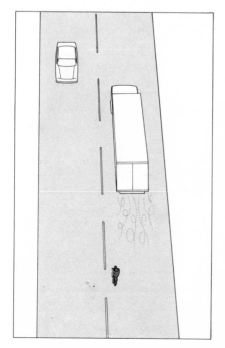

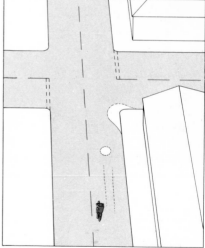

Never follow large vehicles along wet roads: the backwash of dirty spray is blinding. A rider this close has lost his braking space, anyway.

All metal studs, covers, lane markers and some painted markings should be avoided in wet weather: they offer no adhesion whatsoever.

Bad weather/2

Riding on ice calls for delicate control of the machine. Progress should be slow; gear changes must be as smooth as you can possibly make them; braking should be controlled by the rear unit.

Invisible, or "black" ice, which cannot easily be identified, creates an extremely dangerous road surface, either when a wet road freezes or when rain falls on a freezing road surface. As it is clear, not frosted, you may think it is just a wet patch—until you hit it.

Grit, which is laid on icy roads, is usually sprayed to the crown of the road and the gutters by passing vehicles. Depending on the road surface and severity of the weather, the grit should provide better grip for straight-line riding, but *worse* traction for cornering. Salt makes roads slippery.

Remember that ice develops more quickly on bridges, on roads in exposed country or on the shoulders of hills near the top. It also lingers in the shadows under overpasses or bridges. The first warning of ice on the road is often given by the changing noise of the tires, as the hiss of a wet surface gives way to a more muffled sound. An open-face helmet lets warning signals through to the face, which can feel temperature variations. Full-face helmets may be more cozy but they do isolate the rider from the elements.

Never slam the throttle shut when riding on ice — the torque change will lock the rear wheel. Do not brake if you can help it, just lose speed as gently and smoothly as you can. Relax, hold on to the bars and let the bike run its course. Do not try to snatch at the handlebars.

Snow presents few of the problems of ice, except that the two often come together. Virgin snow can be ridden through without fuss. Steer towards the edge or the middle of the road — out of tire tracks which will be hard-packed and slippery. Be wary, however, if you do ride in the middle of the road. When the snow has frozen it presents more

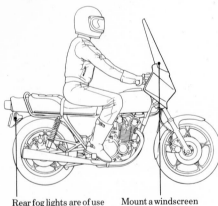

1 Decelerate with gears before brakes.
2 Ride in a high gear at low revs.
3 Keep your feet up.
4 Relax: do not clench the bars.
5 Grit in the gutter provides grip.
6 Virgin snow gives good grip; hard tracks, no grip.
7 Slush causes aquaplaning at low speeds.
8 Salted roads are more slippery than wet ones.

Rear fog lights are of use only to riders who encounter fog regularly. Forward-facing lights should be mounted low and wired to the dip circuit.

Mount a windscreen just below eye level for clear vision.

When riding on ice or snow, a slightly deflated tire provides less bounce and more adhesion. Ride slowly.

Light diffuses and some inevitably bounces back. The diffusion of a

dipped beam is less dazzling than that of the main beam.

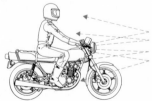

problems. Piled up slush becomes as hard as rock. If you have to cross such a ridge take it at a 90 degree angle.

Try to avoid riding in fog, if this is at all possible. If you do have to continue on your way, stay clear of freeways or other high-speed roads. It should be second nature for all drivers to slow right down in fog but it is amazing how many drivers do not bother. Try to drive on roads with street lighting.

If you drive within the limits of your vision, then a heavy fog will slow you down to a walking pace. Fog not only affects vision but also makes the road surface slippery, thereby reducing braking ability.

The biggest danger in fog, after that of being run down from behind, is running into something yourself. It will be necessary to follow a lane marker or other clue to the direction of the road. If possible stay clear of the verge, where obstructions may be lurking unseen. But bear in mind that riding in the middle of the road is always dangerous.

To avoid goggles or faceshields misting up and restricting vision even further, you can ride without them — this will also help keep your speed down.

Do not follow other vehicles too closely. If you latch on to another vehicle's tail lights, maintain the biggest possible gap between you. Do not overtake unless it is unavoidable. The fog will be clearer around vehicles. At the head of a line of traffic it presents a wall of opacity.

Headlights on main beam will bounce back off the wall of fog. Use dipped lights to be seen and special fog lights to penetrate the gloom. Rear fog lights are useful defensive extras but if you have no additional lighting and still you *must* ride, the rear brake light switch can be cheated so that the brake light remains on. String, wire or tape can be used. This should only be done as a last resort when conditions are so bad that immediate survival is your only concern.

To keep faceshields clean use demister spray, soap, spittle or a potato. Tie a rag around the finger to wipe off spray.

A heated faceshield does not mist up and keeps the rider's face warm. It is run off the battery, using about 40 watts.

Do not follow rear lights too closely but keep them in sight to enjoy the safety of a clear lane.

In fog on a familiar road do not be lulled into a false sense of security. Expect new hazards.

A car parked against the traffic flow with its lights on could make you drive off the road.

When visibility is reduced, reaction times are increased.

Night riding

When darkness falls, new conditions arise. Not only is your vision restricted but your visibility to other road users is reduced.

The judgement of speed and distance is drastically altered by both the incomplete vision of other vehicles and the inability to judge perspective and dimension from roadside objects.

A solo motorcycle, as it passes behind an obstruction, can be overlooked by another road user sitting at a road junction. Even wearing a reflective jacket, if you are physically out of view, you will not be seen by others and will not enter into their consideration and judgement.

See and be seen is, therefore, the motto when driving in the dark, more so than at any other time. Start with basic considerations. Never take it for granted that your lights are all in order. Check them thoroughly and regularly. Terminals can get dirty; wires can work loose and nothing is more dangerous than all the lighting blacking out on a dark or dimly lit road. Even a dirty headlight lens will cut down the limit of your vision ahead and reduce your visibility to other road users. A motorcyclist has less excuse than a car driver for not noticing a light failure — and more reason to rectify it. The efficiency of lenses can deteriorate imperceptibly with the daily build-up of road dirt and the resulting decline in light value may go unnoticed. A clean machine is not only a more reliable machine, as defects are found as a matter of course during regular cleaning, but shining paintwork and metalwork will reflect the surrounding light. If your bike has side-mounted amber reflectors, keep them clean.

Set up lights correctly, always bearing in mind that a pillion passenger will alter the line of your light beam. Remember that on a bumpy road, particularly on some lightweight motorcycles, the headlight beam can bounce up and down

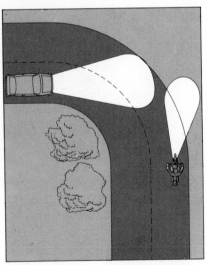

Oncoming traffic is heralded by headlight glare. Flash ahead to warn of your approach and dip your lights to see better and to avoid blinding oncoming drivers. Vehicles on the inside of a bend create dazzle before the lights of a vehicle on the outside.

Expect to be dazzled by the lights of vehicles approaching over the brow of a hill, on a bridge or undulating roads, whether they are on main beam or dip.

If a driver refuses to dip slow down and look away—to the right preferably. Do not try to out-dazzle him; he may have badly adjusted lights which are already dipped and which he could flash with blinding effect.

Drive within the iluminated braking distance

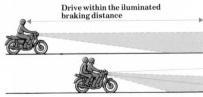

At over 70 mph the main beam will not illuminate the braking distance. Readjust the beam when carrying a load or passenger.

quite considerably. Always set a dipped beam to cut in well to the right to save others the discomfort of being dazzled.

Whatever message you want to convey, *never* flash your main beam into the face of other road users. A dazzled driver becomes disorientated and may quite rapidly collide with you or another road user. Never take another driver's flashed signal for granted. The lights may have been switched on by accident.

Ride so that you are not shielded from view by your close proximity to other vehicles. Keep out from the curb to improve your vision ahead and avoid the risk of colliding with a suddenly-opened car door. Remember that you are less visible at night.

When traffic is approaching you, always dip your headlight and look away from the glare of the oncoming lights. Stay in from the center of the road. The vehicle may have an overhang that obstructs your part of the road or it may be hiding a vehicle running with only

right-hand lights on. This is particularly important when the road is narrow. There is no point being angry about unlit vehicles, loads or road obstructions, simply be alert enough to avoid them and stay alive.

On an unlit road, always momentarily dip your headlight as you approach a bend or corner. This will enable you to detect the glare of an approaching set of headlights. This early warning could be denied you if your main beam has out-flared them.

Always dip lights on the approach to the brow of a hill. If the main beam shines into the open sky ahead, and is bounced back as a white glare, vision is lost.

Remember to read every clue at night. Take nothing for granted. If you cannot see, then don't go. If you are not sure of the situation, don't go. Never ride into a position from which there is no visible exit. Never overtake when you cannot see what is in front of the vehicle to be passed.

Electrical system faults usually become apparent at night. Check equipment regularly and correct any faults before the onset of winter.

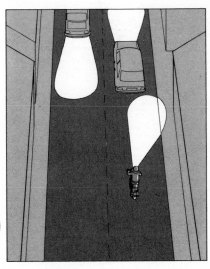

Take care of your lights. If a rear light blows jam on the brake switch. If the headlight blows ride to a garage on the alternative beam.

In an emergency remove amber lenses from front turn signals and wire the circuit direct to the battery.

Do not pass another vehicle until you can see the road ahead of it. Flash a warning before overtaking. Headlights,

particularly a motorcycle light which is high enough to blind drivers easily, should dip to the right.

Conspicuity

Being conspicuous certainly does not mean behaving like a lunatic and drawing attention to yourself by noisy, inconsiderate and illegal riding.

If you are forever being "carved up" by drivers who turn suddenly across your path, stop and think about it. Examine your own riding style and approach to other road users. Can they see you? To stay alive, motorcyclists must be seen — by drivers in the same lane as much as by oncoming and cross traffic.

Motorcycles are comparatively unobtrusive. They can be obscured by lampposts, trees, pedestrians or street furniture at fairly close range, particularly when approaching head-on.

The correct position on the road will vary with the particular circumstances. At a multi-road junction drivers have a great deal to look out for and there is every chance that a bike moving up on the left of a line of traffic will go unnoticed. Never ride squarely behind the vehicle in front, either. You will almost certainly be hidden in one of the driver's blind spots and, if the vehicle brakes, you will probably hit it.

Ride so that the driver ahead can see you in his rearview mirror. If you ride close to the inside your presence is likely to be missed. Right-hand mirrors, when fitted, are quite often ignored and overtakers are not expected along that side. The inside creeper is denied vision ahead and will be boxed in, finding it difficult to avoid parked vehicles. Riding nearer the center of the road makes you more obvious to other road users, and widens your own field of vision.

Daytime headlights, although they are compulsory in some places and frequently recommended everywhere, have a limited value; if the other road users are not looking your way, you will never be seen and if your headlight is set with its beam too high, you will cause aggravation. In poor visibility a dipped headlight is essential. Most drivers find it difficult to judge the speed of

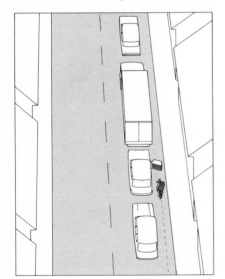

Riders who insist on travelling up the inside of a traffic lane cannot be seen by drivers. Passengers often hop out on the right, usually without looking behind them. To be conspicuous give others a chance to see you.

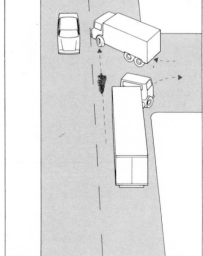

This rider has passed a vehicle without a clear road ahead and ends in a dangerously cramped position. Although he is visible to the approaching traffic, his presence will be overshadowed by the two larger vehicles.

oncoming motorcycles and even though you may be seen, do not assume that your intentions are understood.

Overtake lines of traffic only when you can be seen. You must always be able to stop safely within the distance of the road you can see to be clear. If you cannot pass the whole line safely in one go, then overtake one vehicle at a time, letting each vehicle driver know you are there. Keep in mind all the time that there may be a vehicle moving out through the line ahead, so do not begin to pass unless you can see that the road which you want to occupy is clear. Use turn signals throughout the maneuver.

A flashed headlight or horn note should only be used to inform other road users of your presence behind them, not to burn or blast them off the road. The etiquette varies from country to country, and people's attitudes even more often. Many drivers resent being honked at. Such signals are only of use when given at the right moment. Give the horn signal

from a point behind the vehicle which will enable its driver to notice you and react to your presence. Wait a moment; do not just honk as you pass. If you blow your horn too close to a vehicle you might put yourself in danger as the driver reacts to your close presence.

A clean bike is more likely to be a reliable bike and it is more conspicuous on the road than a dirty one. A well-turned-out machine will attract more than admiring glances from other bikers. Bright paint and metalwork do reflect back sunlight or streetlamp light, but more importantly the condition of a bike is a reflection of the owner's attitude. The rider who operates skilfully, gives good signals and considers others is noticed by more people than you might think.

It is sensible to wear something bright and/or reflective, but remember that to be seen you must also see. Give other road users every opportunity to see you — ride defensively.

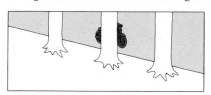

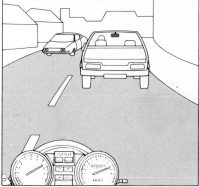

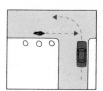

Motorcyclists can be hidden as they ride behind trees or street lights. Turning drivers should double check, but is the cycle visible when they do look?

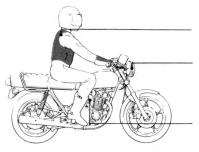

Conspicuous warning clothes do work. They can be seen from a long way off.

Daytime headlights should make bikes more visible. Use them constantly in rain or poor weather.

A clean bike stands out in the gloom and faults can be spotted easily.

Correct positioning means riding where you can see and be seen. Position yourself to the outside of your traffic lane and keep your distance. If you can see the mirrored face of the driver ahead he can see you.

119

Advanced riding

Advanced riding is what all riders should aspire to. Experience might only teach you to ride automatically. Experts ride systematically.

Good riding is done on small bikes just as much as on bigger machines, and it does not depend on achieving high speeds or looking spectacular.

An advanced rider should be able to handle and control his machine skilfully through its entire performance range — this requires practice with every new machine, particularly one bigger than ridden previously. It takes a skilled rider to ride safely and slowly under full control in heavy traffic. Great maturity is indicated by a rider holding back and not blasting through a closing gap in traffic when the less skilled would think it was the right thing to do.

Because a rider has a big bike and can claim high average speeds for a journey, he or she is not necessarily any more qualified as an advanced rider than the motorcyclist on a 125 who can commute safely and unobtrusively week in, week out, through city traffic. Unfortunately, press road-testers spend too much time writing about top speeds and rates of acceleration, too little about a machine's low speed abilities. They seem to make nothing of the dangerous lack of braking potential of many disc brakes in the wet, so the young motorcyclist could be forgiven for believing that the opposite were true.

The advanced rider can, of course, travel at speed safely, can handle a machine safely in heavy traffic and ride considerately. To attain a peak of skill the rider must have a large amount of basic bikecraft; he will have to rely upon more than the power of a machine. The advanced rider will adopt a riding position which suits his frame, and is comfortable over a long distance, giving complete control at all times. This may well be a semi-racing crouch, but no intelligent person would sacrifice comfort for style — would they?

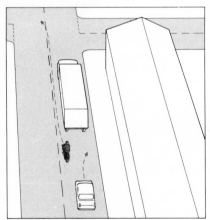

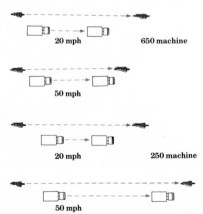

20 mph   650 machine

50 mph

20 mph   250 machine

50 mph

Prior knowledge of the route and the road conditions allows a rider to anticipate. By riding in the correct position he does not have to make last minute adjustments to his chosen course. Give other road users as much room as you take for yourself.

The differential in passing speeds for bikes of different sizes varies a lot. At 20mph, a sporty 250 and a slow 650 can both pass a big truck in about 6.6 seconds. But to pass it at 50 mph, the 250 takes 12 seconds and almost 1,300 ft; a 650 bike takes only 8 seconds and less than 1,000 ft.

danger zone 410 ft.

If you are travelling at 70 mph and anything steps into your path within 410 ft you will hit it.

The advanced rider will demand good lights to see and be seen, and smooth operation of all controls; will know the characteristics of the machine inside out; will know, for instance, that even a sporty lightweight will need more space to complete safe overtaking at high speed than a bigger bike.

It will also be ingrained into the advanced rider's thinking that a big bike can get its rider into trouble more quickly because, as speed rises, so the limits of safety diminish. Reaction times remain more or less constant (depending on your state of health and degree of concentration), but braking distances and distances covered to execute a maneuver can vary frighteningly. Therefore, just as your position in the road, speed for the situation and correct gear must always be spot on, so, as the road speed increases, your vision ahead must be projected that much farther in front.

At 70 mph (115 km/h) a rider's attention is focused on a point about 2,600 ft (800 m) ahead. It will take only 23 seconds to cover this distance. As the combined thinking time and braking distance is 410 ft (125 m) it is unlikely that the rider will either see in time, or be able to miss, anything intruding into this vital stretch of road directly ahead.

It is a fallacy that safer riding is guaranteed by assuming all other road users are unpredictable idiots. A superior attitude will do no good. Most other road users are as sensible as yourself. In view of the high degree of driver conformity, the trick is to locate the drivers who do not conform to normal behavior patterns and treat them with great caution. Attitudes and road manners differ widely between big cities, industrial districts and rural areas; and even more so between nations. Advanced riders will familiarize themselves, when possible, with the conditions to be encountered.

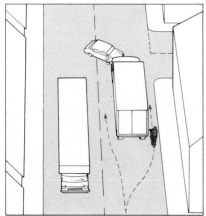

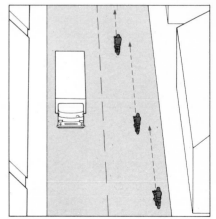

The advanced rider will ride in such a way that he is never boxed in, in unforeseen circumstances. Correct positioning on the road provides him with alternatives to use if the need arises. After this accident, the inside lane is the only clear way through.

When motorcyclists are riding together the leader should adopt the best position on the road and those following take up the next best. Never ride in the wheel tracks of another bike. The riders on the inside have more braking distance to compensate for poorer vision.

point of focus 2,600 ft.

Riding two-up

A two-way responsibility exists when a rider takes a passenger. The rider must be aware of his responsibility to the passenger and the passenger must know what is required of him or her.

The machine must be properly prepared to carry a passenger. A rolled up coat on the luggage rack and feet resting on the mufflers are unsafe and illegal. Pillion passengers need the same equipment as the rider: a comfortable seat, a bar to hold and thoughtfully positioned footrests. Uncomfortable passengers make dreadful travelling companions who rarely return for a second dose of "punishment." At worst, they are dangerous.

Few pillion footrests are in the right place on standard motorcycles. Modify them to suit the needs of your pillionist by placing the footrests on simply made brackets wherever the passenger's feet naturally fall. Most pillion rests are too high and too far forward. Make sure the pillion rider leans forward on to you in the touring position when the footrests are relocated.

The additional weight of a passenger must be taken into consideration. Always increase both tire pressures. Most manufacturers will publish the required increase in the handbook. About 0.28 kg/sq. cm (4 psi) front and 0.42 kg/sq. cm (6 psi) rear would be a safe average on a machine of about 650/750cc carrying a 77 kg (170 lb) rider with the addition of a passenger. Most motorcycles have an adjustable spring preloading system fitted on the rear suspension. Alter it to suit the load. Failure to trim the machine will lead to negative steering and a wallowing ride as the bike rolls about on under-inflated tires and overloaded suspension springs.

For the passenger to become an integral part of the machine he or she must be instructed to sit as close as possible to the rider and not to move around on the seat. When cornering or maneuvering, the passenger must assist

A visor on a passenger's helmet will peck at the rider's neck.

Adjust tires to the maker's recommendations.

Adjust rear suspension to a preload position.

Passengers sit in an area of high turbulence, especially on machines fitted with weather shielding. The quality of the passenger's clothing should match that of the rider's. Passengers become bored and cold more quickly than riders because they have nothing to do. Be considerate.

Pillion riders with no handlebars need something to hold. A rear grab handle should be provided for passenger security.

If a regular passenger is carried, the pillion footrests should be modified to suit his or her comfort.

Passengers should lean slightly forward to come into light body contact with the rider. A backrest which

encourages the pillionist to lean back upsets the balance of a machine—except on the biggest heavyweight cruisers.

increased breaking effort with passenger

normal braking distance

the rider by leaning with him; otherwise the balance and stability of the machine will be upset.

The passenger should sit with hands on thighs, with hands resting lightly on the rider's waist, or gripping some fixed part of the machine — whichever is the most comfortable. He should never hang on with a vise-like grip as this will almost certainly upset the balance of the machine.

Correct pillion carrying requires no extra effort on the part of the rider unless the passenger sits bolt upright on a bend when the rider will be required to fight a battle with an unstable machine.

The rider must acknowledge that a load is being carried and that no machine handles as well or as nimbly as when ridden solo. The effective power of the motorcycle will be reduced. The extra weight of the passenger will reduce acceleration, nimbleness and all machine responses including braking power. Ride accordingly, remembering that braking effort will have to be increased. Read the road well ahead and allow even more time/space in which to reduce speed and to overtake.

Remember that, however experienced your passenger is, a sudden and unexpected change in course will easily shake him or her loose. Experienced riders frequently make nervous passengers. Their riding technique will be different and they have no control. Remember this, and ride in a deliberate and predictable manner.

The rider is responsible for the passenger's life. Take care of it. So often in an accident it is the passenger who comes off worse: the rider has a pair of bars to hold on to but the passenger gets thrown off.

Two-up riding is an enjoyable pastime, if both operate in unison. The rider must never try to be a racer with someone on the pillion. A passenger is much more impressed by a safe, enjoyable ride.

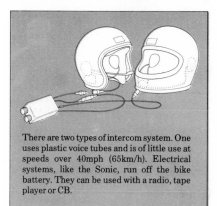

There are two types of intercom system. One uses plastic voice tubes and is of little use at speeds over 40mph (65km/h). Electrical systems, like the Sonic, run off the bike battery. They can be used with a radio, tape player or CB.

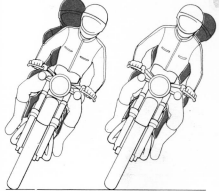

The ideal position for a passenger is tucked in directly behind the rider. The two should ride as one. The actual attitude is a matter of preference, but it should remain constant. A passenger looking over the right shoulder provides the rider with better vision for backward glances. By leaning to the left, the weight is distributed better for riding on a camber. Cornering clearance is reduced by the extra weight.

Accident analysis

Seventy-two per cent of motorcycling accidents involving other vehicles are caused by another vehicle maneuvering into the path of a motorcycle travelling straight ahead; 65 per cent occur at road junctions; 59 per cent of collisions are frontal ones for the motorcyclist. Just over half the other drivers involved claim not to have seen the motorcyclist; this includes other motorcyclists.

In 50 per cent of all motorcycle accidents involving other vehicles the motorcycle is travelling at normal traffic speed; 75 per cent occur under 30mph (50km/h) and 93 per cent under 40mph (65km/h).

Some 80 per cent of these accidents are in urban or built-up areas and wet roads contribute to 31 per cent.

Novice riders 17 to 19 years old make up 43 per cent of the total motorcycle accident casualty rate. Machines in the 149cc-250cc category form 43 per cent of the same total.

Leg injuries account for 62 per cent of all types of non-fatal injuries; 30 per cent of these are to joints or close to joints, and many of them are complicated by dislocation.

One to two per cent of all motorcycling accident injuries are fatal among habitual users of crash helmets. Approximately half the fatal total is caused by chest injury.

A minimum of 22 per cent of all motorcycling accidents involve no other vehicles. As few of these accidents are reported, however, it is assumed that the actual contribution of single vehicle motorcycle accidents is probably around 50 per cent of the total. Expert opinion is that many of these occur after loss of machine control at speeds above 40mph (65km/h). These accidents are responsible for over half of all motorcycling fatalities.

Whatever orthodox protective clothing is worn, it is impossible for a rider to survive direct body impact collision with an unyielding obstacle at speeds above 40mph (65km/h).

A typical novice on a 200cc motorcycle is riding along at normal city traffic speed when a car pulls into his path just 130 ft (40 m) ahead. The rider freezes, then panic-brakes, skids, and slams into the front corner of the now stationary car.

As the rider is still travelling at 20mph (30km/h) his own body weight of 54.5kg (120lb) flings him up and over the front of the car. This breaks the shin bone and dislocates the hip.

Numbed by shock, the 18-year-old nevertheless remains hopelessly aware of the terrible reality and prays for unconsciousness, even death.

The ambulance takes 20 minutes to arrive.

The car driver is fined the equivalent of one week's earnings for dangerous driving, and then complains to his insurance company which has increased his premium by 20 per cent.

He is entirely to blame. Everyone, even the court, said so.

But is he? What actually happened?

The young novice rider had relaxed his vigilance because he was conscious of the fact that he was wearing a crash helmet, was within the speed limit, and had the right of way. It was a dangerous, yet sadly typical, case of legality removing an individual's self-responsibility.

When the car appeared ahead of him the nervous system operation of the new rider was literally suspended by shock. It lasted for one second, which carried him 50 ft (15 m). A further half-second passed before the brakes took effect, by which time another 25ft (7.5 m) had passed—a total of 75 ft (22.5 m). Over-reaction locks the wheels instantly, so the motorcycle continued forward toward the car virtually unslowed, and with eventual loss of stability.

At a speed of 30 mph (50 km/h) a motorcycle is generally considered to require 100 ft (30 m) to stop safely.

The novice's motorcycle was small, with no easily discernible frontal profile. He was dressed in a dull-colored one-piece suit. The bright detail of his meticulously hand-painted helmet merged into a dirty-looking camouflage at a distance. The young rider no more saw the stationary distant car than the car driver saw him.

An experienced rider would immediately have noticed the car and its threat from afar. He would have been wearing brightly colored clothing. He would have moved carefully across his traffic lane, after checking his mirror, to attract the car driver with lateral movement. He would have looked for the face of the car driver peering his way, and tooted his horn and prepared himself for sudden braking if still in doubt.

As he whiplashes across the car, three ribs are broken on the bonnet, or hood, and his face smashes into the unyielding wing, or fender. This breaks the nose and the lower jaw.

The rider rebounds to the ground.

The broken shin heals well, but only after the surgical removal of a quantity of shattered bone that has left the leg 40mm (1.5in) short.

The most serious damage is psychological.

Accident procedure

Anyone involved in an accident will be affected by it. Even those who are not injured, but are close at hand when someone has taken a tumble, will probably suffer from shock.

Shock can produce a sense of panic and the fear that all is lost. It is, therefore, essential that you have a program of sequential action stored in your mind, ready for such an emergency. Many riders seem more concerned about damage to the chrome and paint on the motorcycle: skin grows for nothing, paint and chrome cost!

1 The first step is to deal with any casualties — even if they are complete strangers. The casualty might even be an animal; remember an injured animal, ignored at the roadside, may suddenly find new strength and run off into the traffic causing another accident. DO NOT drag casualties to the side of the road. Attend to them where they lie.

2 If there is any potential danger from other traffic, send someone back along the road to warn oncoming vehicles. If there is no assistance available, try to protect the injured party with some physical object, like the bike parked in the roadway with its lights on.

3 Place a warning obstruction far enough away to give the traffic time to stop before reaching the scene of the accident.

4 When, and only when, the injured have been dealt with, concern yourself with clearing the obstruction.

5 Details of any witnesses to the accident should always be sought.

6 If there has been personal injury or if an offense would seem to have been committed, the police must be informed as soon as practicable and, in any case, within 24 hours.

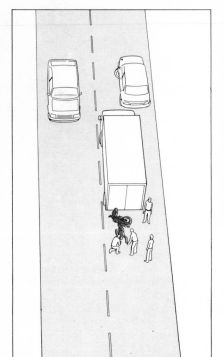

Brief checklist
Brief checklist 1 Ensure that casualties are breathing and lying in the recovery position. 2 Warn other traffic of the danger before sending for help. 3 Identify witnesses before they leave the scene. 4 Take notes and/or sketch the location. 5 Obtain the names and addresses of anyone involved. 6 Make arrangements to have your own vehicle removed.

However minor the accident, it will constitute a hazard for other vehicles. To prevent a chain reaction of events, place a warning sign in the road or have someone wave-down traffic.

Hazard-warning triangles or flares are compulsory equipment in some countries. They transmit the message without ambiguity.

7 The same applies in the case of damage to a vehicle or damage to roadside property — even if you have escaped unscathed.

8 If the emergency services have not been called to a minor accident, take a note of the exact location; name of the road or street and distance and direction to the nearest junction. It may be useful for later reference to make a sketch plan of the accident, with the positions of vehicles involved measured to some fixed street furniture such as a lamppost, telegraph pole or telephone box.

9 Before leaving the scene of an accident always ensure that you have obtained the name and address of the driver(s) of the other vehicle(s) and have given them your own particulars. Note the license numbers of other vehicles involved.

10 It is the responsibility of the driver/rider to remove his vehicle from the scene of an accident, not to leave it there at his/her own convenience. Quite apart from the security problem, a damaged vehicle left at the scene can be a potential cause of another accident or of injury to a pedestrian. The local police will have their own arrangements to deal with vehicles which are the property of someone who has been taken to hospital or who can make no arrangements of their own. Do not go home and take it for granted that someone else will take care of your vehicle. Ensure that arrangements are made, either by yourself or the police. Do not forget that you must pay the costs of having your bike removed.

11 Once at home, inform your insurance company of the incident as soon as possible. If the other party makes a claim before you have informed your insurers you may be in trouble.

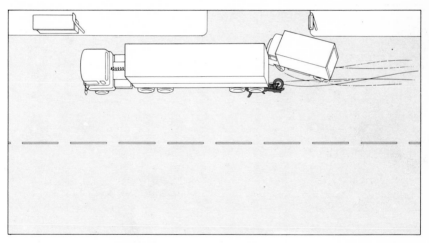

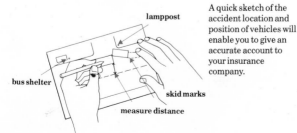

lamppost

bus shelter

skid marks

measure distance

A quick sketch of the accident location and position of vehicles will enable you to give an accurate account to your insurance company.

Move debris or anything obstructing the road only when the injured have been cared for. If anything prevents you riding your machine home, make your own arrangements for its recovery. Do not expect the police to organize its removal.

First aid

Let us consider the victim of a serious accident — it could be anyone, God forbid, even you.

The casualty is sprawled on the road, motionless and obviously unconscious. You have to ensure that he or she is able to breathe. Before you do anything else turn the injured person into a semi-prone position — half on the side and half on the front, with the head turned to one side. If possible, use the arm on the higher side as a support for the head. Bend it at the elbow to form a crook.

Unless there are obvious limb injuries, draw up the leg on the same side, bending it at the knee. Leave the other arm lying straight and in line with the body. Clear the mouth and ensure that the air passages are clear.

As long as he is breathing properly, NEVER attempt to remove a crash helmet from an injured motorcyclist. Remove goggles or faceshield only. The crash helmet might be acting as a useful splint for a broken skull.

The first step in first aid is the most important. The casualty may have internal or other injuries but if breathing is not restored or maintained you will soon have a dead body to deal with. Every second counts, so do not hesitate or wait to ask for the opinions of others before you act.

Make the injured person as comfortable as possible. Shock sets in quickly so keep the casualty warm. Insulation under the body is as important as cover over the top. Loss of body heat accelerates the onset of shock and other problems. If the arrival of emergency services is likely to be delayed, find a blanket, coat, plastic cover, or something to roll up and lay alongside the body of the casualty.

When turning over an unconscious body you might compound any internal or spinal damage, so to prevent movement in the trunk, use about three pairs of hands to support the underside of the body evenly. Lift together, taking

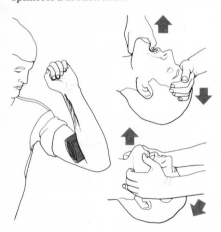

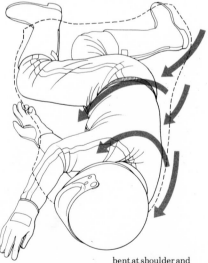

To inhibit severe bleeding, apply pressure to the wound. Blood from a deep cut in the forearm or hand can be stemmed without assistance by flexing your elbow against a pad.

If breathing has stopped or is obstructed, *carefully* remove the helmet. Turn the head to one side if there is fluid in the mouth. Tilt the head back to open the throat; push the jaw forward to pull the tongue clear of the windpipe.

If the casualty is breathing DO NOT remove the helmet. Turn him to one side with the head facing down and the neck bent back. The upper arm is bent at shoulder and elbow; the leg bent at hip and knee. The lower arm and leg are stretched out behind. Do not raise the head with a supporting pillow.

your cue from one person chosen as the leader, just enough for the blanket to be unrolled under the body. Lower together carefully.

Even though the injured person may seem to be unconscious, calm words of comfort and encouragement will be of great benefit. To be in a state of helplessness while still aware of events is a most frightening experience. If the casualty's limbs will not respond and he can perceive little, a voice which seems to be concerned about him might lessen the feelings of anxiety and alienation.

If the injured person is able to communicate, be guided by him or her on how to place limbs in the most comfortable position. If the casualty says that your tightly secured splints, copied from some text book, are causing extreme discomfort, remove them and arrange the limbs so as to minimize the pain.

Do not rely on hearsay advice or books read some time ago. First aid is constantly being updated as medical knowledge increases.

The sight of heavy bleeding can cause panic and over-reaction in the victim. Do the best you can to prevent or reduce the flow with some firm pressure, preferably by tying a clean scarf or handkerchief around the wound. If the problem is more serious, grasp the wound with your hand and hold on. Again, we are talking of *first* aid; it is no good keeping a deep wound clean while the casualty bleeds to death. Blood is warmth, blood is oxygen supply — blood is *life*.

Remember that these first steps at the scene of an accident are the most critical. Do not stand back in terror, even if you have no medical training. The casualty needs your immediate help more than any later expert attention. Take action, and use your logic and commonsense.

Learn some first aid. Perhaps one day you will be injured and will have to instruct a panic-stricken helper how to save your life.

Profuse bleeding can be stopped by applying pressure to various points. The pressure must be applied continuously to the point nearest the wound, and between it and the heart. Bleeding should slow down immediately, but it will take at least 10 minutes for a clot to form and stem the bleeding. If the blood is pulsing an artery has been severed. The traditional tourniquet method has lost favor recently because it is easy to forget it is on tight — pressure must be relieved regularly.

Bleeding from a cut in the palm of the hand can be stemmed by gripping tight on a piece of clean cotton.

pressure points

The standard method of artificial respiration is now the "kiss of life." The neck must be supported and the head tilted back. Clean the mouth and hold it open. With the casualty's nostrils held shut, clamp your mouth over his and breathe out into his lungs. Lift your head, breathe in, and repeat. Natural pressure on the chest aids the clearing of the lungs.

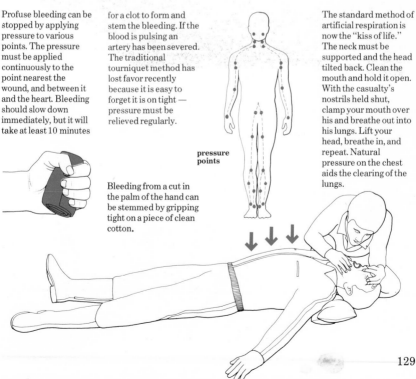

Mike the Bike

Mike Hailwood was probably the greatest grand prix road racer of all time. He won 10 world championships, 77 grands prix and 14 Isle of Man TT races. During his professional career he raced for the major factory teams of the period, MV Agusta (1962-5) and Honda (1966-7).

Without doubt, "Mike the Bike" was something of an enigma, made so by journalists who saw only part of the man and then reported on the whole. This appeared to satisfy the good-natured Hailwood who treasured his private life and resented intrusions into it.

All manner of ingredients contribute to the spirit of a champion, but in Hailwood's case it was a highly developed competitive instinct that formed the major part of his success.

Before he raced in his first TT in 1958, Hailwood practised ceaselessly until he knew the 37¾ mile circuit properly — riding a Triumph at night when the road was uninterrupted by daytime distractions. In that first visit he finished third on his 250cc NSU, not far behind the works MVs of Provini and Ubbiali.

Hailwood's determination to win was never more apparent than in the Senior TT of 1965 when he crashed his MV Agusta after skidding on a slick of wet oil. After bump starting the bike he rode to the pits and stopped for almost 70 seconds before rejoining the race. With a bent and stiff gear change lever, twisted handlebars, a sticking throttle and a missing footrest, Mike forced his way through driving rain storms back into the lead.

Mike left MV to ride the unstable, yet super-fast Honda racers which could only be tamed by a few top riders. When Jim Redman broke an arm and retired, Hailwood was left with the responsibility of winning all classes. He took the 250 and 350 titles but the Senior (500cc) eluded him. Had Honda adopted a more rational approach then Mike would probably have beaten MV Agusta's new home-grown hero, Agostini, to the 500cc crown.

Possibly his finest accolade came in 1967 when Honda retired from the grands prix and paid Mike a salary, in keeping with a world champion's requirements, *not* to race. If their ex-rider returned to MV Agusta he could only prove one thing. . . .

An insight into the essential humanity of Hailwood is illustrated by an incident during his brief car racing career. During the 1972 South African F1 Grand Prix, Clay Regazzoni's car caught fire after a crash which trapped the driver. Hailwood abandoned the race to rescue Regazzoni from the inferno. The action won him the highest British civilian award for bravery, the George Cross, to add to the MBE he received in 1968.

Exactly 10 years after his retirement from full-time bike racing, Mike returned to his favourite circuit, the Isle of Man, to win the Formula One TT on an 864cc Ducati; his race speed was a record 108.51 mph. With the prize was awarded the one-off TT World Championship. The following year (1979) he won his final TT race, the Senior, on a works Suzuki.

Motorcycling's most respected figure, Hailwood won races on five continents against strong opposition. On the following pages are shown some of the classic bikes, his most respected rivals, and other giants of motorcycle sport.

Hall of Fame

Hailwood, the hero of
the Isle of Man—in
1965 he struggled to
win on his battered MV.
In 1978 he returned
with a F1 Ducati.

Hailwood's rides and rivals

Norton

Manx Norton
In 350cc and 500cc versions, the Manx was the mainstay of British racers throughout the 1950s and 1960s. It remains one of the best-loved of all British bikes. Geoff Duke won world titles on it, but its biggest claim to fame was the legendary Featherbed frame introduced in 1951.

NSU Rennmax, the German bike, was one of the classic 250 twins of the 1950s. It featured a sohc engine and one of the first dolphin fairings.

NSU

One of the finest racers of lightweights was **Carlo Ubbiali** who led the MV Agusta lightweight spearhead for most of his road racing career. Between 1951 and 1960 he won six 125 and three 250 world championships— all but one of them on MV machines.

132

HONDA

Jim Redman was admired and feared by most racers but the English-born Rhodesian, who won seven world titles, was idolized less than many of his contemporaries.

As Honda's team leader from 1960 he dedicated himself to their success rather than his own. He won races by the smallest possible margins to avoid unnecessary risks.

AJS 7R
The 350cc "boy racer" was developed in 1952 from the R7. It was a favorite of private racers, frequently proving faster than the 350 Manx. Many riders

included a 7R and a 500 Norton in their stables. The G50 Matchless was an almost identical, yet less successful, 500cc version.

Rides and rivals/2

Giacomo Agostini has the finest road racing record of all time. Between 1966 and 1975 he won 15 world titles. Some claimed that his success was due to Hailwood's and Honda's retirement but in the 350cc class he was competing against Yamaha's top aces. In 1975 he rode a 500cc Yamaha and he beat everyone, including Read who had replaced him on the MV Agusta.

John Hartle was as fast and consistent as any rider of his time. His style was probably the finest in post-WWII years—clean, fluid and beautiful to watch. He was over-shadowed initially by John Surtees, whom he backed up faithfully. Hartle refused to retire, and was killed in a crash in 1968.

Derek Minter was one of the best grand prix racers of the 1960s but he would not adapt to the restrictions of a works team. He was practically unbeatable in Britain with his Manx Nortons, on one of which he rode the first 100mph lap of the IoM TT circuit to be achieved on a single. Minter did join the Gilera team in 1963 but the bikes proved uncompetitive.

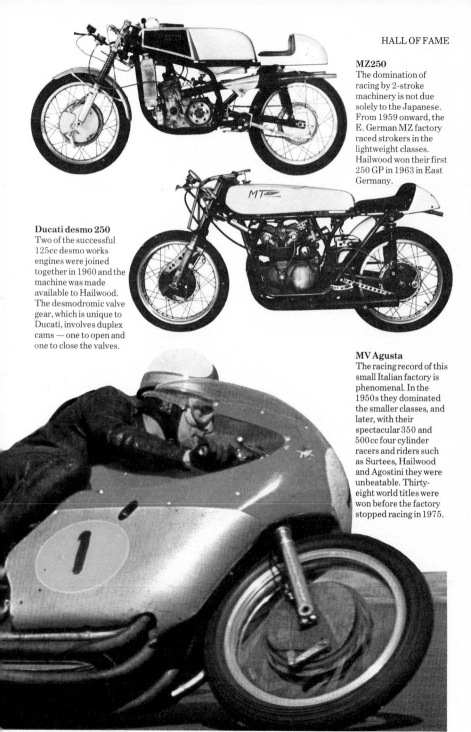

MZ250
The domination of racing by 2-stroke machinery is not due solely to the Japanese. From 1959 onward, the E. German MZ factory raced strokers in the lightweight classes. Hailwood won their first 250 GP in 1963 in East Germany.

Ducati desmo 250
Two of the successful 125cc desmo works engines were joined together in 1960 and the machine was made available to Hailwood. The desmodromic valve gear, which is unique to Ducati, involves duplex cams — one to open and one to close the valves.

MV Agusta
The racing record of this small Italian factory is phenomenal. In the 1950s they dominated the smaller classes, and later, with their spectacular 350 and 500cc four cylinder racers and riders such as Surtees, Hailwood and Agostini they were unbeatable. Thirty-eight world titles were won before the factory stopped racing in 1975.

Three-wheel hero

Sidecar racing is, perhaps paradoxically, a sport for individuals; there have been very few works sidecars and most machines are built to individual requirements, often by the riders themselves.

The achievements of the German rider Helmut Fath, however, have never been equalled in any form of motor sport.

Fath was BMW's top runner in 1960 when he won the world championship. He crashed in 1961 and injured himself severely. In 1963, he planned to return but the Munich factory would not provide him with one of their racing engines.

Riders had frequently built their own motorcycle frames but Fath set about designing and building his own four-cylinder engine, with which, in 1968, he took the title from BMW.

Aided by eminent engineers and neighbors from his home village, Fath built no more than half a dozen of the 500cc motors. They featured 90° crankshafts and fuel injection.

Helmut Fath delighted British crowds in the 1960s with winning rides on his home-made URS outfit.

BMW rider Max Deubel and passenger Emile Horner **right** won four consecutive world titles in the early 1960s. They lead Chris Vincent, who was the last rider of the URS outfit.

When it comes to monopolizing one single class of motorcycle sport, few manufacturers have come within sight of BMW. Their racing engines were only available to a select few, yet BMW's dominance of sidecar racing after WWII was so complete that it became boringly predictable.

Between 1954 and 1974 only two world titles were won by non-BMW riders; one by Fath and the other by Owesle on Fath's old machine.

Of the BMW-mounted multiple champions the most successful were Deubel, with four championships, and Enders with six.

Straight line fever

The fastest man on two wheels rides inside a projectile which has little in common with a conventional motorcycle except, perhaps, the motive unit(s). Since his early manhood, Californian rider Don Vesco has been making runs on the Bonneville salt flats in Utah. He has held records in many of the stream-liner categories, but his ambition to break the absolute world speed record was achieved in 1970 with an average speed of 251.9 mph (405 km/h).

That first record was established with two 350cc Yamaha racing engines, but when Vesco returned in 1975 with a double-750cc engined machine, he became the first man to run at over 300mph. His record then was 302.92 mph (487.5 km/h).

Changing his allegiance to Kawasaki, Vesco returned in 1978 with *Lightning Bolt,* on which he achieved a two-way average of 318.598 mph (512.7 km/h). He has been able to run faster times but never in both directions, which is the criterion for an FIM record.

Vesco is, not surprisingly, an ace tuner and, apart from his Bonneville rides and occasional races on classic bikes, he is more often found turning a torque wrench than a throttle.

Drag racing came from California, which is still the home state of the most exotic machinery made.

Twin-engined bikes have been seen on the drag strips for almost 20 years. The originals were paired-up twins, using Triumph or Harley-Davidson power. But when Russ Collins unveiled his 858lb (389kg) Honda concoction, the *Atchison, Topeka and Santa Fe,* in 1975, spectators needed three hands to count the cylinders. Twelve of them lay across the frame in three neat rows.

Drag racing is a matter of clipping hundredths and tenths of seconds from previous times, and each complete second is a momentous barrier. In 1976 Collins broke the sevens barrier with a run of 7.86 and a terminal speed at the end of the quarter mile of 178mph (288km/h). Later that year the 500bhp triple looped in spectacular style and Collins returned to the relative simplicity of a double engined bike, *Sorcerer,* which he supercharged for good measure.

Collins, whose business is making tuning equipment for other people's Hondas, goes drag racing for its promotional value. Consistently the fastest rider on the drags he is a good salesman.

Vesco poses beside his record breaking cycle on his beloved Bonneville salt flats.

The *Sorcerer,* **center,** may be the smaller of Collins' bikes but it is hardly a simple machine.

Off-road maestros

Ulsterman S. H. "Sammy" Miller is arguably the most talented motorcycle sportsman. He revolutionized his chosen sport and recorded over 900 major event wins. He retired from serious competition in 1975 after a 20-year career.

Miller began riding grass track and moto-cross in Ireland, then turned to road racing and rode for the FB Mondial, NSU and Ducati teams.

In spite of his success, Miller chose to become a professional trials rider at a time when the sport was little more than a peculiarly British, part-time activity.

He turned a ponderous 500cc Ariel into an all-conquering award-winner and then moved to Bultaco. By designing the Sherpa, a remarkable lightweight trials machine, Miller changed the face of observed trials. Sections became more severe, even dangerous, just to test the new combination.

Miller on the Bultaco and (inset) on the Honda TL125 which he also developed.

Belgian Joel Robert was the first man to ride a Japanese machine to a moto-cross world championship.

Robert, who began his moto-cross career on a converted 500cc Matchless, won the 1960 Belgian Junior Championship, and by 1964, riding a CZ, he had managed to beat Hallman, the Swedish master. Despite his obvious talent, Robert was a wild man who would entertain the crowds with frightening and unnecessary aerobatic displays.

By 1967 most experts dismissed Robert as a beaten man. In 1968, however, he fought back with determination and a more disciplined riding style to win the 250cc World Championship.

By the end of 1969, the CZ machines were past their best and Robert signed up for Suzuki. He won the next three 250cc World Championships in 1970, 1971 and 1972.

Robert won six world titles, first on CZ and later on Suzuki works machines.

King Kenny

With the possible exception of the late Jarno Saarinen, the finest road racer of the 1970s has been Kenny Roberts, as famous for becoming the first American to win a road racing world championship as for his dashing riding skills. In wet conditions, especially, Roberts has few challengers.

The Californian rider was apprenticed in the hurly-burly of American championship racing, where he quickly worked his way through the Novice and junior championship gradings, to win the Grand National Championship in 1973 and 1974. He won races in every class of AMA racing.

Roberts has always ridden Yamahas but he left the official works team in 1974 to campaign under a private banner. The machines were supplied by the factory but the team management was left to himself and Kel Carruthers. From 1974

Roberts is a dedicated professional who makes a difficult job look simple yet exciting. His presence draws crowds to tracks all over the world and, as a spokesman for GP riders, he has earned the respect of promoters and rival competitors.

onwards he captained the American team at the British match race series. He was an immediate success with the European race fans.

In 1978 Roberts entered the grand prix series as Yamaha's main contender and won the 500cc world crown, a feat he repeated in 1979 and 1980. It is probable that the small, energy-packed, tough and spectacular rider will go down in history as America's finest motorcycle racer.

Roberts's assault on the world championships was not single-handed. Behind the yellow and black colors was a whole team, led by Kel Carruthers, whose own moment of glory was in 1969, when he won the 250cc world championship on a Benelli-4. Carruthers, an Australian, was the first road race champion to move *to* America where he became an inspiration to many young riders.

All-time classics

MOTO GUZZI

Henderson four
Henderson set the pace
for sporting luxury in
America. In 1922, Wells
Bennet covered
1,562.54 miles
(2,514.54 km) at an
average speed of
65.1 mph (104.7 km/h)
in 24 hours.
Vincent Black Lightning
Was there ever a more
evocatively named
motorcycle? Built
around 998cc Black
Shadow roadster
components, it turned
out 60 bhp. Top speed
was over 140 mph
(225 km/h).

Moto Guzzi V8
The 500 cc V8 of 1956/7 was brilliantly engineered: weight was similar to the 320 lbs (145 kg) of a Manx Norton. The dohc water cooled engine developed 80 bhp. Top speed was 167 mph (270 km/h).

Harley-Davidson KRTT
Harley's classic road racer boasted a 65 bhp 733 cc, four valve head, side valve, V-twin engine. It was raced until as late as 1969. A flat track model was also made.

BSA DBD34 Gold Star
The 120 mph (193 km/h) Goldie clubman's racer holds a legendary place in British motorcycle history. It delivered 42 bhp plus from its 499 cc pushrod engine.

Honda GP six
Honda first raced their 250 cc dohc six in 1964. The 53 bhp engine revved to 16,500 rpm; top speed was almost 150 mph (241 km/h). In 1966 an improved 296 cc six won the 350 world championship.

Road racing

The origins of road racing, perhaps the most prestigious of motorcycle sports, are linked with the first pioneers who, in order to test their puny engines, were paced against each other over public roads.

Speed *and* reliability were tested in those far-off trials; since then the speed interest has been concentrated into circuit racing, and the reliability test has undergone a metamorphosis into the modern trial. A wide range of specialized sports has also evolved.

Today motorcycle sport around the world is controlled by the FIM (Federation Internationale Motocycliste), which was founded in 1949. Its predecessor, the FICM, became a solely European organization when the other great motor-cycling nation of the time, the USA, withdrew almost as soon as it had constructed its own nationally representative body, the AMA (American Motorcycle Association) in 1924.

The AMA considered that competitive motorcycles should be based closely on roadsters and disagreed strongly with the ultra-specialization that, even then, was becoming the European custom. Later, commercial interests intruded into and corrupted the laudable ideals of the AMA, and, in effect, home products were allowed the advantage of a 33⅓ per cent larger engine.

In 1968 the AMA rejoined the FIM, which with South American, Asian and the Eastern bloc membership, is now a truly international body. In 1979 42 countries were represented.

Until 1959 the FIM's headquarters were in London, but in an effort to widen its influence in a polarized world, the office was moved to Geneva in neutral Switzerland.

Each motorcycling nation has its own FMN (Federation Motocycliste Nationale) as its controlling body. The FMNs are divided into conveniently manageable sections, or centers, each with its own specialist sub-committees.

The Sport

Grand Prix

The absence of a single Champion of the Year (awarded to the individual who collected most points regardless of class) has led to understandable confusion among the non-motorcycling public about the number of two-wheel champions clambering on to various winner's rostrums.

Grand prix road racing capacity classes are 50, 125, 250, 350, 500cc, and sidecar (500). This results in a minimum of six World Champions. There are also road racing championships not connected to pure grand prix racing.

The first international road race championship was the European Championship initiated by the FICM in 1938, competed for in 1939, and then withdrawn during World War II. It was revived in 1949 by the new FIM as the World Championship, although this was still without support from the USA.

By 1969 so many nations were hosting grands prix that an eventual winner was likely to be the man with the most time, money and stamina. So a compromise was reached in which a rider scores from his best seven rounds, regardless of his total number of races. Points are awarded on a 15, 12, 10, 8, 6, 5, 4, 3, 2, 1 scale.

Traditionally many grands prix were held on true road circuits, but in recent years some of these (including the Isle of Man TT) have lost their status in favor of short circuit events.

In 1981 thirteen countries hosted grands prix, although few of these meetings included races for all six classes.

Sidecar

Road racing outfits are far removed from the shape and performance of their road-going counterparts. No longer are they the fascinatingly biased union of motor-cycle and sidecar, but three-wheel racing cars in which the second partner is virtually reduced to the role of live ballast.

The three strongholds of sidecar road racing have always been Britain, Germany and Switzerland. When sidecars were brought into the grand prix fold in 1949 and awarded their own championship, Britain's Eric Oliver and his rival Cyril Smith dominated on their Norton Watsonian outfits.

German Willhelm Noll spearheaded the BMW factory attack by winning the championship in 1954. The reason for BMW's determination to succeed on three wheels lay in the uncompetitive-ness of their flat twins in solo racing. They retained the manufacturer's sidecar championship award for an unbroken 19 years from 1955 to 1973, although BMW riders won championships the year before and the year after.

Strict regulations prohibit three-wheeled cars of geometrically balanced layout although constructors are continually introducing radical designs. The maximum engine size allowed in sidecar grands prix is 500cc. At national level, however, engines up to and over 1000cc are frequently allowed.

These days most grand prix racing outfits are Yamaha-powered. In general, they achieve race speeds similar to solo 125 grand prix machines.

Production/Stock

Production, stock or road-machine racing is the purest form of road racing, and is the direct descendant of the early speed trials in which roadster motorcycles were compared, and which led to their eventual improvement.

Unfortunately, despite the AMA's attempts to retain them, the old ideals have been corrupted by the quest for speed, and grand prix racing has become the most prestigious sport.

One problem is that anomalies exist in the specifications of production racers. In the USA they have evolved into little more than touring-*styled* grand prix machines, as best exemplified by the Superbikes at the 1981 Daytona event.

In this championship series, commercially built roadsters must retain their original appearance; have a top engine capacity limit of 1025cc; weigh no less than 416lb (188.6kg); retain their original carburetors, major engine components, frame, seating and control layout.

For all the road bike gestures, winner Wes Cooley's Yoshimura-modified Suzuki GS1000 turned out just over 140bhp at 10,000rpm (standard model 90bhp at 8,000rpm)—sufficient for a race average speed of 107.74mph (173.38km/h) and a lap of 108.52mph (176.63km/h).

At the same meeting Dale Singleton won the 200 Mile race on his TZ750 grand prix Yamaha at an average speed of just 108.52mph (176.63km/h). It is plain, from the similarity of performance, that appearances can be deceptive.

British production machine racing and the American stock class are closer to the real thing. In Britain the ACU allows the adoption of clip-on handlebars, rear-set footrests, raised exhaust systems and fairings but, by insisting on original mufflers, it virtually precludes any attempts at serious race tuning. And electrical equipment must be retained in full working order.

Australia goes a step farther and allows no modifications whatsoever on their stock racers. While this does at least prove machine quality in the long run, there are drawbacks. Of necessity, riders must bend footrests during the first few laps to aid cornering clearance, a practice which results in frequent mishaps. In some instances, protests against a winning machine have been upheld for as little as a missing tank badge or side panel.

France introduced 24-hour endurance racing with the famous Bol d'Or at Le Mans. This sport, for all its exotic overtones, is closely associated with production racing because the majority of endurance bikes are privately owned one-offs, using roadster engines.

The closest thing to the spirit of internationally recognized stock bike racing should have been the FIM's F750 Championship, which simply required that competing machines were restricted to 750cc and used major engine components from a commercially built unit. Unfortunately these specifications included TZ750 Yamahas, which are purpose-built racers.

Every race meeting is run under the responsibility of a Clerk of the Course, who must be a representative of his national governing body, or federation, of motorcycle sport.

He is assisted by timekeepers, who attend to the starting, lap scoring and timing, finish of a race and notification of lap and race times. Although the timekeeping apparatus may be electronically powered it is usually hand-controlled. This apparently archaic method is unavoidable when so much lapping (race leaders overtaking the slower tail enders) occurs. Timekeepers usually operate from a control tower by the start, or from a penthouse above the main grandstand.

All manner of marshals must be in attendance. They control pit and paddock movements of machines and riders and, as flag marshals, communicate vital information to riders on the circuit about slower riders ahead, hazards, oil spills and everything connected with rider safety. Riders who disobey flag signals face probable disciplinary action, such as loss of placings and, thus, cash prizes.

A doctor and full medical team including ambulances must be available at every race meeting; helicopter ambulances commonly stand by. A fire tender and crew is also present. Fire marshals accompany flag marshals at certain points of the track to provide instant fire-fighting when necessary.

Most race meetings rely heavily for their manpower on volunteer enthusiasts, without whom there would be no racing at all.

Before a rider can race his machine it must be inspected in the scrutineering enclosure. The scrutineers are highly experienced motorcycle race-mechanics or engineers, who ensure that all machines conform to the FIM's internationally agreed code on race-machine construction.

The standards they apply are: to ensure safety by checking such items as tires, lock nuts, handlebar and footrest clearance, fuel tanks and lines and brakes; to restrict machine design and thus ensure that the richest manufacturers do not have an unbeatable advantage (no machine may be equipped with more than four cylinders or six gears, for instance).

Finally, the scrutineers check that the machine is equipped with the items the rider stated in his application: by this means sponsorship is fairly controlled. A rider might be paid to use, or be supplied free with a certain oil or spark plug, but then decide secretly to use an alternative brand. The rider's protective leather clothing and helmet will also be subjected to scrutiny.

Grands prix are usually organized, and always controlled by the host nation's FMN, although sometimes the meeting is actually organized by the track owners, an experienced major club, or a combination of both or all three.

To compete in any international race a rider must hold an international racing license, which is granted only to those who have achieved a specific level of skill and experience by scoring points in national races.

Grand prix starts are awarded to riders who are included in an international grading list. A jury of representatives from the organizing and administrative bodies judges each application on past merit and future potential, and negotiates start money with the applicants. Grand prix prize money is paid at a level set by the FIM.

If a competitor thinks he has been treated unfairly, or that another competitor has cheated, an official protest can be lodged, which is then considered by the jury of senior administrators. If it concerns a machine the scrutineers will make a check: a refusal by the owner or rider to agree to this check results in automatic disqualification. If the protest cannot be resolved on the spot, an official enquiry will be organized for a later hearing.

50cc & sidecar

350cc

125cc

500cc

250cc

750cc

Racing number plates
are color-coded for FIM
events. For races run
in darkness numbers
are white on black.

1300cc

FIM specifications for
the dimensions of a road
racing machine.
Minimum weight for a
500 is 100kg (220.5lb).

Clearance between
fairing and motorcycle
must be at least 20mm
(¾in) in all places.

Clearance between the
(prone) rider's head and
fairing must be at least
100mm (4in).

Maximum tank capacity
for GP racing is 32 l (8.5gal).

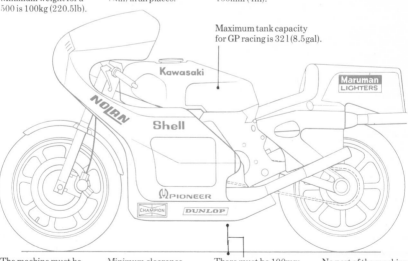

The machine must be
able to bank to 50°
without grounding.

Minimum clearance
between tank and bars
on full lock is 30mm.
Bars must be at least
450mm (17¾in) wide.

There must be 100mm
(4in) minimum ground
clearance.

No part of the machine
may project beyond the
edge of the rear wheel.

Moto-cross

Moto-cross is the most demanding of wheeled sports, requiring a degree of physical stamina, concentration and capacity to endure stress unparalleled in any sport except, perhaps, professional soccer. A pulse rate of 200pm is not uncommon among competing top-line moto-cross racers.

In many countries moto-cross is as popular a spectator sport as road racing. During recent years Americans have promoted indoor stadium events and a women's league.

As a participation sport at club level, it is accessible, exciting, and safer than road racing. It is a sport for young riders who these days start early: competitions exist for riders as young as six years old.

In the market-place there is a wide range of impressively powerful moto-cross machinery available from many countries.

Moto-cross is now a specialized, highly commercial sport but it began as an informal affair. The story goes that in 1924 a trials club in Surrey, England, was inspired by the Scott time trial to organize a fast cross-country competition, without any speed-restricting observed sections. The ACU, Britain's FMN, pointed out that without observed sections it could not be a trial, so the first rough country race was publicized as offering participants "a fine old scramble"; after which the sport spread rapidly through Britain.

After World War II scrambling was adopted on the Continent under the new name of moto-cross, from the French word "moto," as in motocyclette, and "cross" from cross-country. Some people erroneously assume that a difference exists between scrambling and moto-cross. It is a mistake that arose from the near simultaneous adoption of the new name in Britain and a two-leg points scoring system. Under these rules a rider must finish in two legs of a race. The winner is the one with the best aggregate position.

The first international moto-cross competition was organized in 1947 as the Moto-Cross des Nations. It became an annual team event which Britain dominated until 1967.

In 1952 a 500 cc European Championship series was instigated, at which period all competitors rode the heavy, docile and ponderous trials-based 500 singles from FN (Belgium), Monark (Sweden), BSA and Matchless (Britain). By the time a 250 cc European championship and later a World Championship series had been organized in 1957, the age of the 32 bhp, 330 lb (150 kilo) 500 cc banger was over, and the day of the highly strung 2-stroke had dawned.

In Britain, Brian Stonebridge, working for BSA, developed one of their plebian 2-stroke utilities, the Bantam, into an astonishingly successful scrambler. BSA refused to acknowledge their protégé, but directors of the Greeves motorcycle company gave Stonebridge his head. Their radically designed 197 cc machine so thoroughly trounced the ponderous 500 cc 4-strokes, that manufacturers (except BSA) turned to the successful development of a brand-new type of lightweight moto-crosser, powered by the highly strung, stretched 250 cc 2-strokes.

With the advent of Japanese interest, encouraged by the huge potential American sales awaiting moto-cross success, European factories like Husqvarna, KTM, Maico and CZ found themselves up against the formidable technology of the entire Japanese industry. Belgian Joel Robert moved with the times when he changed camps from CZ to Suzuki in 1969. He was followed by fellow countryman Roger de Coster who was to be the 500 cc World Champion five times, also on a Suzuki.

In 1980 six of the top nine places in the 125, 250 and 500 cc class Manufacturer's Championships were filled by Japanese machines. A similar domination occurs in the individual championship lists.

ANDRE MALHERBÉ ON A 500 cc HONDA

Moto-cross/2

The best moto-cross circuits are on dry, undulating terrain, incorporating artificial ditches to be jumped by fast riders and at least one freak climb; undulating graded steps and a steep downhill turn are usually included. A favorite with spectators is some sort of a water-splash, usually at the bottom of a big gulley, which turns to mud.

Those who assume that mud is the focal point of moto-cross could not be further from the truth. Wet conditions ruin good racing by clogging the machines, exhausting riders and largely negating their skills. Mud can turn a race into a slimy, slow-moving shambles.

In northern Europe, the stronghold of moto-cross, wet courses are common, and this has for long delayed the eagerly-awaited American challenge (apart from appearances by Jim Pomeroy, first American to win a moto-cross grand prix, and Brad Lackey, first to win a world championship). The fast sandy circuits of France might have assisted American riders familiar with such going, and handicapped European riders due to the peculiar techniques required. But French moto-cross is almost wholly commercial, with money rather than grand prix points at stake.

Moto-cross is not a clean sport, inasmuch as a lot of leaning goes on, especially during cornering in the first lap or two while the pecking order is established. The hardest riders use any means to clear themselves a path, from shouted curses to elbowing and handlebar clashing, and intentional squeezing out at the hazards.

For all the violence of the sport, deaths in moto-cross are rare, and serious injury is restricted to broken bones, dislocations and torn muscles, usually in shoulders and knees. Riders protect themselves with crash helmets, eye shields, face guards, plated or molded boots, gloves, trousers and jerseys approved by their own FMN, according to FIM requirements. Chest, shoulder, knee and elbow armor is also worn.

CLOSE RACING IN THE 250cc CLASS

Moto-cross/3

Moto-cross machines are short circuit racers as specialized as road racers. The main difference is that moto-crossers are designed to cope with natural hazards of all types.

Natural conditions vary between circuits and an average race-duration speed limit of 50 km/h (31 mph) is applied to discourage the sport's degeneration into a flat-track type of pure speed event.

Contrary to popular opinion, modern moto-cross machines are not ruggedly over-built, as they once were, but are designed to the bottom limits of anticipated racing stress requirements, in order to reduce dead-weight to a minimum. Despite the rugged terrain they are expected to tackle, moto-cross engines are as finely tuned as those of road racers, and require no less skillful attention by expert race-mechanics. Because of the terrain the cycle parts are ingeniously designed.

Significantly, the excessive power being developed by current moto-crossers has led to a complete and welcome, if belated, reappraisal of suspension systems. The Suzuki type of variable rate, rocking-link, rear suspension and the Valentino Ribi double link front suspension adopted by Honda may benefit roadsters more than recent road race developments.

Due to the powerful modern engines that drive them, knobbly moto-cross tires can actually wear courses out after a couple of meetings. It is paradoxical that while the knobblies are required for grip, the engine must be powerful enough to break rear wheel traction, when required, for fast cornering. Honda's little NR125 twin produces 35 bhp.

Spectators, deafened by endless and harsh 2-stroke noise, might be surprised to learn that no grand prix moto-cross machine is allowed to exceed a noise level greater than 110 dba.

Specified dimensions for moto-cross machines.

The width of handlebars must be between 600mm (23.5in) and 850mm (33.5in). The length of lever, its angle and the diameter of the ball end are also specified.

The fender ends are rounded to a radius of at least 8mm (0.3in). Front fenders can be removed on authorization of the jury.

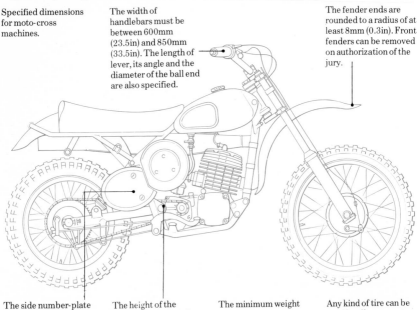

The side number-plate must be above a horizontal line drawn through the rear wheel spindle.

The height of the footrests (with rider) may not be more than 50mm (2in) above the wheel spindle.

The minimum weight for a 500cc moto-cross machine is 95kg (210lb).

Any kind of tire can be used legally on a moto-crosser. In practice the deepest available tread is preferred.

Moto-cross is a tough sport in which hard knocks are inevitable. Protective clothing is essential equipment but, until recently, moto-crossers went racing in thinly padded jerseys.

Jerseys should be chosen for freedom of movement. Approved material should be chosen with weather conditions in mind. A kidney belt should also be worn to protect internal organs from harsh jolts.

An open-face helmet is lighter and cooler than a full-face type.

A visor deflects flying stones and mud from the rider's face.

Goggles should be chosen to fit the helmet. Tinted lenses and tear-off types are available.

Face masks offer protection from flying stones, and incorporate a dust filter. Mask and goggles may be an integrated unit.

Body-armor vests, incorporating a chest protector with shoulder pads are available in a wide range of styles. The J-T model is made of ventilated polythene over a padded vest.

Trousers must be leather or an acceptable substitute to comply with international regulations.

Moto-cross gloves are padded back *and* front to prevent blisters. The best are tailored to fit a grasping hand.

157

Trials

No vehicle sport demands a greater degree of machine control than trials riding; and no other vehicle can cross more rugged terrain than a trials bike in skilled hands. Improbable as it might seem, an experienced trials rider can negotiate terrain that would defeat a horseman or even a walker.

Any youngster who assumes that trials riding is for old men because of its lack of speed has only to stand on a set of footrests and look over one of the terrifyingly steep descents common in modern competitions to appreciate his mistake.

Trials is the only motorcycle sport that relies on neither the heat of personal combat nor the stimulating effect of adrenaline. All hazards are tackled alone, under the scrutiny of other knowledgeable riders, and in cold, calculating fashion. The physical dangers are limited to little more than bruising and the occasional torn ligament or dislocation.

Trials bikes share a common ancestry with road racers but, whereas the pavement scratchers metamorphosed into singularly impractical motorcycles built only for high speed use, trials irons held faith with roadsters.

Until the mid-1930s, trials bikes were little more than privately modified roadsters. But with the demise of the road-based trial and the increasing popularity of off-road special sections, the first purpose-built machines with low gear ratios, high ground clearance and control layouts suited to a standing rider began to appear; so did knobbly tires, which the ACU quickly banned. They specified what was then the tread pattern of a typical road tire for trials use and, by doing so, ensured the trials machine's status as a legally equipped roadster.

By good fortune, the tread pattern of trials tires has proved to be an ideal compromise which satisfies most people. Modern roadster tires offer no useful adhesion off road, and moto-cross tires provide so much that special sections would need to be made unnecessarily dangerous to tax the top riders' skills. And, of course, in many places, motocross tires are illegal on public roads. Modern trials tires are soft, frequently of two-ply carcass construction, in order to provide their users with maximum traction on soft or loose going, at which times rear tire pressures may be lowered to 0.28kg/sq cm (4 psi).

The classic events were firmly established in motorcycling lore before World War I, although they were limited primarily to Britain which, apart from outposts of minority interest, enjoyed the peculiar fascination of the sport alone. The Scottish Six Days Trial (SSDT) began life in 1910, and is still by far the toughest of all observed trials. Three years later, the International Six Days Trial (ISDT) started in Cumberland, as a British event, and the Scott trial, by far the fiercest one-day timed trial in the calendar, started up.

It was not until 1968 that a European Championship was organized for observed trials. In 1975 trials became the last major motorcycling sport to be accorded a World Championship. The first champion was Martin Lampkin, one of a family of Yorkshire trials experts. Since then riders from Finland, France and USA have challenged the British supremacy.

Observed trials measure the ability of competitors to negotiate observed sections. Although riders have to complete the entire trial within a given time, this is only to ensure that everyone manages to get home that night.

Timed trials also include observed sections, although there are generally fewer of them. Participants have to complete the entire course within a given time; penalty points are awarded to those finishing outside it.

Not surprisingly, timed trials have much in common with enduro events and some, such as the ISDT, have become so much like enduros that moto-cross based machines are necessary for the serious competitor.

A FANTIC RIDER AT THE SCOTTISH SDT

Trials/2

The most common trials are the observed type. They last the best part of one day and incorporate approximately 40 sections on private ground, usually joined by stretches of public road. A section is a plainly marked hazard or series of hazards, which might be anything between 25m (82ft) and 1km (0.6 mi) long.

Acute gradients form the basis of most sections, which are usually interrupted by adverse cambers, fallen logs and tree roots, loose rocks and rock steps, deep and frequently water-filled gulleys, mud and sand. Riders are routed up, down and across gradients by the most difficult path.

Generally, all trials should incorporate a balance of wet, dry, soft and hard going, but warm climate events are usually dry, with sand and rocks; mid-European events are wet, with woodland conditions, and north-European trials are wet, with rocky conditions.

Competitors leave the start singly at timed intervals and are given a period in which they must finish the event or risk penalty points. However, time is allowed for every competitor to stop and inspect each section before he or she rides it.

If a competitor dabs—places a single foot down for balance—just once, one penalty point is awarded; three points are given for footing—assisting progress by walking; and five points for stopping—or breaking through the section limits. Sharp-eyed observers attend each section to inspect the progress of every rider. The rider with the fewest penalty points at the end of the day wins the trial.

Planning and marking out sections is a skilled job for experienced trials riders. The Clerk of the Course is usually a semi-retired expert who tries out each section. He does not necessarily have to clean each section himself—a few impossible sections are usually included to test the abilities of the top runners.

As trials motorcycles have to conform to road vehicle legislation, all are equipped with two brakes, a chain guard, lighting equipment, a speedometer, a horn, license plate, road-legal tires, fenders and a fully muffled exhaust system.

The chief reason that trials bikes look so odd by comparison with roadsters is that they are constructed to provide maximum control with the rider standing on the footrests, from which position balance and steering are most sensitively controlled. The wheelbase is ultra-short at no more than 1270mm (50 inches); ground clearance is high at around 355mm (14 inches), and weight is as low as 90kg (200lb). All these factors contribute to uncanny maneuverability.

Trials engines are tuned for maximum low engine speed torque development. Although the Bultaco 350 Sherpa T develops only 20bhp at 6,500rpm, its torque is more than enough to put proper control beyond the ability of a novice. It is said that Sherpas can climb walls on idle revs.

A six speed gearbox is usual, with the wide ratio gears starting at a super-low crawler first gear. A top road gear is included for use between sections.

Suspension action is long, with very soft springs and damping rates to absorb low speed shocks. Tires are usually run at extremely low pressure.

Fuel tanks rarely hold more than 4.5l (1.2gal) for the sake of lightness and for a slim profile to suit a straight-legged, standing rider.

Sidecar trials outfits are invariably based on the largest (350cc) versions of popular solo machines. Special one-piece outfit chassis are usually adopted in place of the original frames. At club level, many outfits are quite simply modified solos with lightweight chairs bolted on to them. In most events incorporating sidecars, the three-wheelers follow a similar, but less rigorous, series of special sections after the solos have passed through. As in all sidecar-based sports, the passenger plays a vital role in competitive progress.

Trials machines have evolved from road bikes which, technically, they still are. However, they are now highly specialized with certain ideal characteristics.

Seats are minimal, as most trials riding is done standing up.

Speedometer and horn are compulsory for use on public roads.

Martin Lampkin, the first World Champion, in 1975.

Handlebar dimensions are the same as for moto-cross—600 to 850mm wide, although the bend is modified.

Where lights must be fitted by law they are small and run direct from the engine, without batteries.

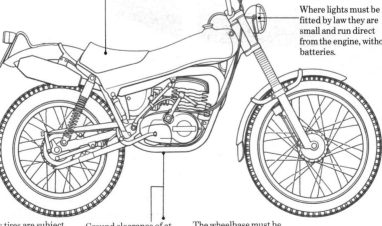

Trials tires are subject to restrictions governing road use. The width may not exceed 115mm (4.5in).

Ground clearance of at least 300mm (12in) is considered essential.

The wheelbase must be extemely short for optimum maneuverability.

Drag racing

Drag racing originated on the West coast of the USA, where the sport began in earnest during the late 1940s. It arrived in Europe as late as 1964, via the intentionally American-sounding Santa Pod Raceway in Bedfordshire, England. Britain and Holland are now the strongest European rivals of America in the drag world, although American riders still dominate the sport.

But however modern drag racing appears to be, it is simply a commercialized version of sprinting—a traditional form of acceleration, or lapsed time, competition, which is as old as motorcycling.

The difference between the two is that, in sprinting, a single rider starts in his own time and accelerates alone over a ¼ mile. This distance (402.3 m) is the basis for sprint and drag competitions across the globe. Sprint buffs claim with justification that theirs is the purest motor sport of all: one rider against the clock without artificial or commercial impediments.

The different characteristics of drag racing were devised to add spectator interest and, thus, make the sport commercially profitable. Pairs of riders compete in a series of knock-out heats, the faster competitors moving through a succession of eliminating rounds until, at the end of the day, a final run-off is made.

In dragging, unlike sprinting, there is no guarantee that the competitor covering the ¼ mile strip in the shortest elapsed time of the day will win the event. The fastest rounds may be those run early in the day.

As acceleration is not consistent, there is also a distinction between the fastest and the quickest. A machine may come in second at a higher terminal velocity than the one which got there first.

Moreover, drag racers are required to start at a given light signal, which places great emphasis on initial quick reaction. Standby and start signals are given by lights on a post-mounted device on the line which is known as a Christmas tree.

HENK VINK ON BIG SPENDER

163

Drag racing/2

Most public interest is centered around drag racing's fuelers, in which engines are limited to 3000cc, or 2000cc if blown by super- or turbocharger. The most commonly used fuels are various brews of oxygen-rich liquid chemicals such as nitro-methanol. Fuel is pumped into engines in such huge quantities that there is a danger of hydraulic locking in the combustion chamber—so much fluid is injected that the spark is extinguished and the piston will not move. This results in a blown cylinder head at least.

Burning fuel or "dope" is frequently ejected from machine exhaust pipes, which leads to the impressive display of pyrotechnics so much appreciated by spectators.

In some cases the fireworks are deliberately exaggerated by riders attempting to soften their slick rear tires to a sticky, and therefore more adhesive, consistency. The 10-inch-wide slicks are spun in household bleach, generating thick smoke.

Smaller machines have their tires burnt as the clutch is let out while they are held against a wall. Larger ones are usually given a rolling burn-out. At night meetings, an inflammable mixture may be ignited to give the spectacular effect illustrated on the preceding page by Dutchman Henk Vink.

Tom Christensen is one great drag exponent who, with his double-engined Norton, *Hogslayer,* proved that technical innovation could produce better results than brawn alone. He equipped his bike with a controlled-slip clutch to reduce initial wheel-spin wastage and to allow the useful adoption of a two speed gearbox. In 1973 when he introduced this device, Christensen won every event he entered.

The first rider to beat the eight-second barrier, known in drag circles as breaking the sevens, was Russ Collins on his triple Honda-engined machine in 1976. He reached a terminal velocity of 178mph (286km/h) at Ontario, California, in a time of 7.86 seconds.

Within the range of FIM sanctioned standing start competitions a total of 81 world records waits to be broken at any time. These range from the 50cc ¼ mile (held at 15.5685 sec by A. Toerson on a Krielder since 1968), to the 24-hour 750cc solo (held since 1977 by an American team riding a Z650 Kawasaki at 117.125mph [188.494km/h]). Twenty flying-start world records also await breaking, and these include the world land-speed records such as the one Don Vesco holds in the Group F (solo 3000cc) class. Also included are records like George Brown's 1300cc sidecar record of 1966—when his Vincent outfit achieved a velocity of 149.733mph (240.972km/h)—which is asking to be broken by almost any competent racer these days.

The FIM controls sprinting, and all records have to be calculated from the mean time of two runs, measured in both directions with FIM timekeepers present. Drag records are accepted, by their more commercial associations, from only a single run measured by timing equipment controlled by regular meeting officials. These do not count as official world records.

A popular supporting class in drag racing is the pro-street or pro-stock category in which modified road bikes compete. The rules stipulate that they must run on ordinary pump fuel and must retain the appearance of their origins. For all their restrictions, these machines are now covering the standing quarter in under 10 seconds and will undoubtedly be battering at the door of the nines before long.

The wheelie bar is a precautionary device to hold the bike down when the front wheel paws at the sky. Without such devices riders have been left standing as the cycle flies out from beneath them.

Street solo motorcycles can be ridden on the road, but few riders actually drive them to meetings.

Major modifications include engine tuning, the lightening of certain cycle parts and the

fitting of security clamps to some components—and the wheelie bar.

The double-engine bikes of Danny Johnson (H-D) and Tom Christensen (Norton) gave European fans a thrill in 1975.

Stands must be wired up or removed.

The wheelbase must not exceed prescribed limits.

Speedway

Speedway was developed into an identifiable form of motorcycle sport by commercially-minded Australians during the early 1920s. Prior to that, dirt-track racing was peculiar to the shale or sand and clay tracks of America.

Australia adopted the sport under American guidance, but reduced the track length from ½ to ⅓ mile. Before long, the surface of loose cinders encouraged a new riding style. The rider balanced the machine by applications of excessive power to the rear wheel and opposite lock to the front wheel. The crowds loved it, which influenced British sports promoters to adopt speedway in 1929.

Shortly before World War II a World Championship was organized and, while American riders have occasionally made their mark, Australian, British and Scandinavians have since virtually dominated the sport, although they were joined during the 1950s by riders from Eastern Europe.

Most speedway nations run leagues with professional teams from various towns, each with their home stadium.

No gears are fitted to speedway bikes; and brakes were soon banned when it was realized that their use on the approach to bends was leading to serious crashes.

Rudy Muts, a Dutch rider, demonstrates the speedway style of cornering. Grass trackers **right** chew up a field in southern England.

Grass track

Grass track is a natural development of speedway, with which it shares much, including many riders who find that the transition from one to the other requires the smallest of style changes.

The sport began during the 1920s in most European countries where grassy

Speedway machines have no brakes, no gears and only minimal front suspension.

Grass track bikes are equipped with rear swinging forks, brakes and gearboxes.

fields were abundant. Not surprisingly, one meeting rips up a field quite badly and recovery periods require the venue to change regularly. Probably for this reason, the sport has remained low-key, and very much an amateur affair, with most meetings relying on help from friends and families to assist in their continuance.

Most grass tracks are approximately ½ mile long, and races usually last for at least six laps.

The FIM organize a European Championship but it is not highly regarded among grass track nations. In most cases the national championships are considered to be of greater importance. Classes are for 250, 350, 500 cc and sidecars.

In recent years grass track sidecar outfits have started to equal the popularity of solo machines and, while championship events incur a capacity limit of 500cc, national restricted meetings allow the use of 1000cc machines. The exciting racing these provide is popular with spectators, but there is regular criticism of the unnecessary danger and of the destruction these monsters cause to the course.

US Nationals

To non-American eyes the US Grand National Championship is a medley of mystery race classes which bear no resemblance to the sharply defined, and quite separate, international sports such as trials, moto-cross and grass track.

America is arguably correct in requiring its national champion to prove his mettle in five different classes of racing, in which three styles of riding are required.

The AMA broke with the FIM (then FICM) almost as soon as the AMA had been formed in 1924, because they reasoned that motorcycling would be best served by race machinery based on commercially available roadsters. The FIM preferred the super-specialist approach. Even as long ago as the early 1930s, exotic pushrod and overhead camshaft engines were penalized by a 33⅓ per cent lower capacity limit when competing with 750cc common-place side valvers—as used then by most road-going American riders. The Nationals are still outside the FIM jurisdiction.

Today the National Championship has lost some of its prestige, due to the re-awakening of interest in international championships (particularly as US riders have begun to win the titles). But even so, the American riders who by-pass their traditional route to success are few: Kenny Roberts came through the system; Bernie Schreiber (trials) and Brad Lackey (moto-cross) are unusual men.

Road racing was no more important than the other championship classes, until BSA/Triumph 750cc pushrod triples began competing on level terms against Harley-Davidson at Daytona in 1970. The entire championship system changed shape as American road racing and Daytona rose to an internationally pre-eminent position. Daytona had become to American racing what the Isle of Man TT was to the European championships—if you did not win there, then you were an also-ran.

Without doubt the most spectacular of all forms of motorcycle competition is the flat track mile. The track is an extended oval, frequently with a half-mile straight, surfaced in oil-damped, compacted shale and clay. Around this, 25 starters force their heavy machines in close proximity at speeds up to 130mph: they corner at 100mph leaning into the curves with steel-shod boots and rear wheels drifting crazily.

Unlike speedway circuits, these fast dirt tracks become rutted and broken, and this stresses machines and riders to their limit. Machines buck and pitch, apparently wildly, under the control of riders who rely on raw courage no less than skill. A typical mile race will run for a duration of 50 miles at a race leader's average speed of over 100mph.

The half-mile flat track events are similar, but about 10mph slower. Not surprisingly, body contact among competitors is more severe, with clashing elbows and wheel-trapped feet among the commonest causes of accidents.

Gene Romero leads a mile track race on his Harley. The bikes have close-ratio gearboxes but no brakes.

Short track racing takes place on circuits under ¼ mile in length, and on machines under 250 cc. Many riders consider it to be the roughest of all championship events because of the after-me-Jack riding style, imposed by the ultra-close proximity of a lot of big riders hurling small motorcycles around a short track.

Finally there is TT steeplechase racing. Unlike flat track courses these contain both right- and left-hand turns, and a couple of big jumps.

During an average AMA National Championship series, the schedule will consist of approximately 23 races of all types. Of these, six will be road racing, with each heat approximately 75 miles long. Mile tracks are few in number now, but three or four events will still be incorporated, along with six or seven half-mile events and four or five TT races. Half a dozen body-bruising short track events will complete the season.

Ice racing

The origins of ice racing are obscure, but by the 1920s speedway machines were being raced on ice in Scandinavia.

By the early 1930s spiked tires had been adopted, together with an improved riding technique in which the inner leg trailed behind the rider.

So far down do these speedway-based machines fall during cornering that their short, inside handlebars are raked upwards to aid clearance. Even so, crushed and amputated left-hand fingers are the trade mark of professional ice racers. So, too, are scars left by the punctures and rips caused by the 25-28mm (1in) sharp spikes. But while lacerations are common in ice races, serious injury is not.

Each rear tire is equipped with 105 spikes, and each front tire with 65, most of which are biased toward the left; the ¼ mile tracks are ridden counterclockwise.

During the 1960s Russian riders began to challenge the supremacy of the Scandinavians; now Eastern bloc riders virtually dominate the sport.

SWEDISH RIDER CONNIE SAMUELSON LEADS ROLD THYS ON ICE.

Desert racing

Desert racing is a particularly American pastime which achieved popularity during the 1960s. Although speed is involved, the overlying principle is that of individual satisfaction and family fun.

Riders follow routes indicated by columns of smoke from piles of burning tires. Sections between the fires are from 10 to 40 miles (16-64km) long. Although speed plays a part, the best riders are those with an ability to read the country and its contours, and who have developed a strong sense of direction.

Most modern desert racers are modified enduro or moto-cross machines. The most famous desert event is the Baja 1000, in which competitors race, in open competition with cars and jeeps, for 1,000 miles (1,600km) down the sun-scorched length of the Baja (Mexico) desert peninsula.

The French have recently inaugurated a trans-Sahara race. This epic run, from Paris to Dakar, is over 10,000km (6,200 mi) and, like the Baja, it is open to all classes of vehicle.

EXTRA LARGE TANKS FOR XR HONDA RIDERS HEADING FOR DAKAR.

Hill climbing

There are many different hill climb traditions. American climbs are either of the freak type (unclimbable gradients won by the rider who gets farthest), or they are dirt-road speed trials. Most British hill climbs are a type of short and twisty sprint.

The European Mountain Championship, which reached maximum popularity following Switzerland's banishment of road racing in 1955, is the most seriously organized. Championship tracks are paved roads approximately 2 to 4 miles (3 to 6 km) long.

Competitors leave at 10 second intervals and race against the clock. Classes for 250, 350, 500 cc and sidecars are catered for; most machines are road racers. Spain, Italy, Switzerland, Belgium, Austria and France are the principal contesting nations.

One of the most impressive climbs is at Pike's Peak in Colorado, USA. Each year on July 4, car and motorcycle competitors tackle a narrow, winding dirt road that climbs from 9,500ft (2896m) to 14,110ft (4301m) through 156 bends along a total of 12.42 miles (20km).

The race was inaugurated in 1916, when aces like Cannonball Baker and Floyd Clymer hurled their heavy Indians, Excelsiors and Harley-Davidsons up the graded dirt road.

Although cars used the run annually, the bike classes were abandoned for long periods until, in 1971, motorcycles were invited back again. Unlike the cars, motorcycles are started in groups, much to the delight of the crowds. But a serious multiple pile-up in 1976 worried the organizers, and not until 1980 did the AMA sanction the climb again.

The winning time in 1980 was 13min, 44.73sec (average speed, 64.9mph [104km/h]), set by Lonnie Houtchens on a flat track-styled Yamaha XL 750, in the open pro class. This is more creditable than it sounds, since thin air at high altitude reduces the power of the machines, which require compensatory tuning for a range of altitude effects.

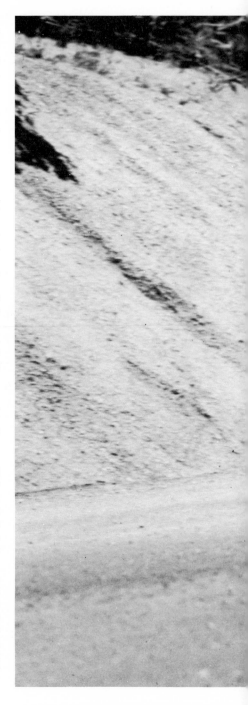

STEVE SCOTT, SIX-TIME 250 CLASS WINNER AT PIKE'S PEAK, ON A BULTACO.

Enduro

Enduros are the newest sporting events in off-road motorcycling. Some of the current enduros were once time trials, complete with observed sections, while others are brand-new. All take their lead from the ISDT, which is not a trial but a cross-country race, relying on timed, rather than observed, sections to evaluate competitors. Enduros are participant events with little access or interest to spectators.

Enduros are not moto-cross events; whereas moto-cross takes place around a prescribed short circuit on private land, enduros rarely cover the same ground twice. They are run mainly on public land, roads and tracks, often covering many hundreds of miles.

Major enduros are usually two-day events. Most European nations contest the European enduro championship, in which awards are made in 50, 75, 100, 125, 175, 250, 350, 500 and over 500cc classes. There is no sidecar award and no major sidecar enduros are run.

In America, where there is easier access to open land, enduros are frequently informal fun events, catering for a wide range of riding experience. Distinctions between enduros and desert racing are often blurred.

Because enduros are usually run along at least some sections of public road, the machines themselves are required to conform to the minimum legal requirements of road-going motorcycles. Many riders find this restricting, especially where tires are concerned, for the use of moto-cross covers is considered to be vital by the majority of serious competitors; yet these are illegal in some countries.

An enduro motorcycle is, strictly according to FIM regulations, a trials machine. But as the use to which enduro machines are put presupposes the capability to absorb a great deal of heavy punishment, and as machines must afford riders maximum comfort and control when seated, few bear any relationship to trials bikes. Most have close kinship with moto-cross machines and, for this reason, demand firm and skilful handling. The power of the larger models limits their effective use to experienced and brave riders. The larger, expert's machines, such as those from KTM and SWM, generate up to 50bhp.

The top speed of the best enduro machines is over 100 mph (160 km/h), and to cope with that sort of performance along a rutted forest track after six hours of strenuous riding, competitors have to be in peak physical and mental condition.

However, a good enduro rider nurses his machine gently, trials fashion, rather than forcing it brutally, moto-cross style. As mileages are high, riders remain seated for all but the most difficult terrain. The best riders are exciting only to experts, for they move at a deceptive pace with controlled style in which body movement, and violent machine maneuvering, including power-sliding, are rarely observed.

Enduro competitors are supplied with route cards, time cards and schedules by the event organizers. When they check in at the start, each rider determines the route speed he must maintain to arrive at time checks within the allotted time: a leeway of two minutes is usually granted, during which time minor machine adjustments are allowed.

The maximum average speed allowed by FIM regulations is 40km/h (25mph), and the minimum depends on the severity of the course, according to the opinion of the organizers. Different engine capacity classes run to different times; the smaller machines are set a slower pace.

During a multi-day event, machines are impounded by officials in a special *parc fermé*. Before the night's enforced rest, riders only are allowed to carry out 15 minutes maintenance work to their machines, when tires, cables, chains, spark plugs, and other specified parts may be replaced.

FLORIDA'S ALLIGATOR ENDURO PROVIDES DEEP MUD TO REVEL IN.

ISDT

The International Six Days Trial (ISDT) is the most important event in the motorcycling calendar — but only for manufacturers, it would seem. A win ensures improved sales and great prestige, but individual riders from western nations appear to treat the event casually.

Unique among motorcycling events, the ISDT demands that competitors relinquish individuality for the sake of national team success, and this comes hard to sportsmen who thrive on intense rivalry. Individuals are awarded gold, silver and bronze medals according to their points (gold medallists must lose no points), but no individual ever wins.

Two prizes are contested: the World Premier Trophy, and the Silver Vase. Each nation is allowed one Trophy team which must consist of four men on machines of identical make, although each model may be different in size; two three-man Trophy teams per nation are allowed, and these can use different makes of motorcycle. On top of this, manufacturers and club teams are also encouraged; thus it is possible for one country to put 16 participants and motorcycles into the trial, without employing numerous club teams.

Since 1954 the ISDT has been firmly in the grip of the Eastern bloc manufacturers, but since the rise of the new Italian industry, and the availability of top quality and inexpensive machinery from Japan, a revival of western resolve has occurred. The most surprising aspect of the ISDT is that Japan has shown such disinterest as a nation, when they obviously appreciate the commercial rewards awaiting any major sporting success, let alone an ISDT win.

As with all enduros, ISDT competitors are expected to maintain their own machines from parts carried with them on route; no outside assistance whatsoever is allowed.

Punctures are common, and the machines are rigged for wheel removal without tools. Good competitors can replace an inner tube in four minutes.

Trail riding

Following hard on the early 1960s success in America of heavyweight street scramblers from companies like Triumph and Matchless, Suzuki built the 125 cc 2-stroke Trailcat in the early 1970s, and opened the floodgates of wild enthusiasm for on/off-road, go-anywhere, fun bikes.

The early, clumsy little machines improved markedly, until currently the best trail bikes are barely distinguishable from genuine enduro machines. And most of them are much more pleasant to ride. At club level, machines like the Yamaha DT175MX are as successful at putting their owners in the front of a dirty bunch of mud-pluggers as they are at placing them ahead of a line of traffic.

Between these two extremes, those trail bikes that are used off-road (90 per cent wear their block-tread tires flat on paved highway) are opening up great tracts of countryside which, previously, had remained undiscovered. While this pleases motorcyclists, who may or may not be the paragons of environmentally-considerate virtue they claim to be, it certainly does not please the dedicated conservationists.

If the only motorcyclists who took to the empty places were, indeed, the users of moderately ridden, properly silenced (muffled) machines, few would even notice them. Resistance to off-road motorcycling has arisen mainly from the bitter experience of naturalists, farmers and country people after the passage of a few howling hooligans playing motocross.

In America and Australia the problem is mainly the destruction of terrain; wheel tracks create scars that assist erosion. In Britain and the rest of Europe the threat is mainly to agricultural interests — gates left open, crops ridden through, animals frightened, and so on.

In all areas, movements have been started by responsible groups of aware motorcyclists, who are doing much to heal, or at least halt, the. antagonism caused by the two-wheeled bandits.

Unless you anticipate travelling over very rugged terrain, deep sand or thick mud you do not need a special trail bike to go trail riding. But unless you can handle a bike well, restrict yourself to tourers below 400cc.

Trail riders should follow these guidelines.

1 Ask local dealers or the AMA for the address of a trail riding organization in your area.

2 Do not assume that paths and tracks, whether marked on a map or not, are a right of way.

3 When you do find a suitable route, ride slowly and quietly; if you meet anyone, or pass occupied houses or farms, stop and pass the time of day, explain what you are doing.

4 If you come upon horses, pull over, stop your engine and make no sudden moves that might frighten them. Give the riders a wave.

5 Carry some tools and spares, including an inner tube, a pump and ½gal (2l) of spare fuel in a can.

6 NEVER venture into sand dunes. On flat sand, ride at a moderate to fast pace in third gear, with tires deflated to around 12psi (0.82 kg/sq cm).

7 Deep mud should be tackled in second gear on a small throttle opening. Never ford rivers without knowing the depth of the water.

8 Tires should be left hard in rocky country.

9 Never ride into something you cannot ride out of — there may be no alternative exit.

10 Inform someone where you are going and when you expect to return.

Long distance fun

The best way to learn about the necessities of touring is to go touring. After travelling say 600 miles (1,000km) in a single weekend you will have learned most of the basic requirements.

Any two-wheeler can be toured, but the less suitable the bike is, the more adaptable (uncomfortable) you will have to be. Mileage is less significant than time, so attempt nothing more than six hours' riding at first. Split the day with a good, long lunch break.

Speed

The top speed of a tourer is unimportant. Its ability to maintain high average speeds comfortably and economically is paramount. A powerful/sports machine cruised at 100 mph (160km/h) at 25mpg (10.5km/1) on a 3.5 gal (13.51) tank has a non-reserve range of 90mi (145km). A less powerful but comfortable machine cruised at 80mph (130km/h) at 45mpg (18.5km/1) on a 3.8 gal (14.51) tank has a non-reserve range of 250mi (400km). The second motorcycle is the better tourer and has an overall average speed potential greater than the sports model.

The rule for high average speeds is to maintain a relaxed, steady rhythm at all times. Stops, for refuelling and rest, destroy a good average.

Comfort

Unless you are abnormally average your machine will require ergonomic tailoring to fit you properly. If you plan to travel habitually at over 75mph (120km/h) you will have to adopt either a slim, windcheating, forward inclination and/or fit a fairing, or suffer from aching arms and neck and numbed fingers.

Let the bike take all the load! All motorcycles can be power-steered. Truly heavy machines like the Z1300 can be swept through bends as effortlessly as a lightweight if the right technique is employed.

Try it yourself: ride along a straight, wide and empty road and gently pull on the right handlebar. This will have the effect of pitching the motorcycle to the left. Return to straight ahead by lightly pulling on the left-hand bar. You are employing the gyroscopic force of the front wheel to move the weight of the machine laterally.

A little practice will soon have you dropping your heavy, luggage- and pillion-laden tourer into mountain road S-bends, and then picking it up out of them like a boy on a bicycle.

Passengers

It is a fact that long-distance pillionists suffer greater discomfort and cold than riders because generally they have nothing to do and less opportunity to move around. It is a serious mistake to assume that pillionists can make do with inferior clothing because they are shielded by the rider. Pillion riders with job responsibility have a much better time. They are ideally positioned to help with navigation.

Cold

In cold climates never ride far without a good meal inside you. The nervous system will deteriorate dangerously as a result of hypothermia in a body without an energy source — food.

Heat

A combination of wind and sun will lead to sickness from dehydration unless a lot of water is drunk. Alcohol, fruit juice, sugar and milk-based liquids are absorbed as food by the body, and do not quench thirst.

Spares

Learn how to fit the usual breakdown parts and carry electrical and ignition components, control cables, chains and links, inner tubes and puncture patches. Tubeless-tire users should carry a tube for emergency puncture repairs — deflated tubeless tires cannot be inflated with a hand or foot pump.

The pleasures of the wide open spaces: America provides a fast empty highway for the BMW rider **above** and a peaceful haven for author David Minton and his Morini.

Touring

Equipment

No amount of bolt-on equipment will ever improve a fundamentally poor design, but a few carefully selected items will turn a commonplace machine into a surprisingly good tourer.

Bear in mind that you are trying to improve your motorcycling, and keep extra equipment down to the minimum; turning a motorcycle into a Christmas tree overloaded with every conceivable goody will destroy its agile and responsive character. Be practical in your choice and calculate the effects on handling of every piece of equipment you add.

Before buying anything make a point of getting to know some older, experienced tourists with at least five years of motorcycling holidays behind them. Do not let yourself be influenced by those full dressers who find greater pleasure in accessories than they do in touring.

On the assumption that your machine is already reliable, quiet and smooth, you should first aim to improve its comfort. This can be done by fitting an alternative seat, handlebar and footrest arrangement. Very few, if any, alternative suspension systems actually improve rider comfort.

The best luxury seats are the firmly padded, body-contoured models, which provide low back and thigh support. The seat you choose should be specifically tailored to fit your machine; large enough to let you and your pillion rider shift position occasionally, yet snug enough to support you and firm enough to stop you sinking through the padding to the seat pan. Seats that feel soft do not provide long-term comfort. In hot weather the fitment of a heavy white cotton cover, which reflects the heat of the sun, adds greatly to rider comfort. Habitual fast riders also benefit from seats which hold the body firm and comfortable against the buffeting slipstream.

People who tour slowly without fairings usually prefer a generously proportioned handlebar in the American style, while faster riders are better equipped with a lower, narrower bar such as that fitted by BMW. This is not simply a question of fashionable style, but is a matter of ergonomics. To insist that one is better than another is to display motorcycling ignorance.

If you do decide to fit a different handlebar, you will probably also have to fit different control cables and hydraulic brake pipes to conform to the new length, whether this is longer or shorter. In some instances, electric wiring will require modification and mirror-stem length may need changing. Alas, motorcycling is no longer the simple pleasure it once was . . . .

Take great care about placing your feet comfortably. If you want to ride fast, then move your footrests back from the standard position by 70-130mm (2¾-5in); this will demand a completely rearranged gear and brake lever system.

American owners of European machines might do well to compare their foot control arrangements with those of the home-market models: many are changed over to comply with American law and the frequently crude modifications spoil an otherwise good movement. Most dealers in the USA can supply the original European control layout as spares.

More relaxed tourists may benefit from the adoption of footboards. These are widely available to suit most popular touring machines in the USA and can add enormously to rider comfort. Europeans tend to dismiss footboards, although practically none of them has any experience with such equipment, which is their loss, because on a long trip there is nothing to beat the comfort of being able to change foot positions.

Pillion backrests are unsuitable for all motorcycles because they alter the weight distribution of a machine and disrupt the close relationship between rider and passenger. They should never be used on machines weighing less than 270kg (600lb).

Alternative riding gear
Sightseeing tourists require walk-about casuals as well as specialist motorcycle clothing. The finest option is heavyweight denim jeans and sleeved jacket. Denim provides good abrasion resistance in case of a tumble. The material is reasonably windproof, which is vital for cold and warm weather riding to stop chilling and dehydration.

The best of sling-over saddle bags is that they are cheap and easily transportable. Choose only those with covered, weatherproof seams, and make sure before buying that they drape fully laden without touching hot parts of the machine.

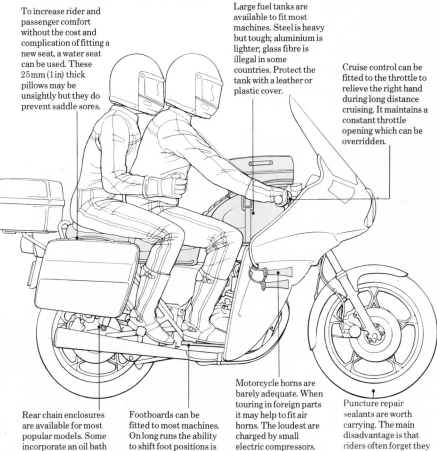

To increase rider and passenger comfort without the cost and complication of fitting a new seat, a water seat can be used. These 25 mm (1 in) thick pillows may be unsightly but they do prevent saddle sores.

Large fuel tanks are available to fit most machines. Steel is heavy but tough; aluminium is lighter; glass fibre is illegal in some countries. Protect the tank with a leather or plastic cover.

Cruise control can be fitted to the throttle to relieve the right hand during long distance cruising. It maintains a constant throttle opening which can be overridden.

Rear chain enclosures are available for most popular models. Some incorporate an oil bath to protect against chain wear.

Footboards can be fitted to most machines. On long runs the ability to shift foot positions is a blessing for rider and passenger.

Motorcycle horns are barely adequate. When touring in foreign parts it may help to fit air horns. The loudest are charged by small electric compressors. Less expensive types use air cylinders.

Puncture repair sealants are worth carrying. The main disadvantage is that riders often forget they have been used, and drive too far on damaged tires.

181

Packing and loading

Packing motorcycle baggage is a craft. If you don't make an effort to learn it you may lose a fortune in damaged goods. Every method of luggage carrying requires special attention.

Top box (trunk)

Nothing heavy and nothing fragile should go into one of these: heavy goods will upset stability and fragile items like cameras will be unnecessarily shaken about because of the positioning of the box behind the rear wheel axle. On the other hand, they are convenient to dip into, so carry spare riding clothing, picnic supplies, toiletries and suchlike in them.

Hard saddlebags

Use these to carry the bulk of your gear. Pack the waterproof inner bags lying flat, or they will be too swollen for the saddle-bag to shut around them. Put heavy clothes that resist creasing low down, followed by lighter clothing. Rigid bags with top loading lids should be equipped with a strong inner bag. This should also be packed when flat, and then lowered into the rigid outer. An inner tube partially inflated inside a saddlebag can be used to protect fragile objects or to fill empty space and protect contents from being shaken excessively.

Soft saddlebags

No soft saddlebag is completely water-proof, so these, too, should be lined with a tough, waterproof, inner bag, which should be taller than the saddlebag to leave room for a generous, water-resistant fold-over. Unless they are already fitted, add a stiffener and inner guard of hardboard or something similar on the inner side of the saddlebag. Check to see where the bag rubs on the machine, and then apply linen-backed adhesive tape to the machine and the bag to stop scarring abrasion and wear patches.

Take care that the bags do not touch the hot engine or exhaust system; if they do you will lose your property along the road as the bag melts through. Pack the bags upright.

Tank bag

Carry the really heavy stuff in this—large tools, books, drinks. Fold a towel in the base for protection, cover it with a clean cloth or plastic bag, then pack the hard pieces among socks and other small, soft items. If you must carry your camera on your machine then do so in this bag. Use the clear top pocket for maps. Buy only a bag that can be quickly released from its permanently attached fixing harness, which must incorporate a filler cap hole. Zips should be generously fly-covered.

Rear carrier (luggage rack)

A good all-purpose general carrier can be used for carrying orthodox travelling bags, camping rolls, tents and other bulky objects. Keep the load light for the sake of stability.

Back-pack

In a word—don't! Unless you plan to travel slowly, with an aching back, have your bike carry the load, not you.

Cameras

These should really travel in a weather-proof bag around your neck to absorb the road bumps and to keep them isolated from engine vibration. Special kidney-shaped, motorcyclists' camera shoulder bags are available, with waist straps.

Locks

Lightweight, pressed metal locks are useless. If they are not already fitted, then have car-type locks fitted to your

Glass fibre (fiberglass)

The only weakness of handsome, molded plastic saddlebags is that if their quick-release fastenings slip, the bag hits the exhaust pipe and melts. The best saddlebags are made from glass fibre, which effectively resists heat, thieves, impact and abrasion. Choose only saddlebags that are smooth-sealed inside, as well as out, or everything stored in them will stink forever of resin, and be dusted with ground glass fibres. If you do get internally unfinished saddlebags, paint them with at least three coats of polyurethane lacquer to seal them.

Five basic rules will help towards easier travelling.

1 Arrange the items you will require most frequently at the top of the saddlebags.

2 Wrap fragile items in soft ones and pack them as high as possible.

3 Place heavy items as far forward as possible.

4 Leave no room for luggage to shift.

5 Disregard all waterproofing claims and pack everything in heavy-gauge plastic bags.

Camping

A touring holiday under canvas is not a simple matter if you travel on a solo machine with a friend.

If your adventure takes place entirely in warm sunshine, then all well and good, but if you half expect inclement weather, consider the possibility of changing your route, adding a sidecar, or hauling a trailer if it is legal to do so. Anyone who has been caught out in Scotland or Norway, for example, during an August mini-winter, with saturated riding gear, a dismally small bivouac tent, damp fresh clothes, and a rained-out ignition system, will acknowledge the potential discomfort.

If you find yourself in this situation then stay at a hotel until you are dry and warm again: this is *not* cheating, it is just good commonsense. Prolonged exposure to damp and cold is not only bad for morale, but it lowers resistance to infection.

The first requirement is a good tent. This should obviously be large enough to sleep two people *and* to contain their luggage. Choose a light, ridge-pole type that incorporates a *waterproof* sewn-in groundsheet, and that does not rely on a fly-sheet for waterproofing. If you expect to camp on open ground in hot climates, then a fly-sheet is vital to prevent the tent becoming unbearably hot. Some of the better tents incorporate heavy flaps, or tongues, on which rocks, rather than pegs, can be used for security on unusually hard or soft ground. Ignore tents with lightweight zipper openings: these should be heavy and robust.

Tents are heavy. The best place to carry them is on the fuel tank, either on a special rack or inside a big tank bag. A fuel tank will carry a surprisingly bulky load, so experiment.

After a good tent comes the need for comfortable sleeping equipment. Good air beds are difficult to pack small, so check out lightweight safari beds with break-down frames. Since they fold up into long hard cylinders, these lend themselves to easy stowage around

upper fork legs, below luggage racks, or behind saddlebags.

Sleeping bags insulated with synthetic fibre are tougher than those with natural down, and less expensive than kapok. Line the bags with cotton liners for hygiene and warmth. Hang them to air whenever convenient; wadding them into plastic carrying bags directly after use will cause eventual dampening from condensation.

Camping gas refills are available the world over, so rely wholly on these. Two single-burner cookers are easier to stow than one larger twin-burner. They also make excellent heaters or driers.

Rely on locally purchased fresh food and a reserve supply of dehydrated foods; canned foods are heavy and bulky.

The best water carriers for motorcycle campers are the old canvas buckets, or modern collapsible plastic jerrycans, which can double up as on-route water containers. A collapsible washing bowl is also necessary. This is best stowed in an exposed position on the bike where it can dry out and remain fresh.

One deep non-stick frying pan and one saucepan will be enough for cooking. Tough plastic plates and mugs, and a knife/fork/spoon canteen each will be sufficient. Take along a heavy, general purpose knife also.

Before you leave, make up half a dozen wire hooks that will fit on to your tent poles; they will prove invaluable for hanging utensils on.

Lighting is a matter of choice. Modern fluorescent tubes use only a little battery power but gas lamps, or even candles, are a light source independent of the motorcycle, which can be a blessing.

Always take along water purification tablets if you plan to travel where these are needed and do not forget insect repellant and/or sting balm.

Motorcyclists can take camping holidays in isolation or clustered together with like-minded enthusiasts.

Navigation

Once out of the primary stages of motorcycle riding, many enthusiasts gravitate toward two-wheeled exploring. But direction-finding from the windy saddle of a motorcycle is not as simple as it is from the sheltered and spacious seat of a car.

Lack of space and exposure to the weather more-or-less preclude the luxury of on-route, unfolded map-reading for the average motorcyclist. Yet maps are essential if real satisfaction is to be achieved from touring.

For the best possible motorcycle touring you will require four route-finders. A planning map is vital. It should cover the entire country or countries you expect to ride through. It should be small scale and incorporate all major roads and topographical and geographical characteristics. This map will give scale to your trip at a glance, as well as displaying features of the countryside such as mountains, rivers, forests and beaches. Plot your route and leave the map at home.

For the ride itself rely on a top-quality touring map, which displays such details as altitude. The best sources of maps are national motoring organizations, which will frequently provide a planned itinerary should you request it, and government-sponsored national carto-graphers, such as the British Ordnance Survey and the US Geological Survey. These maps should include all villages, minor roads and useful tourist infor-mation such as campsite, hotel, national park and tourist office locations. The scale should be approximately 1:250,000 (1 inch:4 miles or 4 cm: 10 km).

Cut this map into sections that correspond with convenient routing; mark the route in colored pencil (ink runs when it gets wet); seal each section inside clear plastic film; then place them in sequence inside your map case.

Alternatively, if you are covering a big mileage quickly, write out route cards directly from the first map. Either draw your route as the idealized road (with all others shown as turn-offs) complete with road numbers, or write a sequential list of towns, road numbers and turns you will require to use. With both methods it is vital that each card is weather-sealed, covers at least half a day's run, and can be read at a glance.

Use a code to simplify matters: straight on as SO in green; turn right as TR in blue; turn left as TL in orange; major urban intersection in red and towns in black. Use numerals such as 2TL, rather than second TL. Indicate the numbers of joining roads for reference.

If you plan to tour from a base, buy a large scale map(s) of the area before your arrival. Choose something about 1:50,000 (approximately 1 inch: 1 mile or 2 cm:1 km). This map will illustrate contours, footpaths, farms, hotels, places of historical interest, small streams, forests, coastline features and all topographical details. Used carefully, it will reward you well.

If you ride with companions, then alternate the navigating duty, and if you are lucky enough to carry a pillionist, use him or her as navigator. Adopt a code if you wear full-face helmets and/or have no intercom; 1 tap left thigh: TL; 2 taps left thigh: 2TL; tap on helmet: SO; tap between shoulder blades: stop.

Make it a rule to follow the navigator's instructions implicitly and to argue only once you have stopped, when it is safe.

Between riders on separate machines a simple finger code can be used: left forefinger upright followed by a jerked thumb to the left: 1TL; two left-hand fingers upright and jerked thumb: 2TL. These will not be mistaken by other road users for hand signals if the arm does not project.

The best places to put maps are: on the rider's back inside a bandolier-type map case for the pillionist to use; inside a flexible case around the rider's thigh; inside an envelope-type case taped or tied to the fuel tank, or clipped to a board clamped to handlebars or fairing interior.

Rallying

Every rider is a participating motorcyclist but, even so, the average biker without the desire or means to start competitive riding usually wants to put his skills to some sort of use.

Rallying is becoming an increasingly popular recreation, with riders of all types of motorcycles organizing their own get-togethers—often in the most obscure locations possible.

Most nations have their own important rallies. Norway has its aptly named, midwinter Crystal rally; Britain, its Dragon rally and America has several, including the Harley-Davidson Sturgis rally. These non-sporting events are nothing more than gigantic motorcycling jamborees, most of which are loosely organized and offer little more than in-crowd gossip as the principal entertainment.

To the astonishment of most non-motorcyclists, a good many of the rallies are held in periods of bad weather, for no other reason than that the unavoidable difficulties incurred tax the survival skills of the entrants, and provide a theme for friendly conversation during the rest of the year.

The best rallies are always oversubscribed. This fact leads either to their disintegration—such as has happened to Germany's world-famous Elephant rally held in midwinter at Nürburgring —or to entrance by invitation only. The only way to participate in some rallies is to join the organizing club, or one closely associated.

No special equipment or motorcycles are required. Indeed, a good many rally enthusiasts go to great lengths to log huge mileages on odd machinery, simply to enter into the spirit of things. Awards are frequently made to individuals and/or clubs who have travelled farthest.

At the other extreme from the social gatherings are the sporting rallies. Until a law forbidding them was passed during the early 1970s, map-reading rallies were popular in Britain. Nowadays the French lead the world in competitive motorcycle rallying, although these rallies have more in common with enduros, or even endurance road racing, than anything else.

The toughest of these rallies is the Paris-Dakar Rally. This is an outright race which starts in Paris on January 1, and takes its entrants approximately 10,000km (6,200 miles) south, through France and across North Africa and the Sahara Desert. Like the Baja 1000 desert enduro, the Paris-Dakar encourages two- and four-wheelers to race against each other. In 1980, 287 drivers and riders started out and just 67 finished. Motorcycle winner was Hubert Auriol on a BMW R80/GS, and car winner was Range Rover driver Bernard Giroux.

As rallies go, this is no weekend family romp. Accidents and even deaths appear to be commonplace.

The FIM organizes its own international rally each year, usually in west or eastern Europe. Points are awarded to nations according to their number of national entrants but, according to some riders, the FIM International Rally has little more than a prestigious title in its favor.

If you plan to go rallying, take note of these tips. 1 Ensure you possess the necessary permits and directions before leaving home. 2 Carry a set of carefully planned and accurate route cards and map. 3 Get official meteorological information before setting out; anticipate the worst possible weather, and carry at least one complete set of extra clothes. 4 Know how to repair your bike at the roadside, and carry enough equipment to fix all minor breakdowns. 5 Provide other rallyists with the sort of assistance you hope to receive yourself. 6 Learn how to erect a tent in deep snow, liquid mud, a force 10 gale or driving rain. 7 If the weather is cold carry a heat source, such as a camping gas stove. 8 Expect to cook your own food from your own supplies. 9 Never attempt to ride when you feel sleepy.

Sidecar riding

Who should really be given the credit for inventing the sidecar, no-one will ever know, although in 1903 the world's first commercially built sidecar appeared on the market as "the Liberty social attachment."

Beware, you innocent soloists. Outfits, combinations, chairs or side-hacks are utterly alien to all you have known before. They are crazy, maddening, wonderful, artful things that foil criticism and praise with equal facility.

It is a myth that outfits are safer than solos. Sidecars appear to be so because they are usually ridden by more mature riders (the chair is often added for the benefit of new family members), and there are fewer outfits on the road.

Outfits are not ridden, they are driven. Keep this in mind and you might avoid the dangers that face the foolhardy innocents who imagine that a third wheel will provide them with instant security. It does not! If this seems like a lie then take a fast ride on a child's tricycle and see how you fare on the first bend.

All the power, all the steering, most of the weight, and usually all of the braking, is on one side of an outfit. Ignore advice that a sidecar wheel brake is unnecessary. If one can be fitted, then have it. It will be an invaluable aid to braking stability, which is worth more than braking power alone.

Practise driving on private ground first. Place at least a 50kg (100lb) sandbag on the sidecar seat to act as ballast. This is important. A light chair in the hands of a novice is dangerous. Applied power will accelerate the bike around the

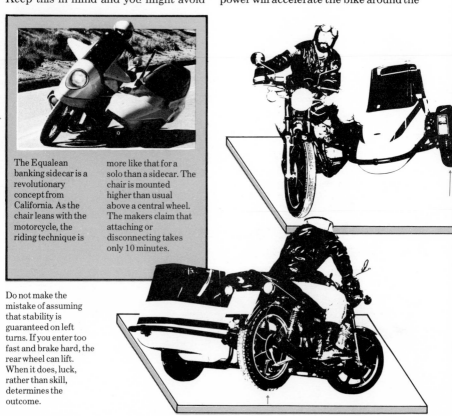

The Equalean banking sidecar is a revolutionary concept from California. As the chair leans with the motorcycle, the riding technique is more like that for a solo than a sidecar. The chair is mounted higher than usual above a central wheel. The makers claim that attaching or disconnecting takes only 10 minutes.

Do not make the mistake of assuming that stability is guaranteed on left turns. If you enter too fast and brake hard, the rear wheel can lift. When it does, luck, rather than skill, determines the outcome.

chair, engine or wheel braking will swing the chair around the bike. Take time familiarizing yourself with this because it is the heart and soul of sidecar technique.

At first, turns into the sidecar will be difficult and you will feel convinced the chair will lift up. It will not, if treated gently. Turns away from the sidecar will fill you with confidence since the bike is supported by the sidecar. With increasing confidence you will corner faster, more easily, understanding slowly that it is possible to steer on the throttle—open up, and go round the chair; shut down, and have the chair come around you.

The real danger period occurs during the first flush of confidence, which will probably arrive after three to six months. Inevitably, the sidecar will lift on the inside of a fast bend and you will be scared stiff, unable to take the curve because you will shut off, which will bring the chair flying around the bike, while you dare not accelerate further to continue the curve. If you are lucky, no traffic will be coming at you.

Experienced and skilled "charioteers" can utilize power to produce high speed controlled drifts in both directions, but this requires different driving techniques altogether. They cannot be taught, merely learned.

Braking hard is not easy, especially with a heavily laden sidecar, which tries to swing around the motorcycle. Steering into the sidecar occurs involuntarily at such times. The only solution is a sidecar brake, which prevents this.

Novices who get into trouble on turns tend to panic; they shy away from the chair and brake hard. The harder you decelerate and the farther out you lean, the higher the chair wheel rises.

If the sidecar wheel lifts on a right turn lean into the chair as far as possible. Do not brake or snap the throttle shut; keep the power on and steer into the bend.

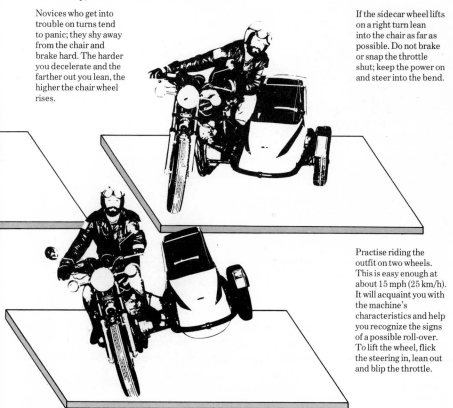

Practise riding the outfit on two wheels. This is easy enough at about 15 mph (25 km/h). It will acquaint you with the machine's characteristics and help you recognize the signs of a possible roll-over. To lift the wheel, flick the steering in, lean out and blip the throttle.

Sidecar fitting

Despite some claims to the contrary, all orthodox motorcycles can be fitted with sidecars providing it is *correctly* done. A well-fitted sidecar will strengthen, not weaken, a motorcycle frame. But the fitting of a sidecar invalidates some manufacturers' warranties, reflecting lack of experience rather than any engineering wisdom.

An unmodified solo motorcycle makes a poor chair tug. Improvements can vary from fitting expensive, car-type, small wide wheels, and special front suspension, to the simple lowering of the gear ratios.

These are the basic necessities, without which an inferior, although possibly acceptable, performance is guaranteed.

1 Overall gearing must be reduced by between 20 per cent (small machine) and 10 per cent (large machine). Most solos

1 Fix the motorcycle securely to an anchor point with negligible lean-out as measured with a spirit level placed vertically down the rear wheel rim. The rear suspension must be jacked right up and both stands folded away. The ground must be flat.

2 Attach the four clamps to the frame: **a** on the front down-tube abutting the steering head; **b** on the front engine mounting; **c** on, or close to, the swinging fork axle nut; **d** on the upper rear sub-frame tube. Take advice from the sidecar manufacturer on this important procedure. The two lower ones are the load bearers, while the upper ones provide rigidity through triangulation.

4 With all alignments complete, ensure that the sidecar chassis is firmly chocked to resist shifting. Offer up the two main bottom fittings for length, and adjust to suit, if necessary shortening with a saw. Insert the two main fitting tubes loosely into the clamps and pinch them closed.

5 Now fit the upper arms in the same manner. Check and double check all alignment measurements. Once you are satisfied they are perfect, tighten up the clamp bolts and nuts hard.

are slightly overgeared anyway, and cannot cope efficiently with a sidecar's increased weight and wind resistance.

2 Heavier suspension springs are necessary. Front fork spacers and jacked-up rear suspension might suffice with a light chair. Thicker damping fluid is no substitute.

3 Flat-section tires should be fitted to provide maximum adhesion. A round-section, ribbed front tire is dangerous.

4 If no front fork slider bridge-piece is fitted to the solo, it must be added with the chair to avoid individual fork leg movement and flexing—walking.

5 Wide handlebars can make up for steering heaviness, and a steering damper combats front wheel fluttering.

6 Tire pressures must be increased by at least 0.35 kg/sq cm (5 psi) with even the lightest sidecar. Check with the tire or sidecar maker on this.

3 Locate the bare, but wheeled, chassis as close to the motorcycle as possible, leaving enough room for necessary access. With a spirit level, ensure the chassis is horizontal and chock it. The sidecar wheel axle should be approximately 230 mm (9in) ahead of the rear wheel axle. Use straight poles and a large T-square to obtain a true parallel alignment and accurate toe-in.

Lean-out refers to the attitude of the bike alongside the sidecar. About 25mm (1 inch) is usually enough to stop the bike steering into the chair.

25mm lean out

20-40mm toe-in

230mm between axles

6 Finally, drop the body into place and connect up the electrics and any other ancillary parts.

Lean-out is produced by motor-cycle suspension compression during loading. Toe-in is vital for straight line-ahead running, but too much scrubs tires. Measured at the front wheel axle it should be between 20mm and 40mm. Rear wheel maladjustment during chain maintenance can produce up to 100mm (4in) of toe-in misalignment.

Toolkit

Successful bike maintenance is only possible with a good set of tools. Two sets are preferable: one to carry on the bike for roadside repairs, and one for the more serious jobs at home, which need not duplicate the roadside kit.

The workshop kit

This kit should be comprehensive enough to allow both servicing and more detailed repairs.

Wrenches form the basis of the kit; buy both box and open-ended types but only those that fit your bike. If more serious engine work is contemplated, complement the wrenches with a socket set, which provides greater adaptability and can be used with a torque wrench.

Two further vital tools are a spark plug wrench and an adjustable wrench. The adjustable should be used only as an emergency option when the appropriate wrench is missing. Mole, or vise, grips are extremely versatile and should also be included in the kit.

Most manufacturers use three different types of screw on their bikes: plain slotted, crosshead (Phillips) and hexagon (Allen). Consequently you need both main types of screwdriver in the appropriate sizes as well as a set of Allen wrenches. More and more manufacturers are using hexagon screws, so a set of good quality Allen wrenches is important.

A set of feeler gauges for checking valve clearances, points and plug gaps; a tire pressure gauge; a pair of pliers and a set of tire levers complete the basic service essentials. Further workshop equipment should include a soft-headed mallet, a chain splitter, and a grease gun. A bulb and a length of wire is sufficient for basic circuit testing, but a multimeter is invaluable.

More specialist service items should include a xenon strobe timing light, a dial gauge (for 2-stroke ignition timing); an impact driver and a set of vacuum gauges.

Serious engine work may necessitate certain special tools such as clutch extractors. Fitting jobs will require a drill, a junior hacksaw and a file. Measuring tools like a vernier gauge or micrometer are essential for measuring small wear tolerances.

The bike kit

This can be extracted from the main kit and should cover minor service needs. Experience of your bike's weaker points generally dictates the size and variety of the bike kit but it should be sufficient to enable you to get home.

Buying tools

The best way to build up a toolkit is to buy only what you need, when you need it. Buy only the best makes; they will be expensive, but they will last and usually come with a substantial guarantee. Cut-price tools are generally of poor quality.

Good used tools can often be bought from garages and from auctions where entire toolkits may be on offer.

Do not buy special factory tools. These are used rarely and are very expensive. Most motorcycle clubs now lend out factory tools for small sums. In emergencies, a dealer may be prepared to lend or rent a tool to a good customer.

Using tools

Keep tools in good condition and they will last. After working, always wipe them clean with a lightly oiled rag to protect them from rust and corrosion.

The way you use tools will determine their life and efficiency. Always use the correct size wrench or screwdriver; using the wrong size will damage both the tool and the nut or screw.

Workshop tools used imaginatively can double their uses; vise grips can serve as a light bench vise, a temporary cable nipple or a brake lever; a small ring wrench can triple the leverage of an Allen wrench, and so on. But, as a general rule, tools should be used only for the job they were designed to do. If not used sympathetically they can cause damage: a screwdriver blade, used previously as a cold chisel, will wreck the head of the screw. So take care of your tools and they will look after your bike.

The bike toolkit should be as comprehensive as possible without being impractically bulky or heavy. Carry only what you may need, including any necessary spares.

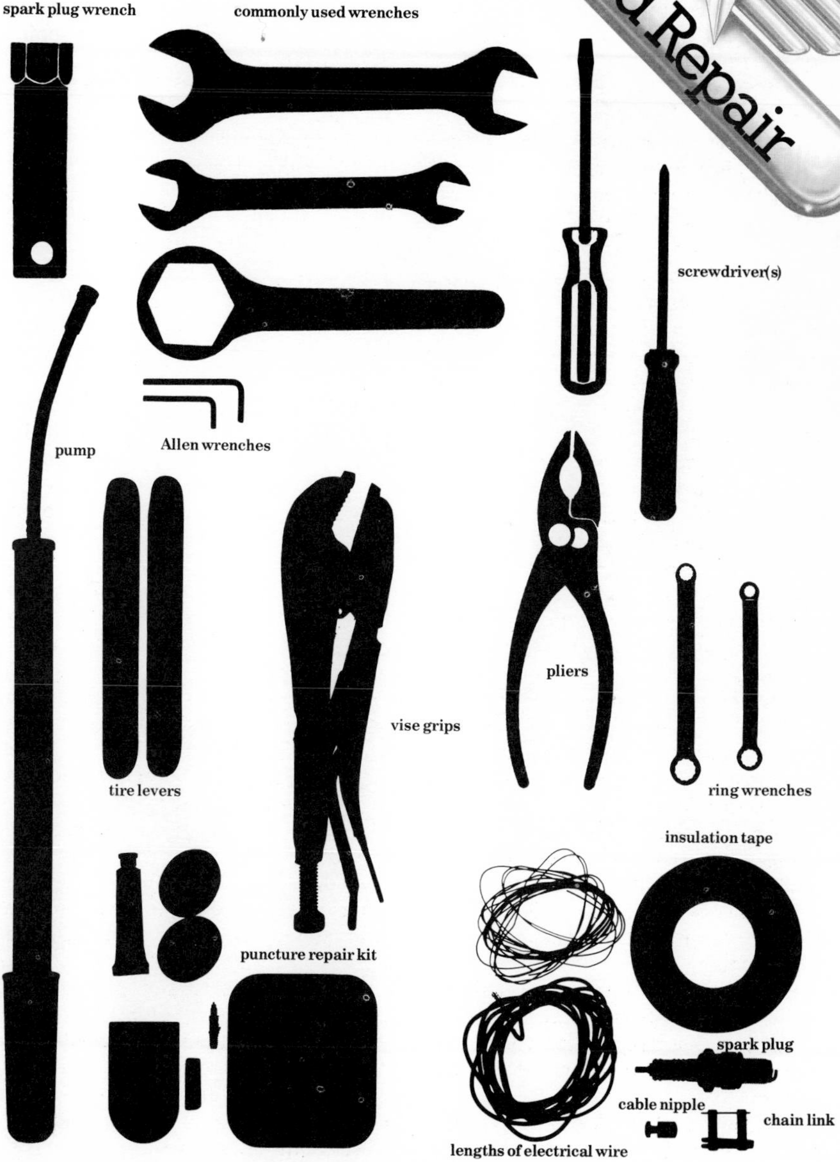

spark plug wrench

commonly used wrenches

screwdriver(s)

pump

Allen wrenches

pliers

vise grips

ring wrenches

tire levers

insulation tape

puncture repair kit

spark plug

cable nipple

chain link

lengths of electrical wire

Daily routines

All too often, owner's handbooks, service manuals and specialist magazines offer motorcyclists nothing more than ideal daily service routines, which none of the writers themselves would dream of practising. Few people can afford the time necessary to check a motorcycle the way they recommend, and most motorcyclists simply cannot be bothered.

Tire pressures do not vary by an appreciable amount from day to day; chains do not wear; wheel axle nuts do not suddenly work loose; oil pumps do not stop working nor fuel lines start to leak. The reason that the Japanese motorcycle became so popular was that it was designed to eliminate the bugbear of intensive and constant rider attention, and this has forced other manufacturers to follow suit.

If you use your motorcycle regularly, you will quickly notice any specific performance defects, and these can be attended to on your return home.

Despite all the recent improvements, however, it is vital that you are fully aware of the need for some sort of daily routine to cover safety and reliability. It involves neither tools nor dirt and very little time. Stick to it for your own sake.

Before riding off

Have a good look at the motorcycle and check for a nicely balanced overall appearance. Then check the following items to make sure nothing is loose or has shifted: wheel axles and nuts; control pivots and clamps; fuel taps and fuel line connections; license plate and side panels; all lights; fuel and oil levels; mirror adjustment. Feel around the machine, and pull on the front brake while bouncing the front suspension up and down. Bounce on the rear suspension; try all the controls; knock the fenders and headlight; rock the fuel tank. This routine will reveal loose, stiff or missing parts.

Once you have started the engine, test

Pre-ride checklist
1 Look at fuel system, fuel and oil levels, brake hydraulics and engine for leaks;
2 control cables and pivots for condition;
3 wheel nuts for tightness;
4 chain for tension;
5 tires for foreign bodies and
6 missing valve caps.

7 Feel fenders, side panels, tank and filler cap,
8 exhaust system, seat, pillion handle,
9 handlebars, headlight, rear lamp and license plate for security.

10 Test, main, dip (dim), parking, brake and turn signal lights, and horn.

11 Final check
IS EITHER OF YOUR STANDS STILL DOWN?

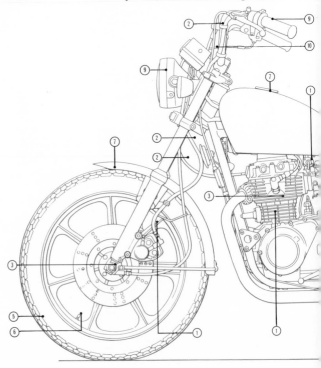

the electrics by using all switches and examining the lights visually. Do not idle cold started engines slowly: this restricts vital oil circulation. Check tire pressures by accustoming yourself to the feel of your machine's tires when correctly inflated, and then ensure that they feel the same way each morning.

While riding
Take careful note of the operation of all warning lights, especially the ignition light; the operation and response of both brakes, clutch and gearchange; of switchgear and lights. Pay particular attention to the intensity of the headlight beam at low engine revs.

Study the behavior of the entire machine during braking, acceleration and especially cornering. In all the above examples any sort of a performance change, however slight, heralds future problems unless preventative maintenance is tackled immediately.

A flickering headlight could indicate nothing more than a corroded earth (ground), partially broken connection or a dirty, dry switch, but if it is not attended to more serious trouble will result.

A different feel to the handling could be due to nothing more serious than low tire pressure from a lost tire valve cap and a slack valve core, but the tire will be flat in the morning.

At the end of a ride
When you arrive home, ensure the engine still idles regularly. One that refuses to do so is off tune and needs attention. First check the spark plug and all associated connections; then check carburetor(s) and all associated components; finally check the entire ignition system connections and parts.

Attend to any problems as soon as you can. For instance, a mild popping on the overrun could indicate nothing more than a loose silencer (muffler) clip. Leave it and your piston(s) could be overheated by a weak mixture.

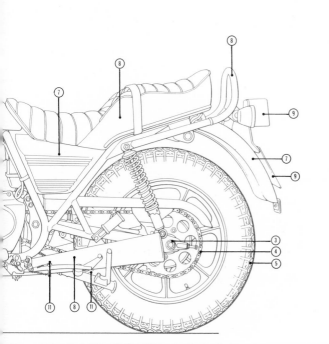

While riding
Develop machine empathy — get to know how things feel and sound when everything is going nicely and use this as your standard.

Feel for irregular handling characteristics, coarse or sloppy controls, excessive engine heat, vibration.

Watch instruments and warning lights — believe them!

Smell for leaking fuel.

Regular service

Don't touch a thing! Stay right away from your motorcycle if you want it to last. Any attempts to fool around with it will result in trouble unless you know *exactly* what you are touching, why you are doing it, and how you should tackle it.

The most important tool in your workshop is your owner's handbook. Study it until you know it well. It may be confusing, so after looking right through it, study the maintenance chart, or service data. Even these may contain maintenance demands that no one would dream of tackling as routine tasks.

For reasons best known to themselves manufacturers, especially the Japanese, recommend regular 3,000 mile checks on valve (tappet) clearances, contact breaker points, idling, clutch, carburetor, throttle, steering head (headstock), and even compression ratios. If you are a big mileage motorcyclist, keeping to this sort of a schedule will ruin your social life. It will also probably upset the nicely settled running of a good bike.

So much depends on how you use your machine. The Sunday morning cruiser will barely have to touch his bike, while the rider who commutes and tours at weekends will have to spend at least three hours a week attending to his machine. A motorcycle used for a lot of short haul city runs suffers much greater wear and tear than the long haul, open highway tourer—whatever the mileage.

All motorcycles produce a gallon of water from internal condensation for every gallon of fuel burned. The average engine takes at least five miles to warm up, and another 10 to burn off the condensation left inside the engine after the last time it was used; 90 per cent of engine wear occcurs on cold engines before the oil is circulating properly. If an engine never gets the chance to warm up, water from condensation is permanently mixed into the oil, which largely destroys its lubricating qualities.

1 For an oil change you will need funnel, tray, wrench, rag, newspaper and 20 minutes time.

2 If you plan to change the oil filter, wash clean the filter area or dirt will fall into it.

5 If you plan to change the filter, remove the filter housing cover while this is draining.

6 Replace the drain plug once the old oil has stopped running from the drain hole.

Oil changing

Carrying out your own oil changes will save time and money, and is probably the first serious maintenance a new rider can tackle at home.

If your machine is used for short trips only, then double the frequency of the manufacturer's recommended oil changes (halve the mileage). Whatever mileage you cover, never leave oil in your bike's engine for more than six months at the most. In cold, wet climates the limit should be three months.

First, make a large drip-tray by cutting the side from a 1 gal (5 l) oil can and lay it to one side. Take the machine for a 10 minute run to wash all contaminants into the old oil. On your return home, collect your equipment together, by which time all loose oil in the engine will have drained into the sump.

You will need a drip-tray of twice the capacity of your machine's sump to avoid spillage; a can of recommended fresh oil;

some old newspapers to park the machine on (oil stains concrete, muddies sand and gravel, dissolves pavement and kills grass); a bundle of rags (the job is a messy one); a funnel and the tools needed to unfasten and replace all components affected.

Park the motorcycle on flat ground; slacken the drain-plug until just finger-tight; place the drip-tray underneath and unscrew the drain-plug; remove the filler cap for maximum oil flow; remove the oil-filter if a change is necessary. Leave to drain. Carefully remove the drip-tray; replace the filler plug and fasten tightly with a spanner (wrench). Clean out the filter-holder (wash out sediment with paraffin [kerosene] and dry with fuel); replace the filter and fasten it to the machine. Wipe away dirty oil drips; fill the engine with the recommended quantity of the correct oil using the funnel; clean up the machine and the surrounding area.

3 Slacken the filler plug/dip stick but *do not* remove it, or things might fall in.

4 Unscrew the drain plug and allow the old oil to drain into the drip-tray.

7 Wipe the filter housing with lint-free rag, check the gasket and fit new filter.

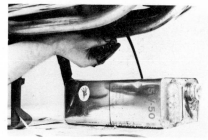

8 Pour in the fresh oil to the recommended quantity. Check with dip stick. Clean up.

Regular service/2

Estimate your annual mileage and then break it down into time intervals. This makes it simple to plan regular servicing. Naturally, if you live in a cold or wet climate, or your bike is garaged out of doors, it will demand much greater attention than this routine.

Weekly

1 Clean the machine. Wash and wax polish, if you have the time.
2 Lubricate all control pivots and cable ends and inspect for fraying; check hydraulic pipe condition.
3 Inspect the tires thoroughly for embedded foreign bodies and remove them. Check pressure and reinflate.
4 Inspect rear chain, check and tension correctly, then lubricate.

5 Check oil circulation and oil tank level. Oil circulation is best seen through inspection windows but can be checked with a flashlight inside filler orifices or inspection caps.
6 Inspect electrical connections under side panels and seat; spark plug caps, battery terminals.
7 Check tightness of major nuts and bolts.

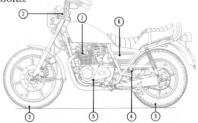

★ ★ ★ ★ ★ ★ ★ ★ ★ ★ ★ ★ ★ ★ ★ ★ ★ ★ ★ ★

Monthly (in addition to the weekly check)

1 Give the machine a really good scrub and polish. Do not use degreasants unless it is unavoidable: they destroy lubricants and encourage corrosion, causing long-term damage to electrical parts, switches, cable ends, control pivots, brake parts, fork seals, grease nipples, and *all* bearings however apparently well-sealed.
2 Dry the bike off by starting the engine and letting it fast-idle for a couple of minutes.
3 Remove the tank and side panels; lift the seat to inspect beneath it.
4 In wet climates lightly lubricate all electrical connections and switch internals—through slackened joints—with silicone oil.
5 Check under front and rear suspension gaiters or seals for dirt and water.
6 Check all brake operations, connections, and adjustment, including stop switches.
7 Check all fuel lines, taps, connections and filters.
8 Carefully inspect the contact breaker points and related wiring and connections. Check the points gap and ensure the cam lubricating wick is *lightly* lubricated.
9 Check radiator and water hoses for leaks and cracks. Inspect coolant level.
10 Inspect the battery and ensure the vent pipe is fitted and open; the top is clean; the filler plugs tight; the fluid level correct (fill only with distilled water, never acid or tap water), and the mounting secure and free from rust.
11 Check hydraulic fluid level and look carefully at all joints and unions for signs of wear.

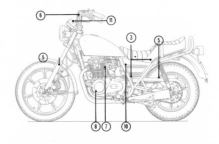

Yearly (in addition to the monthly check)

1 Remove both wheels, inspect bearings for play; check brakes for wear and adjustment; lubricate drum brake bearings, pivots and cams; check wire spokes for tension and inspect cast wheels for cracks; wipe out old grease and wash unsealed bearings in paraffin (kerosene) then dry in fuel, repack *lightly* with recommended grease.

2 Remove and clean under suspension gaiters and outer seals and pack lightly with silicone grease.

3 Remove battery, neutralize acid by wiping its outer case and carrier with a vinegar-damped cloth; repaint and lightly grease.

4 Remove light unit from headlight and check all electrical connections; remove rear light and check it internally. In damp climates lightly touch connections with silicone oil.

5 Replace all filters and check air hoses and connections.

6 Test steering head (headstock) bearings for play and adjust as recommended.

7 Drain front forks, test them for play, and then refill as recommended.

8 Test swinging arm for play as recommended.

9 Carefully inspect all wiring connections, including fuse box, for good condition; pay special attention to all earths (grounds) which must be removed, cleaned and silicone greased if corroded or dirty.

10 Check all nuts and bolts for tightness.

11 Balance the carburetors, or have them balanced.

12 Test the oil pressure, or have it tested.

13 Remove and inspect contact breaker points for good condition.

14 Check valve (tappet) clearance and correct.

15 Remove carburetor float bowls and clean out.

16 Check primary and cam chains for adjustment.

17 Inspect the entire machine for corrosion, paying special attention to engine cover lacquer cracks which must be touched up.

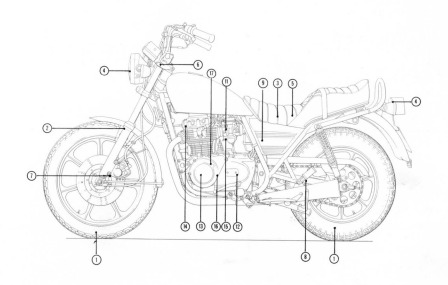

Brakes

Brakes are the primary safety control, and it is vital to keep them in good order. In most countries it is a legal requirement to have two efficient, independent brakes.

Although there are many different designs, all brakes work in a similar way. Operation of the brake lever brings a piece of friction material into contact with a drum or disc fitted to the wheel. The friction causes the wheel to slow, converting the kinetic energy into heat.

There are two main systems—the drum and the disc brake. In the drum, friction material is fitted to two stationary curved shoes inside a drum which is part of the hub. Mechanically controlled levers press the shoes to the drum. The advantage is that the shoes are enclosed and protected from water, which can reduce friction. However, heavy braking can overheat the linings and the drum, causing it to expand, so reducing the braking effect (fade).

Discs are fitted to the wheel and are generally gripped by hydraulically activated friction pads on either side. The main advantage is rapid heat dissipation and less susceptibility to fade.

Three systems are used to transfer pressure from the brake lever to the brakes—hydraulic, cable and rod. Hydraulic operation is largely confined to discs, cable to drums and rod to rear drums.

In hydraulic operation, the brake lever moves a piston, forcing a controlled shock wave through fluid in a line, then into a cylinder which presses the brake pad on to the disc. In cable systems, the lever pulls a cable or rod, operating a lever on the brake to turn a cam and force the shoes outwards.

It is essential that the friction surfaces and the operating mechanism are in good condition. Inspect the friction pads or shoes regularly, making sure they are not worn beyond recommended limits.

Replace drum linings when there is 1 mm of material left above the shoe, or in older machines, the rivet heads.

Mechanisms must be lubricated occasionally. Use high melting point (hmp) grease only, on spindles, cams and pivots.

Twin leading shoe (2LS) brakes rely on the adjustment of the threaded linkage if the shoes are to lift in unison.

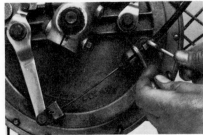

After fitting new linings take up all slack on the brake adjuster and leave the handlebar one for on-route adjustments.

Check the condition of the bearing surface of the drum or disc. Severe scoring can sometimes be skimmed professionally but, if in doubt, replace the disc or have the wheel rebuilt with a new drum. Check too that the drum is not distorted into an oval, and that discs are not warped. Again, replace if damaged, although minor damage may be repairable.

Check for damage if the bike is involved in a crash or if there are signs of binding or uneven application, such as squeaking. With drums, squeaking may also be caused by dust build up. Clean the drums if this is the problem.

Lubricate all moving cable linkages and the cable regularly. Check for wear or damage and replace suspect parts. Keep the cable adjusted so the brake is not binding but comes on progressively as the lever is pulled, with full application before the lever is fully depressed. With rod operation, check that the pivots are free and lubricated.

On hydraulic brakes, check the flexible and rigid lines for wear, damage or kinking. Keep the fluid topped up to the level marked on the reservoir. Watch for signs of leaking and suspect a leak if the level drops rapidly. All worn parts should be replaced.

If the brakes feel spongy, air may have entered the system, and you should bleed it. Attach a transparent pipe to the nipple, unscrew the nipple slightly and squeeze the lever until fluid emerges in the pipe. Keep the fluid topped up and continue squeezing gently until there are no bubbles in the fluid emerging. Then give one final squeeze on the lever, and hold it down until the nipple has been retightened. Check for pressure. Repeat the procedure until pressure returns.

You should change the fluid every 6,000 miles or yearly. Bleed the system, topping up until clean fluid emerges.

Check disc brake pad wear by inspecting the groove around the pads, which should not be worn. Minimum pad depth is 2 mm.

Brake hydraulics should be bled annually or whenever they feel spongy. Use only recommended fluid.

Check slave cylinders (caliper pistons) annually for leaks and corrosion. Smear with brake grease.

If fluid level requires topping up more than twice in succession anticipate a leak. Check all unions, lines and seals.

Electrics

No bike can run without electricity, and although electrical failures cause more breakdowns than any other fault, most riders are painfully ignorant about this aspect of the machine. Electricity provides the ignition spark, which makes the engine run, and the power for many other components, such as the lights, which are essential, and electric starters, which are convenient.

The electricity needed by a bike is produced by an engine-driven generator. On most modern bikes this is an alternator. Other machines may have a dynamo or magneto. The power is regulated to produce 12 volts or, on old machines and most trail bikes, 6 volts.

Most machines have a battery to store this power, so that it can be used when the generator is not producing as much as the bike is using. Occasionally the generator is connected straight to the electrical components, and no battery is fitted. This is called direct electrics and means that the ignition and lighting only work when the engine is running.

Each system is connected to the power source, usually by separate wires. One side of the circuit is made by connecting the component to the metal frame of the bike, which is also connected to the power source. This is called the earth (ground) connection. The ignition switch controls the power to all systems, but each usually has its own switch as well.

The power also flows through one or more fuses. A fuse is a thin piece of wire which burns out quickly if too much current passes through it, stopping the current and so protecting the rest of the circuit.

The ignition system has a separate circuit, switched on by the ignition switch. This circuit includes the contact breaker points (or an electronic trigger), coils and spark plugs. The spark plugs have high-tension leads which are connected with insulated plug caps.

To minimize fuse connection trouble, coat with petroleum jelly or silicone oil.

A bad ground; corroded and coated with engine oil. Remove and clean it.

Clean fouled battery terminals with vinegar; dry, then coat in petroleum jelly.

This sort of electric wire trapping occurs frequently on home-fitted accessories.

Fault prevention

There are four main reasons why electrical systems fail:

1 A circuit can break beause a wire has chafed through.

2 A loose or corroded connector stops power getting through.

3 A short circuit develops, allowing electricity to find an easier path than through the component—usually because a wire has worn through and made contact with the frame to earth.

4 The power source itself can fail.

Protection against the first two faults is easy, and consists of making regular checks to see that none of the wires is strained or rubbing, and making sure that all the connections are sound. If a wire is at fault, bind it with insulating tape or replace it. Trouble with connections is often due to water, which corrodes them or causes short circuits. This can be prevented with a moisture dispersant spray or by binding with insulating tape to keep water out. Always clean the connection thoroughly first. Replace corroded connections.

Generators rarely fail and are not easy to repair if they do. Most power failures are due to a faulty battery, so regular checks are important. Keep the fluid level up to the mark by adding distilled water. If the battery is in a low state of charge, use a battery charger to keep it topped up. Make sure the terminals are clean, and prevent corrosion by smearing them with petroleum jelly.

Check the other components from time to time, and clean or replace them if they are suspect. Pay particular attention to bulbs, contact breaker points and spark plugs.

It is a good idea to carry replacements for the components which are most likely to wear or develop faults. Spare bulbs and fuses are essential, but also carry replacement contact breaker points and spark plugs.

A pre-winter squirt with silicone oil will improve switchgear reliability.

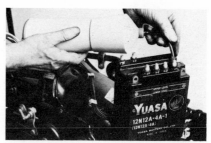

Check battery fluid level monthly in warm climates. Use nothing but distilled water.

A typical under-tank, hidden connection; almost disconnected and corroded.

The same connection, cleaned, refastened, and bound with weather-proofing tape.

Electrics/2

Component faults

Many electrical faults are easy to check and put right with only simple aids. A circuit tester is a cheap and useful checking tool consisting of a bulb, a battery and two wires, fitted with probes, so connected that the bulb lights when the two probes touch across a conductor.

At the first sign of an electrical fault, check to see which circuits are working. See whether all have failed at once, or if the fault is confined to one component.

If only one component, such as a light, has failed, check to see whether the filament has broken, and then check the fuse for that circuit; a blown fuse will stop the power. Check also the rest of the wiring for damage, which may have caused the fuse to blow, and repair it before fitting a new one. If the fuse is sound, disconnect the component and check for faults. Apply the probes of a circuit tester to the terminals. If the tester does not light, the component is faulty and you need to fit a replacement.

If both the fuse and the component are sound, check the wiring, including the switch, for breaks.

Ignition faults

If the engine stops suddenly, remove a spark plug, hold it against the cylinder head and turn the engine over. If there is no spark, check the wiring and plug cap for damage. In wet weather, dry the lead and plug cap thoroughly or treat with a moisture dispersant spray. Check the contact breaker points to see that they are adjusted and operating properly. Electronic trigger mechanisms can only be inspected for physical damage.

To test for a spark start by grounding the plug body against the engine. If the plug is suspect, hold the bare lead 7 mm from the engine. Poor connections and condensation are the commonest defects.

Ignition coils rarely give trouble. Faulty ones often feel warm after use. Check connections at least annually. If corroded, remove 5 mm from the lead tip, oil with silicone and replace with cap.

Dirt, oil and water cause most points trouble. Wire insulation might crack after years of use. This and contact breaker spring shorting against backplate cause lots of trouble.

When replacing HT leads keep them short enough to route away from the hot engine. Carbon core leads are radio-suppressed but less robust. Wire-cored are tougher but create some interference.

Testing requires sophisticated equipment.

Sudden *total* power failure may be caused by a blown main fuse, which you should replace after checking for other faults. It can also be due to a faulty ignition switch, so inspect this carefully, and operate it several times to see whether it works properly. Another cause may be a broken battery lead or loose terminal, so check these and repair if necessary. One of the commonest causes of failure and erratic performance is a bad earth (ground). Locate and check these connections following a fuse inspection.

Gradual total power failure is indicated by the lights dimming and the engine stalling at low revs. It is usually due to a faulty charging system, where the bike is running only on the power reserve in the battery, which will not last long. The charging system is difficult to check, but make sure that the battery connections are sound, and inspect the wiring for any damage where power might be leaking away.

A faulty charging system is also difficult to repair, so the best course is not to stop but to ride on, using as little power as possible by avoiding the use of non-essential systems such as turn signals. At night avoid riding if possible, dim lights are extremely dangerous.

Whenever electrical failure occurs check with a test meter, starting at the component involved—such as a plug cap which might short out when damp. Use your machine's circuit diagram to work through in stages.

Electrical problems (example)

Symptom	Clues	Cause	Remedy
Headlight fails to work	All other electrical components are dead	Possible main fuse blown	Replace main fuse
	Headlight only out of action	Blown bulb	Replace bulb
	Did headlight flicker the previous day?	Faulty connection; bad ground	Check grounds, connections
	Completely dead bike, including engine	Power source failure (battery, alternator, etc)	Have battery, alternator checked; replace
	Both headlight and instrument lights fail to work	Shared fuse blown	Replace fuse
	Sometimes works; appears to be affected by water, vibration	Faulty switch, connections, or ground	Check switch, connections etc.
	Fuse OK, connections OK, ground OK etc.	Possible relay failure, (if fitted)	Check relay, and replace

207

Timing

For combustion to take place in a controlled manner both the valves (of a 4-stroke) and the ignition must be timed correctly. The timing is determined by the factory and its accuracy is crucial to the efficiency of the engine.

Ignition timing

As the piston nears TDC on the compression stroke, a spark occurs at the spark plug, which ignites the mixture as a controlled flame. If the mixture is not ignited at exactly the right moment, the timing of the flame front will be wrong.

On 4-stroke engines, ignition takes place earlier (is more advanced) as engine speed rises, to allow time for the mixture to burn properly. On 2-stroke engines the ignition always occurs at the same point.

It is vital that the ignition timing is checked regularly, even on those bikes with electronic ignition, since incorrect ignition timing—even a couple of degrees out—can have drastic effects, causing holed pistons (a common 2-stroke problem) and damaged big ends.

Checking

In normal circumstances, ignition timing is checked with a stroboscope for absolute accuracy. This also shows whether the ignition is advancing properly as engine speeds rise. The timing can also be checked statically, by aligning a timing mark on the rotor with a static pointer at the moment the points open.

The timing can be checked further with a 360° timing disc; sometimes the timing marks on the rotor can be wrong. This disc will inform you whether the manufacturer's timing recommendation corresponds to the marks on the rotor.

Turn the engine over until the piston is exactly at TDC on the compression stroke. Now stick the timing disc on to the end of the crankshaft or rotor and align the 0° sign with your own static pointer. Turn the engine backwards until the points are well and truly closed. Now rotate the engine forwards (direction of normal rotation) until the points open. You can then read off on the timing disc how many degrees before TDC ignition is occurring. If this is different from the mark on the rotor but corresponds with factory recommendations, you can paint the new mark on the rotor.

2-stroke timing

For the necessary accuracy—2-strokes are touchy about ignition timing—the timing should be checked with a dial gauge. This device measures piston

To adjust points; remove plugs, select top gear and turn the wheel until the cam heel lifts at the cam's first step.

Visually inspect points. Insert clean feeler gauge of correct size and feel for a sliding fit.

A common cause of trouble is shorting across the points' insulating washers. They must be clean and dry. When removing points, take note of washers' order, and assemble in reverse order with great care.

height—a much more accurate figure than crankshaft degrees.

Screw the gauge into the spark plug hole and rotate the engine until the piston reaches TDC. Zero the gauge and connect a multimeter to the points. Now rotate the engine until the points just open as shown on the multimeter. Read off on the dial gauge how far the piston is from TDC, and compare this to the recommendation in the manual. The points can then be adjusted to open at the exact moment recommended.

Remember that the timing must be spot on; it is the most important service check you can make on your bike.

Valve timing

The breathing of a 4-stroke engine is controlled by the valves. Exactly when the valves open and close varies from engine to engine and is dependent on many factors that affect performance.

Each valve is controlled by its own cam on the camshaft, and it is the shape of this that dictates exactly when and how quickly the valves open and shut, and how long they remain open. The higher the performance of an engine, the longer and the wider the valves open, filling the cylinder to its maximum.

The valve timing can only be altered by the insertion of a different camshaft or by having the cam re-profiled. But it is important to get the timing correct when reassembling a stripped engine. Failure to do so could result in bent valves, so it must be spot on.

The job is straightforward, but it does vary in detail from bike to bike. Simply ensure that the timing dots on the camshaft sprocket(s) or gear(s) line up with timing marks on the rotor, or on the drive sprocket or gear from the crankshaft. On dohc engines both sprockets should be checked in the same way.

On some bikes, especially where the cams are driven by chain, check that the recommended number of rollers or links separates the timing marks on the different sprockets.

Before starting the engine at the end of a rebuild, turn it over by hand first to see if there is any resistance to movement. If there is, recheck the valve timing; if you are just one tooth out, it may be sufficient for a valve to hit a piston.

It is not advisable for unskilled enthusiasts to become too involved in the internal workings of their engines. Obtain expert guidance the first time you attempt a rebuild.

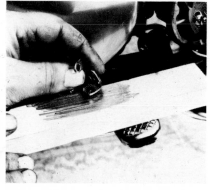

Before adjusting points study which screws do what. Outdoor ones hold the back-plate and can alter timing. Lightly slacken adjuster screws. Look for adjuster slots and insert screwdriver to alter the points' gap.

Grease the felt wick with hmp grease; oil will be flung off and foul the points. Remove the points to clean them.

Clean pitted points by smoothing along a fine oil-stone. Finish on pencil-rubbed wood; wash.

Bearings/bushes

Bearing wear is one of the major sources of mechanical deterioration affecting both the cycle parts and the engine. If left unchecked it will prove expensive and/or dangerous.

Cycle parts

There are normally four sets of bearings in the chassis; wear in any of them will show up as handling problems. Wear is usually due to poor maintenance, especially poor lubrication.

1 Steering head bearings

These may be loose ball bearings running in tracks attached to the steering head and triple clamps. Some makers fit taper roller bearings which are less prone to wear. Wear is indicated by handling vagueness and vibration when the front brake is applied hard.

Check for wear at least once a year. Put the bike on its centerstand, lift the front forks and try to pull them forward and backward. You should not find any detectable movement. Turn the bars from lock to lock. They should fall easily from side to side. Any stiffness or roughness indicates bearing wear.

Dismantle the steering head to inspect suspect bearings. Damaged bearings must be replaced. Pack the bearings with grease, and adjust the pressure on them using the nut on the top triple clamp.

2 Swinging arm

Some machines have taper or needle roller bearings. Others have plain bushes or rubber (Silentbloc) types. Wear is indicated by a tendency to wander off line. To check for wear, put the bike on its stand and, with the rear wheel clear of the ground, pull the swing arm from side to side. Movement means the bearings are worn and must be replaced, or adjusted if taper bearings. Silentbloc bushes always show a small amount of movement.

To prevent wear, lubricate frequently, as recommended, with a grease gun. Many bikes have grease nipples for this purpose, but you can fit them if none exist. Silentbloc bushes need no lubrication.

3 Wheel bearings

Each wheel normally has a pair of bearings, usually of the ball race type, or sometimes taper rollers. Wear is indicated as roughness when spinning the wheel by hand, or play when trying to rock it from side to side. To prevent wear, remove the bearings every 12,000 miles or so, clean them in a fuel bath and *lightly* repack with the recommended wheel

Whether testing for fork or steering head wear, place the bike on its centerstand with front wheel held clear of the ground. Push and pull fore and aft: look and feel for movement between the bottom triple clamp and steering head, and fork tube and slider.

To test for swing arm wear, prop the rear wheel off the ground. Ensure the bike is firmly supported. Grab a leg of the pivot and push and pull laterally. Do this prior to lubrication. Wear will be felt and seen.

bearing grease. **DO NOT OVER-GREASE, AS EXCESS MAY FIND ITS WAY INTO THE BRAKES.** Taper roller bearings can be adjusted for wear. Do not neglect wheel bearings as wear causes serious handling problems.

Engine

The engine is full of bearing surfaces which are worked very hard. All of them depend on the engine oil for their lubrication, so change this and the filters frequently, and use a good quality oil of the right grade. Some wear is inevitable, however, and the more miles a bike has done, the more likely wear is. The three major wear areas are:

1 Small ends

The bearings at the top of the connecting rods may be plain bushes or needle rollers. Wear can be heard as a tapping noise at low engine speeds and, if left unchecked, it will result in increased piston and bore wear. To check for wear, remove the head, barrel and piston, then check the fit of the wrist pin. It should slide through freely but there should be no lateral play. If you find movement, replace needle roller bearing races, or press in new bushes and have them reamed to size. Make sure the wrist pin is unworn. Check the piston and bore before reassembly.

2 Big ends

Big end bearings may be roller or plain shell. Wear is heard as a knocking noise and felt as vibration, and, if it is not remedied, will cause severe damage as the bearings break up. To check for wear, remove the head, barrel and piston, grasp the connecting rod at its highest point and try to pull it up and down. If it moves, the bearings are worn and need replacing. Shell bearings can be replaced by splitting the big ends. Roller bearings need the crankshaft split, which calls for special equipment.

3 Main bearings

Main bearings are either plain shell, ball or roller races. Severe wear will cause vibration and roughness and oil seal failure and will be heard as a rumble. On 2-strokes the movement of the crank will damage the seals, cause gas leaks and combustion failure. On singles and twins you can check for wear by removing the generator, grasping the shaft and trying to rock it up and down. Movement indicates a worn bearing. On multicylinder bikes you should strip the engine to check for wear.

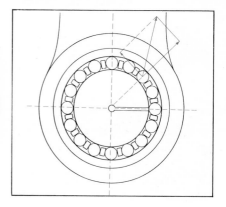

Wheel bearing wear is located by propping the wheel clear of the ground and rocking it at the tire. Look for play at the hub. Remove bearings by heating hub with a flat iron and drifting out. To replace, heat the same way but freeze the bearing overnight.

Ball and roller wear occurs during the scuffing that takes place during acceleration and deceleration. Balls and rollers need a cage to stop them crowding, when rubbing pressure from centrifugal force can be as high as 45 kg (100 lbs).

Chains

Chains transfer power from a driving source to a driven component via sprockets. They are commonly used in cam drive, primary drive, and electric starter systems, as well as in final drive systems.

All chains suffer wear and tear, which results in a loss of efficiency. Regular inspection, maintenance and replacement is necessary to keep them in good working condition. A chain in poor condition can absorb 20 per cent of the power it is required to transmit.

All internal chain systems are run in an oil bath, so life is long and trouble free—as long as the manufacturer's instructions regarding adjustments are followed. Only rarely, or after high mileage, do they need to be replaced; a procedure which frequently requires major engine work.

Final drive chains suffer badly from the conditions under which they operate, being open to water, grit and road salt.

Final drive chain maintenance

Ideally, a chain should be removed every 1,000 miles, washed in paraffin (kerosene), dried and then boiled in a proprietary chain grease.

The second-best treatment is to leave the chain on the bike, brush it clean with paraffin, dry it off with fuel from the tank, then lubricate it with a special chain spray, or paint it with a thick oil (engine oil will do). This is best done at the end of a ride and before adjusting for tension. *Never* ride with a dry chain.

Sealed chains

These contain a sealed-in grease, require less maintenance and last longer than a well-maintained standard chain, but are very expensive. Some types use O-rings between rollers and side plates to retain the factory-injected lubricant. These should not be lubricated by the spray-type greases as they tend to destroy the O-rings, thus allowing the grease to escape. Instead, lightly wipe the chain with a rag damped with kerosene and engine oil so as to remove road dirt, and lubricate the contact between chain and sprockets.

Never pull an old chain off without fastening the new one to it with a spring link. Keep a brake on the rear wheel to stop the chain unravelling.

To clean a chain soak it overnight in paraffin (kerosene) then brush vigorously. Rinse in pump fuel, dry, then boil in chain wax.

Next best to boiling in special wax is aerosol grease. Squirt it between the rollers and side plates on both sides while slowly turning the wheel.

The correct way to insert a spring link clip is by squeezing it over the final rivet with pliers. Any other way can bend the clip, which might come off.

Full chain enclosures protect the chain from the elements and in most cases ensure that it remains lightly lubricated. The life of the chain will be at least doubled.

Adjustment

Poor adjustment is one of the most common causes of severe chain wear. Before a run, always check the chain adjustment. This should be done with the bike on its wheels and at least 220lb (100kg) on the pillion. Use your own weight as you lean over the bike to inspect the chain tension. Total movement measured in the center of the bottom chain run, with the chain at its tightest point, should be ¾-1in (19-25mm). Tight spots are usually caused by eccentric sprockets. Beware of cheap sprockets; they are frequently eccentric.

To find the tight spot, place the machine on its centerstand, and turn the rear wheel slowly through 360°. DO NOT maintain even finger pressure on any part of the chain; it is dangerous, and foreign matter could cut you. Simply stop the wheel every 3in (75mm) of chain travel and lift-test the center part of the lower run.

If adjustment is necessary, loosen the axle nut and the locknuts on the adjuster screws, and then make an equal adjustment on both adjuster screws, or line up the adjusters with their respective markers on the swing arm. Re-tighten the adjuster locknuts, tighten the axle nut and then recheck the chain tension; readjust both ends of the axle equally, if necessary.

Finally, adjust the rear brake to suit, if it is a drum brake.

Sprockets

Keep a regular watch on the condition of gearbox and rear wheel sprockets. They should last a long time but, eventually, the teeth become hooked or even broken. Sprockets in this condition will ruin a chain and absorb power. If the teeth show signs of hooking, then replace the sprocket as soon as possible. If the sprocket is flat, turn it over to use the unworn face of the teeth.

25mm (1in) of vertical movement half way along the bottom run is correct. Less might pull the chain tight during suspension action, and more will cause excessive wear.

Measure for wear after cleaning but before lubricating. A chain is worn out if it curves laterally by more than 1in per 1 foot (25mm per 30cm).

Nothing wear chains out faster than worn sprockets, and nothing wears sprockets faster than worn out chains. These hooked-teeth sprockets are worn out.

Adjust for wear by finding the tight spot before lubricating. Slacken wheel (and sprocket carrier bolts if fitted) and check on wheel alignment.

Cables

Many motorcycle controls are operated by cable linkages which are light, cheap and efficient, if properly maintained. A stiff or worn cable, however, is a potential danger.

Virtually all bikes have cable-operated clutch and throttle controls, and many machines still use cables to the front and sometimes the rear brakes. Every model uses specially made cables whose length, adjusters and other fittings are unlikely to be compatible with other machines; and different types of cable are used in different applications, even on the same machine. Fortunately, the principles of cable maintenance and construction are universal.

Any cable has two main parts—a stranded inner cable, which is resistant to pulling (tension), and an outer sheath, which resists squeezing (compression). The inner pulls against the outer to transfer a force. Both are flexible to follow the curves from the controls to the component and to allow for handlebar movement.

Most cables have an inner made from a simple twist of several steel wires. This is made in different thicknesses—from about 1mm for throttle cables to 2 or 3mm for brake and clutch. Top quality inners are made from thinner wire and are braided. Several wires are twisted into a strand, and several strands are twisted together to form a strong, flexible braid. Some inners also have special anti-friction coatings. Each end of the inner is fitted with a nipple to suit the controls and component. Most have built-in length adjusters.

Maintenance

Cable maintenance is simple. There is hardly any wear in a straight cable, but where it has to bend, friction is introduced. Keep this to a minimum by making sure there are no kinks, tight bends or chafing; reroute, if necessary, to achieve smooth curves. Keep sliding friction down by lubricating with light oil. Attach a pressure oiling tool to one end

If new cables defy normal fitting, remove the tank and slacken adjusters to zero. Slip over any weather-shielding and fit the lower ends of the cable first.

Remove the handlebar lever by unscrewing the pivot bolt. Fit weather-shields over the cable upper end. Pop the nipple into the lever slot. Take care of any shims at the pivot.

Align the cable fitting slots in the adjuster and clean them thoroughly. Drop the outer into its socket, and slip the inner through the fitting slots.

Slot the lever into its operational position but in a wide open angle. Then line up the pivot bolt holes with a closing roll of the lever. Replace the bolt and its shims.

and pump oil through. Otherwise, take off the cable, hang it vertically and dribble oil down the inner until it appears at the other end. Controls will be lighter if you pay attention to these points. Keep cables adjusted properly and check for chafing; check at the ends for a frayed inner. Replace at the first sign of wear.

Even plastic-lined "friction free" cables require oil to prevent inner cable erosion. A few drops of oil applied to both ends once a week is enough. Pump the oil through the cable with lever movement Keep or fit plastic weather-shields in place to stop premature cable wear caused by grit and the entry of rain water. Wipe away excess oil after lubricating; do not forget to oil the nipple.

If the length of a brand-new cable's outer precludes normal fitting, try screwing the adjuster to minimum length and attaching the lower end of the cable to the machine. Remove the control lever by unscrewing its fulcrum screw. Slot the top-end nipple into its correct lever location. Locate the top end of the outer cable in its socket, if necessary by aligning the inner cable access slots. Position the handlebar lever and roll it into operational position. Replace the fulcrum screw.

If the cable is still in tension, then it is at fault and must either be changed, or its outer shortened. This can be done, after precise measurement, with either a junior hacksaw or sharp snips across a single strand of the outer cable coils. If only the inner is faulty, you can replace it after cable removal by fitting in a new length and soldering nipples to the ends.

It is wise to carry spare cables for an emergency. Oil them, coil them loosely and seal in a plastic bag. You can buy spares or make them from inners and outers with the right fittings, and solder on nipples. In an emergency you may also be able to fit a screw-on (solderless) nipple, but *never* use these as a permanent alternative in normal riding.

Replace fraying cables as soon as you notice them. Just a few broken strands can stiffen the control, causing clutch slip, partial brake failure or a jammed throttle.

Solderless nipples are of no use on front brakes or heavy duty clutches—they pull off.

If you do decide to use one, wash the cable free of oil or the screw will not grip.

If you have no cable lubricator (oil filled device attached to a pump) make a funnel from modelling clay, fit it around the cable end and fill with oil. Allow to drain overnight.

Badly routed cables cause a lot of trouble. It is essential that new cables are fitted through sweeping uninterrupted curves, with the fuel tank removed.

Economy

Spiralling fuel costs have made even motorcycle ownership increasingly expensive. This appears to be an unavoidable trend, but there are ways to cut costs, while still maintaining safety standards and broadening the pleasures of motorcycling. After all, paying someone else to do a job you could manage at home for almost nothing is hardly fun.

Make a point of studying your machine and make sure that you play a principal role in its maintenance. This way you get a positive return for the time and effort invested in the bike.

The whole purpose of economy tuning is to maximize your motorcycling resources. It is not simply a tricky way of improving fuel consumption. It employs a range of techniques covering the entire machine, which reduce overall maintenance expenditure.

Rider techniques
The most painstaking economy tuning measures on the machine itself can be totally negated by wild or undisciplined riding. Remember that while safety lies inside the head, economy is held in the grasp of the right fist. Use these few simple rules:

1 Accelerate gently and control the impulse to be first away from traffic lights.

2 Change into a higher gear smoothly and without overloading the engine on shuddering low revs, or by forcing it into screaming high ones.

3 Plan to arrive in top gear without need for further hard acceleration.

4 Anticipate sudden changes in road or traffic patterns.

5 Brake gently, using engine braking as far as possible. Powerful braking, like acceleration, wastes fuel, scrubs tires and increases mechanical wear on all parts of the machine.

6 Avoid prolonged cruising at speeds over 80 mph (130km/h). This can double running costs through increased fuel consumption and exaggerated engine, transmission and tire wear.

7 Never ride in a competitive state of mind.

Machine care
By far the most valuable contribution you can make toward a truly economical motorcycle is regular cleaning. A thorough weekly wash and polish reveals minor defects long before they grow into serious and expensive problems. In a climate where winters are wet and cold, this is particularly important. Salt used on winter roads causes rapid deterioration of paint and chromium plating, and in a single season it can corrode low-grade aluminium to a state of unserviceability. Electrical components and terminals should be lightly treated with silicone oil, such as WD40, once a month.

Servicing must be carried out at the recommended intervals: it is a false economy to delay this. If you service the machine yourself, double check your own

Use your recommended air filter change periods as a rough guide only. Dirty filter replacement is vital to avoid excessive fuel consumption from a choked engine.

Leaks frequently waste more fuel than maladjustment, so check for damp/dirty patches especially around taps and gas-line unions. Gas lines must be clipped.

work to ensure all items have been properly attended to. When servicing has been done by your dealer, inspect the motorcycle on its return to make sure it has been attended to as stated in the owner's manual.

Most of the major contributors to safety are also important economy factors. The two go almost hand-in-glove so pay attention to the following items:

1 Check tire pressures weekly. Low pressures absorb power and increase wear.

2 Look for binding brakes which absorb power and increase wear. Spin each wheel with the machine on its centerstand and watch and listen for a freely turning, silent movement.

3 Inspect carefully all fuel lines and joints, carburetor gaskets and fuel tank filler cap. Leaking fuel is the commonest cause of excessive fuel consumption. Watch for stains and/or dirt deposits at the point of leak.

4 Adjust the chain correctly, then lubricate it with a chain lubricant. Dry, worn and badly adjusted chains absorb power. If the sprocket teeth are worn, buy another sprocket: hooked sprocket teeth will ruin a new chain within 25 miles (40 km).

5 Adjust and lubricate all control cables and control pivots. Stiff ones cause binding, and dry ones corrode.

6 Inspect the air filter and intake system carefully. A dirty and blocked filter causes an excessively rich mixture, while air leaks and breaks weaken it, increasing fuel consumption.

7 Inspect the exhaust system with equal care and, with the engine running, listen for the blat and chuff of escaping gases. Old gas/oil-mix 2-strokes require regular exhaust system decokes. Blocked mufflers cause rich mixture; air leaks weaken the mixture.

8 Inspect contact breaker points for cleanliness and adjustment. Dirt and worn points detrimentally alter ignition timing.

9 Check, or have checked, valve clearances at least once a year. Incorrect ones will prove expensive to rectify eventually.

10 Check, or have checked, wheels for good balance. Unbalanced wheels cause irregular tire wear and can prematurely wear fork bushes, if not corrected.

11 Inspect the spark plug(s) at least once a month and at the onset of all engine trouble. It should be clean and powder grey, with an electrode gap as recommended.

12 Check at least once a year that all the carburetors on your machine are operating in good balance.

13 If a motorcycle is parked in the open, cover it with weatherproof plastic to protect it from corrosion. If the atmosphere is humid, place a cotton drape or sheet beneath the plastic cover to stop condensation.

To stop uneven tire and early fork bush wear, wheels must be balanced by attaching special weights directly opposite the point of imbalance.

Cleaning with hot water and soap uncovers minor defects in their early stages. Strong detergent can attack aluminum, switchgear, and control joints unless rinsed off.

Economy/2

Economy gadgets

If bolt-on accessories worked as useful economy aids, then they would be standard equipment. Most are a complete waste of money at best, while some actually increase fuel consumption.

Fairings can work two ways. The aerodynamics of a scientifically designed model can reduce turbulence and fuel consumption, and even improve penetration. But most fairings will have a completely neutral effect, and some of the biggest luxury touring models might even detract from ex-works economy. Handlebar fairings will, in general, do nothing but upset stability and keep your chest dry.

If modern carburetor kits or conversions are available for older machines, then by all means fit them, and enjoy the benefits of improved carburation and fuel economy.

The same applies to electronic ignition. The more powerful spark and vastly improved timing accuracy can do nothing but good. Whatever goes into the combustion chamber will burn more efficiently. A serious disadvantage is the horrifyingly high price of spares for some of these kits.

A third choice is to fit a different exhaust and muffler system, but this frequently involves vital carburetor adjustments too. Well-designed systems can improve fuel economy because of their less inhibiting gas flow, but as they tend to be excessively noisy, fitting them is frequently an anti-social exercise.

Engine modifications

Contrary to popular inexpert opinion, raising the gearing of a motorcycle does not provide it with an economy overdrive like a car's. Most manufacturers provide their models with the ideal compromise. An over-geared machine requires excessive clutch slip when starting off and the engine will labor heavily in top gear. This wastes more fuel than undergearing although, in extremes, that, too, will prove uneconomical because of fuel wastage and wear and tear from over-revving the engine.

Changing the compression ratio also has its disadvantages. Lowering it reduces certain mechanical stresses, but also drops combustion efficiency. Raising the ratio increases certain stresses but *might* increase combustion efficiency. Fuel economy can be improved but the exercise demands money and skill and is rarely worth the cost.

Never attempt to run an engine for very long without its air filter unless the carburetor(s) are properly modified. Serious engine damage from an over-weak mixture can result.

Home maintenance

Those who know nothing about motorcycles have three options:

1 Enrol at night school classes.

2 Request help from experienced motorcyclists (join a touring club).

3 Proceed, step by step, with a wrench in one hand and the owner's manual in the other—BUT BE VERY CAREFUL AND CHECK AND DOUBLE CHECK THE WHOLE TIME. A high mileage big bike owner could save himself the price of a moped on garage labor charges alone by carrying out his own servicing. Expect to spend as much on a set of good tools as on a good helmet. Rent, rather than buy, specialized tools.

Owner's manuals

Owner's manuals are the bibles of good motorcycle ownership. If you do not own one then get one—quickly. They should be studied in detail until you understand them completely. These days none is written in highly technical style. All contain vital information concerning ownership techniques peculiar to individual models.

Workshop manuals

If you plan to maintain your own motorcycle then buy a workshop manual. But do not assume that everything in print is necessarily correct: some apparently authoritative manuals are inaccurate and confusing. It is worth joining a one-make club, such as the Honda or Ducati owners, to discover their recommendations. Or you can request advice from the service manager or workshop foreman, but *not* the counterhand, of your friendly local dealer. Some manufacturers produce their own workshop manuals for home-mechanics—but do not make the mistake of purchasing the expensive and highly technical factory-trained mechanic's service data.

Spares
Pattern, or non-genuine, spares are usually inferior and should not be used in anything but emergencies. But there are exceptions, coming generally from the specialist manufacturers of tires, brakes, suspension, bearings and lighting parts. Some of these are superior to the original standard parts, and less expensive. Before fitting, however, check with your dealer first, and obtain or read a written recommendation guarantee from the component manufacturer. Be wary of cheap oil filters especially: they can block oil flow.

Savings can be made by cutting your own gaskets when required. The material necessary is obtainable at all good specialist dealers. Simply cut around the shape of the old gasket, or imprint the material around the face edge of the component with a dirty thumb.

Motorcycling handymen even manufacture their own control cables. The materials should be available from the same place as gasket material, but if they are not, all that is generally required is a spare nipple and some inner wire. Why buy a new cable when you can make your own for 10 per cent of the cost? If you can solder you can make cables.

The second-hand market is an invaluable source of cheap spares, frequently in first-class condition, often at less than half the new price. It is also a market where you can haggle or part exchange—they may even buy from you. Visit junkyards, auctions and auto flea markets. Watch the motorcycle press for advertisements and notices of these.

Used spares are not guaranteed, however, so examine them carefully because you will be unlikely to get your money back if they are no good.

One of a biker's best investments is the membership fee of a good motorcycle club. Clubs frequently organize their own spares operations with a discount for members. You will also get to know which dealers are best, which modifications work well, which insurance company rates are lowest and suchlike. A good many clubs also have their own stock of expensive and specialist tools and equipment, which they will lend to members.

Fuel
Always conform to the fuel quality recommended by your motorcycle's makers. The use of superior grade fuel will improve neither performance nor economy because the extra octanes are beyond the digestive capability of the engine. Inferior quality fuel can do nothing but harm. Retarding the ignition timing to overcome pinging caused by the use of inferior fuel should be regarded purely as an emergency expedient: the long-term effect is to encourage the overheating and premature wear of spark plugs, valves, pistons and rings.

Oil
The general rule is to play safe and stick to your machine manufacturer's recommendations regarding the brand and viscosity of oil, and oil change periods. But almost any oil is better than dirty oil in an engine. Engines with ball and roller race bearings require more frequent oil changes than plain bearing engines because the whirling bearings literally chop up the long chains of molecules that provide oil with its unique lubricating qualities. As air cooled engines run hotter than water cooled engines the oil is degraded sooner.

If you run a machine with an air cooled, roller bearing engine then it might pay to use a more expensive oil made specifically for such engines by one of the smaller companies.

Trouble shooting

Trouble shooting is something of an art. It requires logic, experience and a certain understanding of the fundamentals of motorcycle design. But once the basics have been mastered, the principles of trouble shooting can be applied to any problem encountered on a motorcycle. However, this technique will not *automatically* give the answer; a motorcycle will not lightly give up its mysteries.

Always be methodical. Base your assumptions on fact and then follow them up without being diverted to a different line of investigation. Only when the first investigation has proved fruitless should you progress to another.

There are three basic prerequisites for ignition: compression, a spark, and fuel. Without one or more of these, you will have difficulty in starting the engine. It does not matter which system is tested first, but start with the most likely—the one that has given previous problems or where a weakness is known to exist, such as water entering the carburetor.

The technique shown may not lead to the exact cause, but it will isolate the area which requires investigation. It will also establish whether or not a quick repair is possible.

Electrical faults are perhaps the most common of motorcycle problems and probably the most difficult to deal with. The cause of the problem is often difficult to track down and may have the unfortunate habit of coming and going.

The basic necessity for a complete electrical circuit is continuity—that the circuit is not broken. Once the circuit is broken, for any reason, the electrical component will fail to work.

As shown in the chart the circuit can be broken by a number of causes. But stick rigidly to a logical sequence of checks, again starting with what appears to be the most likely cause. A circuit tester can be made from a bulb and two pieces of wire.

Always keep a copy of the circuit diagram handy.

Bike will not start
Was the bike going well the last time you rode it, or has work been carried out on it recently? This will affect your course of action

Mechanical
Rare for mechanical problem to occur overnight

Check 1
engine turns over

Check 2
there is compression

If there is compression, there is no mechanical reason for the engine not to start

Most likely causes

Sticking valve
Broken tappet
Broken cam chain

Electrical	**Fuel/lubrication**
Most common faults are electrical. For engine to start there must be a spark	Fuel faults are also common
Check 1 spark at the spark plug	Check 1 fuel in tank
Check 2 spark at contact breakers	Check 2 fuel reaching float chamber
Check 3 spark on all cylinders	Check 3 fuel reaching spark plug
Check 4 lights for power in battery	Check 4 correct grade fuel being used
Check 5 kill button and ignition switch	Check 5 fuel not contaminated
Most likely causes	Most likely causes
Loose connection(s) Poor spark plugs Poor contact breakers Bad earth (ground) Water in electrics Faulty ignition switch Fault in power source	Water, dirt in float chamber Water in fuel Jets blocked by dirt Blocked filters Sticking float Air lock in tank If fuel is reaching the spark plug, try looking for an alternative fault

Trouble shooting/2

For a breakdown the procedure shown on page 220 should again be used. But in a breakdown there are usually more clues as to the nature of the problem.

The way in which the bike comes to a halt, or the manner in which the engine stops, will indicate whether the fault is electrical, mechanical and/or fuel or lubrication.

However, some symptoms may be caused by faults in any of the three basic systems.

Engine noises
Plain bearing big ends knock heavily when worn out and then break up quickly. In no circumstances ride a bike that is producing regular, engine-speed hammering noises. It will be ruined beyond economic repair very quickly.

Main bearings growl and rumble as they wear out. They will take a lot of punishment and make the most frightening noises for a long time (a few hours sensitive riding) before breaking up.

Ball and roller engine bearings also growl and rumble as they wear, but they do so long before reaching danger point and generally frighten their owners into the repair shop before engine damage occurs.

Strong, regular and light clacking suggests either a sticking valve or broken piston ring. Sticking valves in 4-strokes and broken rings in 2-strokes are serious and can cause expensive damage. Irregular clicking is usually the result of a slack chain somewhere. A coarse and heavy whirring is frequently an indication of worn camshaft bearings or cam lobes.

No engine, however old or worn, should rattle badly, although a light whirring is acceptable.

Engine breaks down	Symptom	Possible problem	Possible cause
	Engine locks suddenly	Mechanical	Seizure
	Strange noises in engine	Mechanical	Broken tappet Broken piston ring Faulty bearing(s) Many others
	Engine runs unevenly, misfires, then stops	Electrical Mechanical Fuel	Faulty earth (ground) Faulty connection Broken, bent, sticking valve Fuel starvation
	Engine fades, then eventually stops	Fuel	Blocked filters Blocked breather hole No fuel Over-rich mixture
	Engine suddenly cuts out	Electrical	Disconnected earth (ground) Blown main fuse Short circuit Faulty alternator or power source

Spark plugs

When an engine stops or refuses to start, spark plugs can be read usefully.

A wet spark plug indicates adequate fuel supply; therefore the trouble source is probably in the ignition system. A dry plug with a good spark indicates an inadequate fuel supply. A wet plug with a good tested spark suggests a probable breakdown of the spark under combustion chamber pressure, or possibly too much fuel.

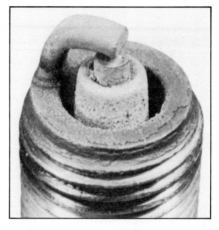

Carbon fouling can short circuit the plug, weakening or eliminating the spark. It is caused by over-rich mixture, possibly due to a faulty choke or clogged air filter.

A normal plug: they should be serviced after 5,000 miles or six months, or half that period on 2-strokes. The gap increases by about 0.0001″ per 1,000 miles.

Oil fouling, common in new engines, may also be caused by worn valve guides or piston rings, or a poorly adjusted 2-stroke oil pump. Cure the oil problem and degrease the plug.

Worn out plugs can be recognized by eroded electrodes and a thin earth (ground) wire. Replace plugs after 10,000 miles or one year—halve the interval for 2-stroke engines.

Roadside repairs

If you look into the tool kit of an experienced rider you will notice that it is filled with what appears to be an assortment of junk. In fact, this stuff is a treasure trove of bodger's delight gathered over many years.

The most usual bits will be: a roll of adhesive insulating tape; 3ft (1m) of single strand locking wire; 6ft (2m) of heavy gauge lighting wire (flex); a length of flexible rubber tube; an assortment of popular sized nuts, bolts and washers; a small cold chisel, a long-nosed, slim drift; a tube of plastic gasket; a tube of resin adhesive; a piece of aluminum foil; a box of waterproof matches; some low-temperature solder tape; a few solder-less cable nipples; a small waterproof flashlight; screwdriver/circuit tester; a file and a few heavy rubber bands.

Add this collection to the chain repair and puncture repair kits, and there is practically nothing a determined and ingenious rider cannot overcome.

The significant fact is that motor-cyclists who lug this lot around with them are not usually those who break down: they know their machines well enough to pick up advance warning of breakdowns long before they actually occur. Component failure is rare; ignorance and carelessness cause most problems.

Of all motorcycle breakdowns, 50 per cent are due to electrical faults. Then follow tire, fuel supply, control cable and chain troubles, in that order. Owners of bikes with "foolproof" electronic ignition, tubeless tires, hydraulic brakes and shaft drive need not feel smug. While such sophisticated machines are probably a little more reliable, they are certainly more difficult to carry out emergency, bodging, roadside repairs on than old-fashioned machines.

Electrics

Poor earths (grounds) and blown fuses account for most failures. Check these first. If the lights fail and defy all repair attempts, route alternative wires direct from the battery to dip (dim) headlight beam and tail light only, and ride slowly, Remove the respective fuses.

Wrap a blown fuse in a roll of aluminium foil if you have no spare fuse. Switch on the circuit incorporating the fuse and feel its wiring: if it warms up, the fault— probably a short circuit—*must* be rectified immediately. Alternatively, by-pass the circuit and wire direct from the battery.

Do not be frightened of substituting non-standard parts if they are of the right voltage and can be fitted. If you adapt a car spark plug, ride slowly to avoid overheating and piston burning. Any car condenser can be made to work in an emergency: use a long wire and fit it outside the housing.

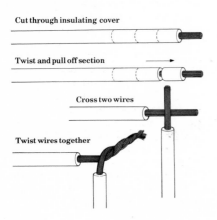

Cut through insulating cover

Twist and pull off section

Cross two wires

Twist wires together

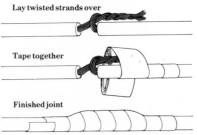

Lay twisted strands over

Tape together

Finished joint

Twisted wire joints are for emergency use only. Remove short sections of the insulation at a time to avoid breakage.

Twist the wire cores firmly together. Use tape to strengthen, insulate and weatherproof the joint.

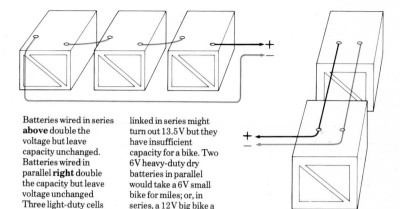

Batteries wired in series **above** double the voltage but leave capacity unchanged. Batteries wired in parallel **right** double the capacity but leave voltage unchanged Three light-duty cells linked in series might turn out 13.5 V but they have insufficient capacity for a bike. Two 6 V heavy-duty dry batteries in parallel would take a 6 V small bike for miles; or, in series, a 12 V big bike a shorter distance.

Take great care with contact breaker insulating washers. If they get lost, make new ones from scraps of plastic and/or paper.

If the charging system packs up, disconnect *all* circuits except the ignition: a motorcycle will cover a few hundred miles like this, providing it is ridden gently.

If a battery packs up completely, disconnect everything except the ignition circuit and run the machine on a couple of 6 V heavy-duty lantern batteries, bought from a hardware store, wired in series. (Any combination of dry batteries to make up the correct voltage can be used; do not be frightened of exceeding your machine's voltage by two or three volts.)

Night riding, with an uncharging system or one relying on dry batteries which refuse a charge, should not be attempted in any circumstances because the battery(ies) will quickly run down.

Fuel

When an engine stops unexpectedly always check the fuel level in the tank. If an engine sparks but will not run, the trouble lies in fuel starvation: the most common cause is a blocked fuel supply.

Remove the lower end of the main fuel line and turn the tap on. If it remains dry the problem lies either in the tank or tap; if fuel flows, check the carburetor float chamber. Take great care, when removing it, not to lose the float needle which may be lightly stuck. If the float needle is lost or the float punctured, it is possible to ride by controlling fuel flow manually with the tap: fill the chamber, turn the tap to the barest possible trickle out of the open-ended line, then secure it over the union and ride off. Check frequently and adjust as necessary.

Fuel taps on 2-strokes must be turned off when the bike is not in use. A leaking system can allow fuel to trickle into the crankcase and cause wet spark plugs.

A split fuel line can be repaired by cutting the split out and lengthening the line by forcing the two ends over a ballpoint pen casing. Make sure first that fuel does not soften the plastic.

When securing a temporary fuel or oil line with wire, bind the wire once around the line union, twist it tight once only, then bring it back to the other side and do the same again, and a third time, if necessary. Most attempts to twist wire really tight in one turn break the wire.

To force a small diameter line over a large diameter union, expand and flex the tube end by gently chewing it for a few moments.

Do not expect plain plastic tubing to resist high oil pressure. Short lengths can be reinforced by binding with adhesive tape and string or wire.

Roadside repairs/2

Broken control cables

Experienced long-distance riders carry clutch and twistgrip/throttle cables with them. They are the two most important cables; others rarely wear out.

Control cable nipples are not often pulled off. If one does break, a solderless nipple will make a short-use emergency standby. If the inner cable breaks close to the nipple, which is usual, try shortening the outer to match. This will enable you to make the cable of operational length again with a solderless nipple.

Unless you have a long ride through heavy traffic ahead, by far the best way to get around cable breakage is to side-step the problem by adopting a different riding technique.

When a clutch cable breaks, change gear without using the clutch by riding carefully and lightly, paying great attention to traffic movement ahead to anticipate speed changes. Use the throttle in a similar but gentler manner than usual, and move the gear pedal smoothly and firmly. Be positive: hesitation will cause bad changes. Change gear at medium revs on light load. If you need to stop, select neutral and coast to a halt. To start, paddle away with your feet and select first gear at idling revs once on the move. Alternatively, kill the engine, switch on ignition, select first gear, press the starter button and simultaneously push with your feet.

The simplest way to ride with a broken throttle cable is to speed up idling on the carburetor screw to around 2,500/3,000rpm, and use gears and clutch to alter your roadspeed.

On some machines it is possible to swap over the choke cable end to the throttle control and to vary roadspeed by moving the choke lever. The easiest to bodge are those with rocker controlled throttle arms: simply tie a piece of string to the cable rocker arm, hook elastic in tension to pull it shut, and control road speed by pulling on the string with the left hand.

Another method is to route the cable up and over a frame tube, and then tie the inner only to a foot with string or a lace. Depressing the foot then increases road speed, but the danger here is that any attempt to put the foot on the ground races the engine. Be careful!

Broken chains

All long-distance riders should carry with them a chain repair kit, consisting of a chain breaker, a few inches of spare chain, three spring links and two cranked links. With this equipment, the worst chain breakdowns can be dealt with.

Should a chain break without this kit to hand, don't panic. In all probability there is nothing more than a missing spring link to be replaced. If you have no spare spring link with you, then you deserve all the trouble that comes your way. But a spring link clip can be reliably duplicated by a twist of wire.

No amount of bodging can mend a

If a chain has to be threaded over a gearbox sprocket, it is frequently

quickest in the long run to remove the sprocket cover plates. If this is

through from below and around the sprocket.

Do not be afraid to
bodge in emergencies.
Short, bent nails make
handy rivets.

A lost spring link clip
can be replaced with a
twisted strand of wire.

chain shortened by breakage unless you have spare links handy. But bent sideplates can be straightened, and rivets relocated and peened over again. Ignore missing rollers and ride carefully on the bare rivets.

Rivets are tough and, apart from using a special tool, the only way to break a chain is to file the head of the rivet down, and then punch it through the sideplate using a slim drift or punch. Do this with the chain wired tight around the rear wheel sprocket, which must be supported at the back.

In dire emergency, it might be possible to bend a nail or thread heavy wire through a chain link to hold it together. This *does* work over a few miles *if* the load carried is light, there are no steep hills and acceleration and gear changing are zero. But a break should be anticipated every yard of the way.

Threading a chain over a gearbox sprocket, with no old chain to guide it through, can cause headaches. Unless a convenient cover plate is fitted beside the sprocket, the best method is to twist a length of wire over the first rivet, and then feed the wire around and below the sprocket until it pokes out of the housing above the sprocket. Get as much light as you can into the sprocket housing, and try to centralize the chain with a long probe before you pull it up and around the sprocket. Do *not* attempt to feed in the wire from the top. You need the chain's own weight to hold it away from

the sprocket so as to give you room to maneuver it into place.

Gaskets

Gaskets are much less important today than they were. Modern machining and silicone rubber jointing compound have largely ousted the old, paper cut-out type. A tube of silicone rubber will solve all roadside sealing problems, except those where extreme heat or pressure are involved—such as at the cylinder head on most machines.

If a cylinder head gasket blows, making the motorcycle unridable, and no replacement gasket is available, be prepared for a long job. The head will have to be removed completely, and the two faces of the head and barrel cleaned of *all* dirt, until they are bone dry and perfectly clean, before reassembling. Any attempt to seal the head joint with anything except the real thing or an identical replacement will fail. A dry joint will leak a little, but it will keep the machine going. Check for reduced piston clearance by hand turning the engine over first: listen and feel for the valves touching the pistons. Never run an engine with a missing cylinder base gasket or the piston rings might hit the wear shoulder around the top of the cylinder.

When gasket replacement is unavoidable use thick paper or thin cardboard pressed with a dirty thumb over the joint to be faced. Then cut around the template so marked.

227

Puncture repair

Removing a wheel can be difficult, and replacement impossible for a novice, unless the wheel is off the ground.

Place the machine on its centerstand so the punctured wheel hangs over a good 100mm (4in) drop, rest the stand on a brick of similar height or lean the machine at an acute angle on its stand against a tree or strong post.

1 Remove the wheel. Deflate the tire by removing the valve core, and break the rim/tire seal by pressing your heels into the tire bead. Remove the valve nut.

3 Pull the tube out, after pushing the valve through the rim. Mark tire, rim and tube in one spot. Lubricate the remaining bead. Hold the wheel vertical, and place a tire lever across.

4 To find the puncture, inflate the tube and listen for it, or hold it to your lips. Search inside the tire for the foreign body, or match up holes in the tire and tube.

6 Rub in a bead of rubber solution until it is tacky, then leave it to dry for at least five minutes. Apply a second light coat of solution and leave it to dry for 10 minutes.

7 Pop a patch over the puncture and squeeze it to the tire using thumbs or a tool handle. Slightly inflate the tube and dust the patch with French chalk or road dust.

9 Lay the wheel flat and kneel the bead, into the rim. Use tire levers curved downwards and lubricate the inside edge of remaining bead. Take care not to pinch the inner tube.

10 Turn the wheel over and repeat. Make sure the bead is continually centralized, deep in the rim-well center. Lubricate it and hold the trapped bead in place by kneeling on it.

2 "Spoon" three tire levers under the bead 60-80mm apart. Lever each one up, lifting the bead. Heel the unlifted bead down into the rim. Extract the middle lever and move it along.

5 Clean the puncture area with fuel and/or spit and dry it thoroughly. Rough the area completely with a scratch pad until it resembles fine suede.

8 With the wheel upright, place the tube inside the tire and rest both inside the rim. Align your marks and put the valve nut in place. Check the direction of the arrow.

11 Inflate and replace the wheel. If the tire is not in line with the rim, deflate it down to around 0.70kg/sq cm (10psi) and slowly ride the bike for 100 metres or so, then reinflate.

Tire fitting tips

The best tire levers are wide, and flat, with tapered ends and are polished smooth. Use cut-down car tire levers with sanded, polished ends. Bind the handles with string or cloth to stop your hand slipping.

When a tire goes flat, check that the valve is not leaking.

Ream out tight-fitting valve holes in rims with a screwdriver.

Punctures cannot be repaired in the rain, so carry a spare tube the diameter of the rear wheel and the section of the front wheel, to suit both tires in an emergency.

Tubes filled with puncture repair or anti-puncture chemical goo cannot be patched.

Most punctures occur in the last 20 per cent of useful tire life.

Place tubes into tubeless tires with care: rim scars cause tubeless tire air leaks.

Discard plastic, acorn valve caps in favor of slot-headed metal ones. They cannot distort and contain a useful valve core extractor slot.

If a refitted tire is not aligned concentrically, ride slowly to a garage and inflate to about 5kg/sq cm (70psi) and then deflate to correct pressure.

A puncture outfit should contain: six large wafer-edged patches; two new tubes of rubber solution; a piece of sandpaper or scratch pad; French chalk; two spare valve cores and caps; a valve repair tool; a tire pump and a spare inner tube.

In an emergency, a split tire can be patched with a piece of clean, unwaxed canvas. Saturate the canvas with rubber solution and apply two coats inside the cleaned, toughened tire wall.

Facts and figures

Hard Facts

There is no such thing as the average motorcycle. For the sake of discussion, however, let us take a 400 cc single cylinder 4-stroke cruising at 70 mph (113 km/h) at 6,000 rpm in top gear.

Its cylinder will fill with fresh mixture in $\frac{1}{130}$ second, the combustion sequence will take $\frac{1}{250}$ second, and both will occur 1,600 times for every 1 mile (1.6 km) travelled.

In that distance each valve will travel in its guide approximately 200ft (60m) and will acquire an inertia force (temporary weight) of close on 140 lb (63.5 kg) during its $\frac{1}{130}$ second opening period. The exhaust valve will dip 1,200 times into a combustion temperature of up to 4,030°F (2,222°C) and in doing so have to operate reliably at a red glow of 1,630°F (888°C). The piston will be subject to an inertia force of about 3,000 lb (1,360 kg) during its moments of direction change.

Torque

Torque is an expression of turning force. The most important standard measurement of engine power is the torque produced at the crankshaft. Maximum torque is produced when an engine is operating at maximum combustion efficiency, although the requirements are different for different types of machine: a trials bike needs maximum torque at low rpm, a tourer at medium (cruising) engine speeds and a racer at racing speeds (high rpm). Torque is measured on a dynamometer, which resists the turning force of the engine with a variable load, or "brake," usually supplied by hydraulic or electrical power.

The British and American standard of torque is familiarly expressed in foot/pounds (ft/lb). The old metric system was indicated as kilogram/metres (kg/m).

The new International Standards Organisation (ISO) method will indicate torque in Newton/metres (N/m). One N/m = the force necessary to lift 1 kilogram 1 metre in 1 second (kg/m/s).

Horse power (hp)

One British and American hp is the force necessary to lift 550 lb 1 foot in 1 second (lb/ft/sec).

1 metric hp (cv) = 1.0139 hp.

The new ISO system will indicate hp and cv as kilowatts (kW). A kW is a measure of work-rate.

1 kW = 1.3596 cv and 1.3410 hp.

Brake horse power (bhp)

Bhp is formulated from torque measurements on a dynamometer. In the future, it, too, will be indicated internationally by the ISO standard, kW. The term bhp is familiar but misleading. If an engine is accelerated beyond the speed of its maximum torque development it will continue to increase its power output because the sheer quantity of combustion strokes overcomes their falling quality. Maximum bhp is achieved immediately prior to the point where quantity can no longer overcome the falling quality.

There are two standards of indicating bhp in common use. Britain and America use the SAE rating, and most metricated nations conform to the DIN rating. There is no means of equating figures of the two systems. Italy alone uses the CUNA system, which is 5-10 per cent above DIN.

The DIN method of obtaining power figures requires the test laboratory to conform to strictly enforced atmospheric conditions, and the test engine to be fitted with all its road equipment, such as air cleaner and mufflers. The SAE rating is more flexible and only requires the engine tester to record what road equipment was fitted during the test.

Power

bhp		kW
0.7457	1	1.34102
18.64	25	33.53
37.29	50	67.05
55.93	75	100.58
74.57	100	134.10
93.21	125	167.63
111.86	150	201.15

Cylinder capacity

To calculate cylinder capacity, multiply the stroke of the crankshaft (measure piston movement minus bearing slack) by the area of the cylinder cross section; or simply use the engine manufacturer's stroke and bore measurements.

As the area of a circle is π (3.1416) $\times$ the square of the radius, divide the bore by 2 for the radius and multiply the square by 3.1416.

E.g. In the case of a Suzuki GS1000 the cylinder capacity is calculated thus:

bore	= 70 mm
radius	= 35 mm
area	= 35^2 x 3.1416
	= 3848.5 mm^2
multiply by the stroke (64.8 mm)	= 249,382.8 cu mm
divide by 1000	= 249.3 cc
multiply by 4 (the number of cylinders)	= 997.5 cc engine capacity

Compression ratio

The compression ratio is simply the ratio between the total cylinder capacity and the combustion chamber capacity.

Having calculated the capacity of one cylinder (A), measure the volume of the combustion chamber (B) with the piston at TDC. Do this by pouring fresh engine oil from a calibrated burette into the engine through the spark plug hole until it reaches the base of the hole. Let the oil settle back into the burette, then note the volume of oil that has been poured.

In the case of the GS1000 this will be close to 31 cc. Add A to B = 249.3 + 31

$$= 280.3$$

and divide by 31 = 9.04 compression ratio

Drag (C_D)

Drag is the resistance of the air to forward motion. It is measured by using a scale which accepts that a flat disc moving broadside along its axis has a nominal rating of 1.00.

A Mercedes-Benz S class saloon car has a C_D of 0.36, while an anti-tank rocket missile might have a C_D of 0.02. A naked roadster motorcycle with rider can have a C_D of approximately 1.3, although a grand prix racing machine with rider in tight leathers in full race crouch can be as low as 0.5 C_D.

Gear ratios

Gear ratios quoted by manufacturers and journalists describe the reduction ratio between the engine and the rear wheel. Thus a gear ratio of 4.776:1 indicates that the engine spins 4.776 times for 1 revolution of the rear wheel.

Overall gear ratios can be calculated by multiplying together the primary reduction, the final reduction and the internal gearbox reduction.

Some manufacturers indicate gear reduction in the form of a sprocket, or gear cog, tooth fraction. The Suzuki GS1000, for example, has a primary reduction of 87/49, which means simply that the crankshaft gear cog has 49 teeth, while the clutch gear cog has 87 teeth. To discover the decimal reduction ratio simply divide the lower number into the higher: 87 ÷ 49 = 1.775 (:1).

Estimating gear ratios

If you have no idea what the overall gear reduction ratios are on your machine use this simple method to estimate them.

1 Remove the primary transmission cover and spark plugs of your machine and select the gear you wish to measure.

2 Chalk corresponding marks on the rear tire and frame.

3 Scribe a mark on the crankshaft sprocket or gear wheel.

4 Turn the rear wheel slowly backwards, to take up transmission slack, counting the number of turns made by the crankshaft sprocket, until the rear wheel chalk mark realigns exactly with its corresponding frame marks after 360°.

5 Using the sprocket, or gear cog teeth, as convenient fractions, the number of revolutions made by that sprocket during the rear wheel's single turn will indicate the reduction of that particular gear. Thus six complete turns plus eight out of 24 teeth signifies a gear reduction of 6,8/24, or a reduction ratio of 6.33:1.

Facts and figures/2

Length

mm		in
25.4	1	0.0394
		(or 40 thou)
50.8	2	0.08
76.2	3	0.12
101.6	4	0.16
127.0	5	0.20
152.4	6	0.24
177.8	7	0.28
203.2	8	0.31
228.6	9	0.35
254.0	10	0.39
279.4	11	0.43
304.8	12	0.47

km		miles
1.6093	1	0.6214
3.22	2	1.24
4.83	3	1.86
6.44	4	2.49
8.05	5	3.11
9.66	6	3.73
11.27	7	4.35
12.88	8	4.97
14.48	9	5.59
16.09	10	6.21

m		ft
0.305	1	3.2808
0.61	2	6.56
0.91	3	9.84
1.22	4	13.12
1.52	5	16.40
1.83	6	19.69
2.13	7	22.97
2.44	8	26.25
2.74	9	29.53
3.05	10	32.81

Cylinder capacity

cc		cu. in
16.387	1	0.061
409.68	25	1.52
819.35	50	3.05
1229.29	75	4.58
1638.71	100	6.10
2048.38	125	7.63
2458.06	150	9.15
3277.41	200	12.20
4096.76	250	15.26
8193.53	500	30.51
16387.06	1000	61.02

Weight

kg		lb
0.4536	1	2.2046
0.91	2	4.41
1.36	3	6.61
1.81	4	8.82
2.27	5	11.02
2.72	6	13.23
3.18	7	15.43
3.63	8	17.64
4.08	9	19.84
4.54	10	22.05
4.99	11	24.25
5.44	12	26.46
5.90	13	28.66
6.35	14	30.86

Pressure

kg/sq cm		psi
0.0703	1	14.2233
0.14	2	28.45
0.21	3	42.67
0.28	4	56.89
0.35	5	71.11
0.42	6	85.34
0.49	7	99.56
0.56	8	113.79
0.63	9	128.01
0.70	10	142.23
0.77	11	156.46
0.84	12	170.68
0.91	13	184.90
0.98	14	199.13

Volume

Litres		US gals
3.78	1	0.26
7.57	2	0.53
11.36	3	0.79
15.14	4	1.06
18.93	5	1.32

Litres		Imp gals
4.55	1	0.22
9.09	2	0.44
13.64	3	0.66
18.18	4	0.88
22.73	5	1.10

Temperature

To convert °C to °F, multiply by 1.8 and add 32.

E.g., $100 (1.8) + 32 = 212$
$100°C = 212°F$

To convert °F to °C, subtract 32 and divide by 1.8.

To convert mpg (US) to km/l multiply by 0.425.
To convert km/l to mpg (US) divide by 0.425.
Metric fuel consumption is now quoted officially as l/100 km (litres per 100km). To convert mpg (US) to l/100km, divide factor 235.22 by mpg.

E.g., $\dfrac{235.22}{52} = 4.523 \, l/100km$

Use the same factor to reverse the process.

E.g., $\dfrac{235.22}{4.523} = 52 \, mpg$

To calculate road speed (in mph)

$$\dfrac{\text{Revs} \times \text{wheel diameter (ins)}}{\text{gear reduction}} \times 0.00297$$

$$= mph$$

E.g., Suzuki GS1000

Diameter of wheel (400×18)
$$= 18 + 4 + 4 = 26$$

$$\dfrac{8,500 \times 26}{4.776} = 46273.031$$

$$\times 0.00297 = 137.43 \, mph$$

Index

A

Accidents, 8, 72, 76, 104, 110, 124-9
  analysis of, 124-5
  casualties, 126-9
  procedure, 126-7
ACU, 64
Advanced riding, 120-1
Adverse conditions, 78-9, 110, *111*, 112-19
  see also Bad weather
Aerodynamics, 28-9, 50-1
Agostini, Giacomo, 130, *134*, 135
Air cleaner, *10-11*
Air filter, *12-13*, 216-7
AJS, 7R, *133*
Alligator Enduro, *175*
Alternator, 204
American Motorcyclists Association (AMA), 76, 146, 149, 168
American styling *10-11*, 80-1
Ammeters, 56
Artificial respiration, *129*
Atchison, Topeka and Sante Fe, the 138
Automatic transmission, 23
Avon tires, 60

B

Bad weather, 112-15
Balaclavas, *67*, 78
Balance, 86-7
Barbour suit, 74
Battery, *11*, 204
  faults in, 224
Bearings, *17*
  faults in, 222
  maintenance, 210-11
Belt drive, 23, 44
Benelli-4, *143*
Bernouilli effect, 51
Big-bore kit, 58-9

Big ends, 210
Bimota, *31*
Bleeding (the brake system), 203
Bleeding (to stop human), *129*
BMW, 50, 136
  R80/GS, 10, 13, *37*
  R100RS fairing, 10, 50
  R100RT, *39*
Body armor, *157*
Boots, 72, 78
Bottom dead center (BDC), 16
Brake,
  cable, *13*
  cylinder, *11*
  fluid, 203
  front, 113
  plate, *13*
  rear, 113, 114
  rear lever, *13*
  rod, *13*
  systems, 202-3
Braking, 90, 92-3
  distances, *93*, 112 120, *121*, *125*
Breakdowns, 222-3
Brembo discs, *31*
British Standards Institute (BSI), 64-5
BSA, 26, 152
  Bantam, 152
  Bombardier, *36*
  DBD34 Gold Star, *145*
BSA/Triumph racers, 26, 168
Bulbs, 205
Bultaco,
  GTS 250 Metralla, *40*
  Sherpa, *36*, 140, 160
Bump start, 83
Buyer's guide, 32-49

C

Camshaft *16-17*, *59*
Camping, 184
Can-Am, 36
Carburetor, *12* *16*, 17
  checking, 217
  kits, 218
  tuning, 58-9

Carruthers, Kel, *143*
Centrifugal force, 90
Chains, 22
  broken, 226
  maintenance of, 212-3, 217
Charging system, faulty, 207, 225
Chassis, 210
Checklist, pre-purchase, 48-9
Chopper,
  hard-tail, *47*
Christensen, T., 164, *165*
Circuit tester, 206
City driving, 96
Cleaning the machine, 196-201, 217
Clothing, 64-79, 112, *113*
  see also individual items
Clubs, motorcycle 146, 219
Clutch, 12, 22-3, 80-1
  cable, 10-11, 214
  control, 82-9
  faulty, 226
  lever, *11*, 80-1
Cold weather, 78-9, 178
Collins, Russ, 139, 164
Collision protection, 28
Combustion chamber, 14, *18*, 59
Combustion temperatures, *18*
Commuter bikes, 32-3, 34-5
Components, *10-13*
  faults in, 206-7
Compression ratio, 18, 59, 231
Concentration, 106
Conspicuity, 76-7, 116, 118-19
Contact breaker points, 18, 59, 205, *208-9*, 217
Control cables, broken, 226

home-made, 218
  maintenance of, 214-5, 217
Cooling, 14-15, 19
Cornering, 90-1, *113*
Country roads, *see* Rural roads
Crankcase, 12
Cranking over, 94
Crankshaft, 12, 14, *16-19*, 22-3, 24-5, *26-7*
Crash helmets, 64-7, 78
  for moped, 75
  intercoms, 123
Crashbars, 56, *95*
Crashing, 94
Cross roads, 102, 112
Cylinders, *14-19*
  configuration, 24-7
Cylinder heads, 14, 59
CZ, 141, 152

D

Daytona, 149, 168
de Coster, Roger, 152
Desert racing, 171
Design (of motor cycles), 10, 12
  future, 28-9
Desmodromic valve gear, 135
Deubel, Max, 136, *137*
Dirt bikes, 32-3, 36-7
Disc brake assembly, *10*
Disc brakes, 92, 112, *113*, 120, 202
DKW, 15
Dnieper MT10, *43*
Dog clutch, 22-3
DOT, 64
Drag, 50-1
  coefficient, 231
Drag racing, 139, 162-5
Drive mechanism, 12
Drum brakes, *13*, 112, 113, 202
Ducati, 25, 130, *131*, 140
  desmo, *135*
  900SS, *40*

Duke, Geoff, 90, 132
Dunlop tire
  company, 60, 62
Dunstall Power
  Exhaust System,
  20
Dunstall Suzuki,
  GSX1100, 41
Dynamo, 204

E

Earoling, 94
Economizing, 216-19
Electrical systems,
  18, 19, 204-7
  failures in, 220-1,
  224-5
  fault prevention,
  204
Electrically heated
  clothing and
  faceshields, 78-9
Elf-X, 29
Enders, K., 136
Enduro, 158, 174-5
Enduro tires, 63
Enfield 350, 42
Engine, 14-19
  braking, 93
  2-stroke, 14-15,
  21, 208-9
  4-stroke, 16-19,
  208
  flat twin, 24-5
  maintenance of,
  208-9
  modifications to,
  56-7, 218
  mutli-cylinder,
  14-15, 26-7
  noises in, 222
  temperatures, 14,
  18
  timing, 208-9
  tuning, 56-7
  vibration, 24
  Wankel, 15
Engine mountings,
  11, 12
Equalean sidecar,
  191
European
  Championships,
  148, 172, 174
Exhaust pipe, 11, 19,
  20
Exhaust stroke, 15,
  18, 19

Exhaust system, 19,
  20-1, 58, 218
  maintenance of,
  217
Expansion chamber,
  21, 21
Extras, 56-7
Eye protection, 68-9,
  113

F

Faceshields, 66-9,
  78-9, 115
Fairings, 10, 31,
  50-3, 95, 218
  fitting, 52, 218
Fantic, 159
Fath, Helmut, 136,
  137
Fenders, 10
Figure-eight test, 88
Filter turns, 104
FIM (Federation
  Internatinaole
  Motocycliste), 65,
  146, 148, 150-1,
  164, 174
FIM rally, 188
Final drive chain, 11,
  22-3, 212
First aid, 128-9
Fluid line, hydraulic,
  10
FMN, 150, 152
Fog, 110, 114
Fog lights, 57, 114
Footboards, 180-1
Footrests, 80-1, 180
Fork slider, 13
Frame, 12
Frame kits, 30-1
Freewheel, 90
Frith, Freddie, 90
Front brake, 92
Front brake cable,
  80-1
Front brake levers,
  80-1
Front fork,
  bushes, 210-11
  Earles Type, 13
  girder, 13
  leading link, 13
  telescopic, 13
Front ribbed tires,
  63

Fuel consumption,
  14-15
  excessive, 217
Fuel injection, 16
Fuel system,
  checks, 225
  faults in, 216,
  220-1
Fuel tank, 10
  large capacity, 181
  teardrop, 11
Full-face helmets,
  66, 67
Full lock turns, 89
Future designs, 28-9

G

Gaskets,
  homemade, 218
  replacement, 227
Gear changing, 84-5
Gear level, 11, 80
Gear ratios, 23, 231
Gearbox, 22-3, 84
  cover, 11
General Electric, 69
Generators, 204-5
Glass fibre helmets,
  64-5
Gloves, 73, 78
Goggles, 68, 79
Grand National
  Championship
  (USA), 142, 168-9
Grand prix racing,
  148-9, 150
Grand Prix, South
  African FI, 130
Grass track racing,
  167
Greeves, 152

H

Hailwood, Mike,
  130-1, 135
Hallman, T., 141
Handlebars, 80-1,
  180
Harley-Davidson, 22,

  24-5, 84, 139, 168
FLT-80 (Tour
  Glide), 38, 54
KRTT, 145
Sturgis, 44
Hartle, John, 134
Headlights, 10, 114,
  116
  adjustment, 57,
  116, 122
  daytime, 118, 119
  dazzle, 114, 116-17
  dipping, 114, 116
  flashing, 118
  flickering, 196
Heat, 178
Helmet liners, 64
Helmet, see Crash
  Helmets
Hemispherical head,
  17
Henderson four,
  144
Henne, Ernst, 51
Hesketh, 25, 45
Hill climbing, 172-3
Honda, 19, 23, 27,
  130, 138
  ATC 110 Trike, 46
  C90 Z-Z, 35
  CB400 AT
  Hondamatic, 35
  CB1100R, 40
  CBX, 24, 45
  CG 125, 34
  CX 500, 24
  dragster, 138-139
  GL1100KA, Gold
  wing, 10, 33, 39
  H100, 42
  NR125, 156

Index/2

racing team, 130, *133, 145*
Soichiro, 13
TL125, *140*
XL500 S-Z, *36*
Horn, *10*, 181
use of, 118
H/T coils, 18, 19, 204, 206
H/T leads, *11*, 206-7
Husqvarna, 152

I
Ice, 114
Ice racing, 170
Identifying (a motorbike), 10-11, 12-13
Ignition switch, 10, 204
Ignition systems, 18-19, 59, 204
electronic, 19, 218
faulty, 206, 220
Ignition timing checking, 208
Inertia (force), 24, 230
Injuries, 124, *125*
Instruments, 10, 56, 111
Intercom (rider/passenger), 123
International Six Days Trial (ISDT), 158, 174, 176
International Standard Organization (ISO), 64
Invisibility (to other drivers), 118-9
Isle of Man TT races, 130, 148, 168
Isolastic principle, 24-5
Italjet 50, *47*
Pak-a-way, *47*

J
Japanese motorcycle industry, 12-13, 49
tires, 61
Jawa/CZ, *43*

K
Kawasaki, 138, *151*

AR50, *37*
KC100, *35*
Z200, *42*
Z1000 engine, *31*, 44
Z1300, 32, 44
Kick start, 22
Kick start technique, 82-3
Kiwi K9, 66
Krauser luggage, 54-5
Krauser MKM1000, *41*
KTM, 152, 174
390 GS, *36*

L
Lackey, Brad, 154, 168
Laminar flow, 50
Lampkin, M., 158
Laverda, 26
Montjuic, *41*
1200, *44*
Leading link fork, 13
Leather touring suits, 70-1
Left turn, *104*
Lightning Bolt, 138
Lights, stop and tail, 11
see also Headlights
Low speed control, 88-9
Lubrication, 14-15, 19
of brakes, 202
wet sump, *19*
Luggage, 54-5, 182-3

M
Machine care, 126, 194-229
Machine control, 8-9, 80-101
see also individual techniques
Maico, 152
Main bearing, 211, 222
Maintenance, 194-219
daily, 196-7
home, 218
periodical, 198-201

roadside, 202-5
Malherbé, André, *153*
Map reading, 186
Marzocchi Grand Prix forks, *31*
Matchless, 141, 152
G50, 133
Megacycles, 33, 44-5
Megola company, five-cylinder engine, 26
Michelin tires, 60
Miller, S.H.
"Sammy," 140
Minter, Derek, *134*
Mirrors, 56-7, 96-7, 118
Moko (Egli-type) frame, *30*
Mopeds, *42-3*
Moriwaki, 58
Moto-cross, 141, 152-7
boots, *72*
circuits, 154-5
clothing, 157
helmets, 66, *67*, 157
machines, 156-7, *157, 174*
tires, *63*, 158
Moto-Cross des Nations, 152
Moto Guzzi, 12-13, 23, *24, 51*
Convert V1000, *39*
850 Le Mans II, *41*
racing fairings, *51*
V8, *144*
Moto Morini, V-twin 25, *183*
Motorway riding, 110-1
Mufflers, *11, 20,* 58-9, 218
Munch 4. 1300 TTS E, *45*
MV Augusta, 130, *131, 132, 135*
MZ
250 racer, *135*
TS125, *35*
TS250, Supa 5, 32, *38*

N
Navigation, 186
Night riding, 116-17, 225
Noll, Willhelm, *51*, 149
Norton, 15, 148
Commando, *25*
Featherbed frame, *30*
Manx, *132*
Novice riders, 8, 32-3, 124, *125*, 190
NSU, *51*, 140
Rennmax, *132*

O
Observation, 96-7
Off-road riding, 86-7, 176-7
Oil changing, 198-9
Oil coolers, 56
Oliver, Eric, 149
Open-face helmets, 66-7
Oversuits, 74-5
Overtaking, 100-1, 118, *119, 121*
on freeway, *111*
Owesle, H., 136
Owner's handbooks, 198, 218

P
Paradoxycles, 32-3, 46-7
Parked vehicles, 106, *107*
Passengers, *see* Pillion passengers
Pedestrians, 106, *107*
Pike's Peak, 172
Pillion backrest, 180
Pillion footrest, *11*, 122
Pillion grab handle, *11*, 56
Pillion passengers, 122-3, 178
Piston, *14*-18
rings, 14, 17
Plugs, two-stroke, 14

Polycarbonate helmets, 64-5
Pomeroy, Jim, 154
Positioning, 96, *97*, *119*
in traffic, 98-9, 100-1, 102-3, 104, 106, *120*
Power failure, 206-7
Power tuning, 58-9
Pre-purchase checklist, 48-9
Primary drive, 22-3
Provini, T., 130
Pulling away, 82, *83*
Puncture repair, 228-9

Q

Quasar, 10, *28-9*, *46*

R

Race meetings, 150-1
Race officials, 150-1
Racing slick tires, *63*
Rallying, 188
Reaction time, 108
Read, P., 134
Rear brake pedal, *81*
Rear carrier, 182
Rear wheel sprocket, *11*, 212
Redman, Jim, 130
Reed, John, 46-7
Reflective materials, *76-7*, 116, 118, *119*
Regazzoni, Clay, 130
Repairs, roadside, 224-9
Rev counter, *see* tachometer
Riding line, 90-1, 98-9
Riding position, 10, 80-1, 112
Riding suits, *see* Leather touring suits; Oversuits; Special clothing, 78-9
Road junctions, 102-5, 118
Road racing, 146-151

Road signs, 96
Road surfaces, slippery, 96, 114
wet, 92, 94, 108, *109*
Roadcraft, 96-129
Robert, Joel, *141*, 152
Roberts, Kenny, 86, 142, *143*, 168
Rocking couple, 24
Rokon 2-wheel tractor, *46*
Rubber tank buffer, *11*
Rural roads, 108-9

S

Saarinen, Jarno, 142
Saddlebags, hard, 54-5, *55*, 182-3
Saddlebags, soft, 55, *55*, 182-3
Scottish Six Days Trial (SSDT), 158-*159*
Scrambling, *see* Moto-cross
Sealed chains, 212
Seats, 10-11, 80-1, 180
Security checklist, 56-7
Selector forks, 22-3
Servicing, 200-1, 216
monthly, 200
weekly, 200
yearly, 201
Shaft drive, *22*
Shifty, *46*
Shock, *125*, 126
Shock absorbers, *23*
Side stand, *11*
Sidecar racing, 136, 148
Sidecar riding, 190-3
fitting, 192-3
trials, 160
wheel brakes, 190
Silencing, 20-1
Simson S 50B, *34*
Skidding, 84, 94-5
Slalom riding, *88*
Slider bolts, *11*
Small ends, 210

Smith, Cyril, 149
Snell Foundation, 64-5
Snow, 114
Solenoid, 12
Sorcerer, the, 138, *139*
Spare parts, *179*, 205, 215, 218
used, 219
Spark arrestors, 20, *21*
Spark plugs, 205
checking, 217, 223
Special clothing, 78-9
Speed, 33, 100, 102, 120, 125
Speedometer, *10*
cable, *13*
Speedway, 166
Sports cycles, 32-3, 40-1
Sports roadster tyres, *63*
Sports tourers, 32-3
Sprinting, 162
Sprockets, 213
Squish band, 14, *18*
Starter motor, electric, 12, 204
Starting, 82-3
Steering damper, *56-7*
Steering head, *10*
Steering head bearings, 210
Stonebridge, Brian, 152
Stopping, 92-3
Stroboscope, 208
Sunbeam, 500cc S7, *25*
Superbike racing, 149
Surtees, John, 134, 135
Survival suit, *79*
Suspension, types, *13*
load adjuster, *12*
plunger, 13
rear unit, *12*
single unit cantilever, 13, *30*
Suzuki, *15*, 156
FS 50, *34*

GS250 T, *42*
GS 1000, 231
GSX 400, *38*
GSX 1100, *44*
moto-crossers, 141, 152
TS 250, *37*
Swagman saddlebags, 55, 181
Swing(ing) arm, 13
see also Swinging (pivoted) rear fork
Swinging rear fork, 10, 12, *13*, 210
Switch cluster, *11*
SWM, 174

T

Tachometer, *10*
cable, *13*, 84-5
Tank bag, *54-55*, 182
Taylor, Dave, *86*
Temperature gauges, 56-7
Test riding, 88-9
Testi Militaire, *47*
Throttle, *10-11*, 80
broken cable, 226
cable, *12*, 214
control, 81, 83, 84-5, 88-9
Timing, 208-9
Tools and toolkits, 194-5, 224
Top bag, 182
Top box, *54-5*
Top dead center (TDC), 16, 208-9
Top engine mounting, *12-13*
Torque, 22, 230
Torque convertor, 23
Touring, 178-87
equipment, 180-1
navigation, 186-7
speeds, 178
Touring bikes, 32-3, 38-9
Traffic circles, *103*
Trail bikes, 36-7
Trail riding, 176-7
Transport and Road Research Laboratory (TRRL), the, 76
Transfer ports, 14-15
Transmission, 22-3

Index/3

Tread wear (tires), 63
Trials (and commuter) helmets, 66, 67
Trials riding, 86, 140, 158-161
Triple clamp, 10-11
Triumph, 26, 139
  Speed Twin 500cc, 24
  T140E Bonneville, 39
Trouble shooting, 220-3
TT racing (AMA), 168
TT racing, see Isle of Man
Tuning, 216
Turbochargers, 58-9
Turn signal relay, 12-13
Tires, 12-13, 60-3
  fitting, 229
  pressures, 122, 196
  trials, 158, 161
  valve, 12

wear, 48, 216

U
Ubbiali, C., 130
Underclothing, 78
Urban riding, 106-7
URS, 136
Used motorcycles, 48-9
Utility bikes, 32-3, 42-3
U-turns, 107

V
Valve,
  disc, 14
  poppet, 16, 17
  reed, 15
Valve overlap, 18
Valve timing, 208-9
Valve train, 16-18
Van Veen, 15
Velocette, 10
Velosolex, 43
Vesco, Don, 138-9, 164
Vespa, 43

Veteran bikes, 16
Vincent, Chris, 137
Vincent HRD, 25, 30,
  "Black Lightning," 144
Vink, H., 163, 164
Vision, 96, 100, 112, 114
  at night, 116
Voltage control unit, 12-13
Voltmeters, 56-7

W
Wankel engine, 15
Water, riding through, 109
Werner brothers, 10
Wet surfaces, 109, 112
Wheel
  bearings, 210
  checking, 217
  replacement, 228-9
  wire-spoked, 12
Wheel axle lock nut, 11

Wheelie, 86, 164
Windjammer fairing, 52
Wiring, 204-7, 224
Workshop manuals, 218
World
  Championships, 130, 134-5, 136-7, 141, 142-3, 148, 152
World speed record, 138, 164

Y
Yamaha, 24-5, 26-7, 30-1
  DT100, 34
  DT175 MX, 37
  Porsche, 29
  RD 250L/C, 40
  SR 500, 38
  TR1, 45
  XS 850, 27
  175 MX, 32-33
Yoshimura, 58-9

——— Acknowledgments ———

The Publishers gratefully acknowledge the assistance and/or material provided by the following:
Champion Spark Plugs
Squire Sidecars
Bimota SpA
Transport and Road Research Laboratory
Lucas Girling
Andover Norton
Vetter Products
Continental Tyres

Metzeler Tyres
Michelin Tyre Co.
Nava Helmets
AGV Helmets
Britover (Continental)
Euro Design
AMF Harley-Davidson
Bill Vero of Everoak Helmets
Mrs. P. Hailwood and Rod Gould of Hailwood and Gould Motorcycles